1994

PROGRAM
EVALUATION

PROGRAM EVALUATION

An Introduction

David Royse

University of Kentucky

Nelson-Hall Publishers/Chicago

Cover Design: Corasue Nicholas
Cover Painting: *Crossing* by David Quednau

Library of Congress Cataloging-in-Publication Data

Royse, David D. (David Daniel)
    Program evaluation : an introduction / David D. Royse.
        p.   cm.
    Includes bibliographical references and index.
    ISBN 0-8304-1245-X
    1. Human services—United States—Evaluation.   I. Title.
HV91.R76   1992
361'.0068'4—dc20   91-29358
                                                        CIP

Manufactured in the United States of America

10 9 8 7 6 5 4 3 2

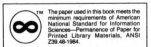

™ The paper used in this book meets the minimum requirements of American National Standard for Information Sciences—Permanence of Paper for Printed Library Materials, ANSI Z39.48-1984.

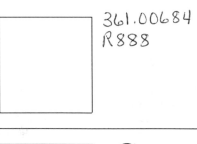

Contents

150, 124

Preface

Program evaluation is necessary in all social and human services to know whether we are making a difference in the lives of the people with whom we work. Accordingly, the purpose of this book is to help students, social work practitioners, and program managers acquire the ability to evaluate social and human service programs. You need not have mastered a certain number of research or statistics courses to find this book helpful. My intent is to provide you with all the essentials you need to understand and to conduct program evaluation in most social and human service settings.

The major focus of this book is to help you to conceptualize the program evaluation effort as a meaningful and understandable set of tasks. Since there is no single way to approach program evaluation, this book will provide you with various perspectives and ways to go about evaluating any program. In the process of developing evaluation skills, you will become a more enlightened consumer of (and potentially a contributor to) evaluation and research reports.

Many former students have contributed to this

book not only through the questions they raised in attempting to design program evaluations but also as they shared unique and creative approaches and resources. While it would be impossible to name all of these students, I am indebted to them. As students attempt to apply evaluation concepts to their various "real-world" programs, an exciting interaction never fails to emerge, which keeps the material fresh for me semester after semester.

I also wish to thank Jacob, Josiah, and Judy for their understanding when I am working on my projects and the wonderful friends who both validate and value me.

CHAPTER 1

Beginning to Think about Program Evaluation

■ Program Evaluation Defined _____

Program evaluation is applied research used as part of the managerial process. Evaluations are conducted to aid those who must make administrative decisions about human service programs. Unlike theoretical research, where scientists engage in science for its own sake, program evaluation systematically examines human service programs for pragmatic reasons. Decision makers may need to know if a program accomplished its objectives, if it is worth funding again next year, or if a less expensive program can accomplish the same results.

Program evaluation is like basic research in that both follow a logical, orderly sequence of investigation. Both begin with a problem, a question, or a hypothesis. Normally, there is some review of what is known about the problem, including prior efforts and theoretical approaches (this is known as reviewing the literature). A research or evaluation design (a blueprint to guide the data collection efforts) is developed, and data are gathered and then analyzed. When thought of this way, both research and evalu-

A program evaluates. lets a person know if

1

ation are similar to the task-centered or problem-solving process known to most social workers.

Rossi and Freeman (1985) have noted that evaluation research involves "the use of social research methodologies to judge and to improve the planning, monitoring, effectiveness, and efficiency of health, education, welfare, and other human service programs" (p. 19). Research and evaluation differ with regard to the expected use or utility of the data. There may be no anticipated need or demand for "pure" research, whereas an assemblage of individuals may anxiously await the results of a program evaluation. Also, the goal of research is to produce generalizable knowledge, while information from a program evaluation may be applicable to only a specific program. However, both are approached with some degree of rigor. Think of program evaluation as a tool—a management tool that you can use to make (and to help others make) better decisions about social and human service programs. Program evaluation helps us to make the best use of our resources as we labor to improve the quality of life of our clients.

Program evaluation involves making comparisons. In fact, Schalock and Thornton (1988) have defined program evaluation as "structured comparison." Few programs can be evaluated without comparing them to something. Programs in one agency may be compared to similar programs in other agencies, to past or prior efforts, or against a stated objective, but without some form of comparison, there can be no evaluation. A major thrust of this text is to help you find or create (to conceptualize) bases for comparison for your own program evaluation efforts.

■ Reasons Why Programs Are Evaluated

There are numerous reasons why program evaluations are conducted. Chelimsky (1989) has observed three broad purposes for evaluation:

1. Policy formulation (to assess the need for a new program and to design it to meet those needs);
2. Policy execution (to insure that a program is implemented in the most technically competent way possible); and
3. Accountability in public decision making (to help decide whether a program should be continued, modified, or terminated).

Quite often, social and human service programs are evaluated because of a need to be accountable to a sponsoring or funding agency, or because competition for scarce funds requires that only one program (normally, the most effective or efficient program), can be funded. Program evaluation is needed whenever new interventions are being tried and it is not known whether they will be as successful as former methods, or when there is a perception that a program could be improved—that it could become more productive or better in some way. We evaluate on those occasions when it is important to have some objective assessment or feedback about the worth of our social and human service programs.

The following scenarios will help illustrate some of the occasions when program evaluations are encountered:

Scenario 1—The Required Evaluation

Your agency is applying for funding from the United Way in your community to begin a new program designed to provide counseling to men who have been prosecuted for domestic violence. You have been asked to prepare the program proposal. As you read the instructions for preparing the proposal, you notice that besides describing the project, listing its objectives, pointing out its uniqueness, and stating the amount of funding that will be required, the proposal also requires a project evaluation. At the end of the project year, data must be presented to show that the project had a successful outcome and an impact upon the problem of domestic violence.

Scenario 2—Competition for Scarce Funds

Your innovative program for battering men has been operating for a year. You have been able to obtain some data (although it is a little weak) that you hope will favorably influence the committee that will make decisions on the continuation of funding for your program. As you prepare your presentation, you discover that a second domestic violence project from another agency will also be making a request to be funded. You further learn that there is only enough money to fund one program.

Scenario 3—Evaluation of New Interventions

Many more clients desire the services of your outpatient counseling agency than you have staff to serve. At a planning session, one of the newer staff members suggests that the agency move from a one-on-one counseling model to a group services model. The benefits are clear—instead of the limitation on each practitioner of seven or eight scheduled clients a day, each therapist could conduct three or four group sessions a day and have contact with twenty-five to thirty clients. In spite of being able to serve more clients, the staff is not very supportive of this proposal, because they believe that individual counseling is much more effective than group counseling.

Scenario 4—Evaluation for Accountability
You work in a large residential agency serving young children. Unfortunately, a child care aide was recently discovered molesting one of the children. The public is in an uproar. Community leaders are calling for the agency director and all key staff to resign. You feel that the agency is a good one—better than other residential programs within the community. Since the agency director knows that you are enrolled in a program evaluation course at the nearby university, she calls you into her office and asks you to find some way of objectively documenting the strengths of the agency. "Can you show," she asks, "that the great majority of our young people have a favorable experience here, a good impression of the agency, and that they go on to do well in school and in life after they leave the agency?"

Why do we evaluate human service programs? Programs are evaluated basically because administrative decisions have to be made, and it is important to know (or to show) that our programs are "good" programs. Individual policy or decision makers may have a hypothesis about a program (e.g., the Free Clinic's counseling program is highly effective). At other times, questions may be raised (e.g., is the Free Clinic's counseling program effective?), and hypotheses or questions provide the motivation for a program evaluation. It makes no real difference whether a question or a hypothesis serves as the catalyst for an evaluation. This can be seen in the following examples:

Motivations for Program Evaluation

We want to show:	We want to know:
1. That clients are being helped.	Are clients being helped?
2. That clients are satisfied with our services.	Are clients satisfied with the services received?
3. That the program has an impact on some social problem.	Has the program made any real difference?
4. That a program has worth.	Does the program deserve the amount of money spent on it?

5. That one program or approach is better than another.

    Is the new intervention better than the old?

6. That the program needs additional staff or resources.

    How do we improve this program?

7. That staff are well utilized.

    Do staff make efficient use of their time?

This list could easily be made much longer. An interest in exploring one question may lead to other areas where information is desired. The evaluator may start off wanting to know if clients were being helped, but in the process of designing a methodology the initial question or problem becomes modified somewhat. The evaluator may want to know not only if clients were helped but also if one approach was cheaper (more cost-effective) than another. Other questions may concern whether improvement has been made in a certain staff's productivity since last year or whether the program has reached its intended target population. On some occasions, administrators may want to use evaluation data to help garner public support for human service programs. (The public is much more likely to support tax increases for those programs perceived to be "good" than those thought to be ineffective or poorly run.) Program evaluation can also be used in terms of marketing programs to the public. (As a program manager or agency director, couldn't you use data showing that 92 percent of your clientele say that they would refer their friends or family members to your agency?)

Social and human service programs have evolved to combat such social problems as drug abuse. Think for a moment of other social problems in this country. We could begin listing such problems as:

Poverty
Homelessness
Unemployment
Child abuse
Domestic violence
Crime
AIDS

Substance abuse
Adolescent pregnancies
Mental illness
Illiteracy
High infant mortality rates
Hunger

For each social problem, there are hundreds if not thousands of programs. Some of these programs work and need to be continued; others are ineffective. If it cannot be demonstrated that certain programs have any impact on these problems, then further evaluative research should be undertaken to discover why the programs were not successful. There may be very logical reasons: the programs could be poorly managed (e.g., the scandal at the Housing and Urban Development Corporation that occurred during the Reagan administration), underfunded, or poorly conceptualized or designed, and there are many other reasons. As social workers and human service professionals, we need to be just as interested in the outcomes of national programs as we are in our local programs. Program evaluation is not to be understood as having application only to the agency that employs us or to the local Red Cross, YWCA, or Catholic Social Service Bureau.

While the examples used thus far have helped us to understand the need for program evaluation primarily at the local level, there remains an immense need for program evaluation of national expenditures and programs. For instance, a recent article in *Newsweek* (June 5, 1989), entitled "Teaching Kids to Say No: How Effective Are Drug-Awareness Classes?" noted that funding for drug prevention programs by the U.S. Department of Education has risen from $3 million in 1986 to $350 million in 1989. However, in exploring the question of whether drug education in the schools works, the article states, "The few studies that have tracked the effects of these programs show no dramatic or long-term reductions in drug use. That finding cuts across race and socioeconomic classes." As a tax-payer, does it make sense to spend $350 million a year on drug education programs that have no evaluative research to show that they work? Given that very little research has demonstrated their effectiveness, is this money well spent? More evaluative research is desperately needed to help distinguish programs that work from those that do not.

Whether at the local, state, or national level, program evaluation often begins with the identification of a problem. Decision makers may have developed a hypothesis or questions about a program because of an indication of some problem with it. This can be a visible, well-recognized problem, or a problem known to only a handful of staff, administrators, or trustees. A problem is any undesirable situation or condition. Sometimes program evaluations are undertaken in order to determine the extent or magnitude of a problem or to confirm a suspected problem. As you think about the agency where you are working or interning, what problems come to mind? (If you do not initially think of any problems, have you seen any recent data suggesting that the program is effective or efficient?)

There are probably as many reasons for conducting program evaluation as there are different programs. In addition to the reasons already given, those in the helping professions also conduct program evaluations because they have a responsibility to improve programs. For instance, the

National Association of Social Workers' Code of Ethics (1979) states: "The social worker should work to improve the employing agency's policies and procedures, and *the efficiency and effectiveness of its services*" (emphasis added). The Specialty Guidelines for the Delivery of Services by Counseling Psychologists (APA, 1981) is even more specific:

> Evaluation of the counseling psychological service delivery system is conducted internally, and when possible, under independent auspices as well. This evaluation includes an assessment of effectiveness (to determine what the service unit accomplished), efficiency (to determine the total costs of providing services), availability (to determine appropriate levels and distribution of services and personnel), accessibility (to ensure that the services are barrier free to users), and adequacy (to determine whether the services meet the identified needs for such services).

■ Overcoming the Subjective Perspective

Any time we have a choice, we find ourselves in a position where a decision must be made between two or more alternatives. Oftentimes, informal (and perhaps even unconscious) criteria guide us in making choices. While these criteria may be more the product of visceral reactions than of contemplation, they aid us in the making of choices. They help us to determine such things as "good" restaurants and "good" movies, and to rate the services of care providers (e.g., a "good" physician). In each of these instances, "good" is defined subjectively and somewhat arbitrarily. For example, my notion of the best restaurant in town may be one that specializes in Italian food. You, on the other hand, may intensely dislike Italian cooking. My notion of a good movie may be *Texas Chainsaw Massacres*, whereas your taste may run to less violence. My notion of a good physician may be one who, although known for a disheveled appearance, answers my every question, while your opinion of a good physician requires that the physician dress appropriately and look distinguished. Because appearance is important to you, you may have no confidence in a physician who does not look the role (whether or not your questions get answered).

What does this have to do with program evaluation? Just this: every day (sometimes many times a day) human service professionals must direct people to their programs or refer them to other programs based upon their subjective impressions. When we make referrals, we want clients to go, not to the poor programs, but to the "good" programs. We want them to have the best possible chance of succeeding or doing well in that program. We have a professional responsibility to avoid making referrals to ineffective or deficient programs. We also want the programs we direct or that employ us to benefit our clients. But, how do we recognize a "good" program? A poor program?

How do we know when our programs are effective? We like to believe that we help our clients, but what actual evidence do we have that the majority of our clients are helped by our programs? Most helping professionals have had clients that have made giant strides as a result of skilled intervention. We feel rewarded by these successful clients. They help us feel that we are competent and that we have chosen the right career. Unfortunately, there are also those clients with whom we are unsuccessful. These clients, despite our best efforts, drop out of programs, make a mess of their lives, or seem to have gained nothing from our interventions. Think of all the clients who have made their exits from your programs. What is the proportion of "successful" clients to "unsuccessful" clients? Are you more successful than unsuccessful with your clients? What evidence could you present of your success?

I have raised these questions to help you understand that program evaluation involves a different perspective than you may normally employ when thinking about your clients. Clinicians and practitioners tend to evaluate their practice subjectively and in terms of selected individual cases. They think of Mrs. Smith (with whom they were successful), Mr. Arthur (who was a model client and who now comes back to volunteer his services), or perhaps Kathy M., with whom they were not a success. However, this "case focus" does not facilitate the aggregation of data at a program level so that an overall determination can be made about the effectiveness of the program as a whole. While "one bad apple" may spoil an entire bushel, one client who doesn't succeed doesn't mean that a whole program needs to be overhauled.

The problems with attempting evaluation using a "case focus" with a single client can be demonstrated easily. Consider Mrs. Smith. While you felt that you were successful in helping Mrs. Smith to quit drinking, others may not be so quick to shower accolades upon you. Those who are skeptical of your abilities as a clinician may point out that Mrs. Smith may no longer be actively drinking, but that the rest of her family is in turmoil. Her husband has left home; a teen-age daughter has run away. Mrs. Smith is now living with another recovering alcoholic and working for minimum wage as a waitress, although she was previously employed as a registered nurse. You reply to these critics, "She's not drinking. She feels good about herself. I think she's shown great improvement." While it may be possible to argue that any given case was or was not a success, a manager needs to look at the program as a whole. Are the clients (as an aggregate) better or worse off as a result of participating in the program?

Consider the case of Mr. Arthur. Everyone in the agency agrees that he has made significant changes in his life since becoming a client of your program. However, upon closer inspection, it is revealed that you spent twice as much time with Mr. Arthur as you did with the average client. Was he a success because he got twice as much attention? Would he have been a success if he had received only as much time as the "average client" receives? (Did he get so much time because he was an "easy" client to work with?)

We've already admitted that the program was not successful with Kathy M. However, is Kathy the typical client or the unusual client? Perhaps Kathy was the most severely disturbed client that your program has ever admitted. Given her previous history of multiple hospitalizations, perhaps no one really expected her to make any significant gains.

We can see from these examples that our perspective as practitioners often involves subjective evaluations. That is, we believe that a client has improved or not improved. The problem with subjective evaluations is that they may not be shared by others. While you think of Mrs. Smith as an example of a successful client, perhaps your best friend and co-worker thinks of Mrs. Smith as something less than a success. While you are quite pleased that Mr. Arthur has overcome a great many of his problems, perhaps your program director has sent you a strongly worded memorandum suggesting that the program's waiting list is such that you are not to spend as much time with the rest of your clients. Although Kathy M. made no progress in treatment, the same program director is not disappointed. "We learned something," she says. "We learned what won't work with clients like this. Next time, we'll try something a little different."

Subjective experiences are not always verifiable and therefore can be problematic as evidence. For instance, suppose I claim to have a severe headache. Most headaches cannot be observed by other persons. Therefore, you either take my word and take a chance that I might be lying or you seek further corroboration. If you felt it was important to establish that I really did have a headache (suppose you were my boss and I had been abusing my sick leave), you might ask any or all of the following questions:

1. "Have you taken any aspirin for it?"
2. "How long have you had the headache?"
3. "Have you seen a doctor about these headaches?"
4. "Have you told anyone else about these headaches?"

Knowing that someone had taken aspirin, had told co-workers about the headache, or seen a doctor about recurring headaches provides some objective evidence of the possible existence of a headache (although it may still not constitute enough "proof" for the boss).

Subjective evaluations about the success of individual clients are very much like the initial examples of a "good" movie and a "good" restaurant. We can expect differences in opinion. Within most groups, if someone says, "That is not a good restaurant!" there are sure to be others within the crowd who will disagree. Someone else may say, "Well, it is my favorite restaurant!" Or, "That's interesting. We were just there on Wednesday and had a wonderful meal." The problem with subjective evaluations is that everyone is usually right. The person who had a bad experience with a restaurant probably got poor service or an improperly prepared meal. The person who ate there on Wednesday could have just as easily have had a wonderful meal. The individual who boldly proclaimed the restaurant to be his favorite restaurant might be quite willing to forget an occasional bad meal because he goes there for the atmosphere, he is personal friends with the proprietor, or his girlfriend works there. Another possibility is that he just does not have that discriminating a palate.

To become evaluators, we need to adjust our perspectives so that we are able to see beyond a single meal or a single client. We need to see the larger picture. We need to go from a micro focus to a macro focus. What are the experiences that most of the restaurant patrons or clients have? In a sense, we need to forget the individual and broaden our perspective to focus on the most common or frequent experience. What percent of the patrons would not return? With what percent of our caseload are we successful? We need to look for corroborative evidence that might convince neutral observers. (For instance, counting the number of patrons leaving meals unfinished or leaving in the middle of a movie might substantiate rather powerfully one's own subjective experience.)

As evaluators, we want to be able to **objectively** conclude that this program is a good one and that another is not—based not on our own personal opinion but on factual evidence. When we go beyond our own personal experience or opinions and collect information about the experiences that others have had, we have begun to develop an evaluative stance—we have moved from subjectivity to objectivity.

An objective stance tends to place faith in numbers and counting. As a rough rule of thumb, the more individuals we are able to interview, survey, or contact, the more confidence we can place in our evaluative findings. Numbers constitute objective data. When, for instance, 97 out of 100 clients indicate that they would recommend our services to their friends, this constitutes objective data. Anyone examining the responses of the 100 clients and sorting them into piles of "would recommend" and "would not recommend" services ought to arrive at the same conclusion.

Evaluators are, in some respects, applied scientists. Scientists seek to understand and explain the world around them. However, it is not just explanations that scientists seek, but *correct* explanations. Whether we think of ourselves as program evaluators or as applied scientists, our findings must stand independently, apart from our claims or persuasive oratory. Our findings must be replicable (reproducable); others must be able to independently arrive at the same conclusions. If someone did not like or agree with the findings from a particular program evaluation, then this person could repeat the evaluation using the same methodology. Assuming that no major changes occurred within the agency in the interim and that the original evaluation methodology was sound, findings from the second study should be the same or very similar to those of the first study.

Objectivity demands precision. Evaluators must be precise about the program they are evaluating, what they will be measuring, how they will collect and analyze their data, and who they will be interviewing or observing during a given time period. Such matters require specificity. Vagueness is rarely tolerated in research or evaluation. Note the lack of specificity in the following: "This evaluation will determine if specialized in-service training on the use of empathy helps social workers perform their jobs better." Do you find it too vague? The statement is vague because we are left wondering: What social workers are being discussed? Has it been established that empathy is necessary to perform their jobs? What jobs are under consideration? What does it mean to perform better? How is empathy to be measured?

One way that evaluators become more specific and precise is by using **operational definitions**. An operational definition is the way a variable or concept (such as empathy) is to be defined and measured for the purposes of the evaluation. The evaluator may use a standardized scale to measure level of empathy. Or, the evaluator may use some sort of behavioral measures, such as the number of times during a session the social worker nods affirmatively or makes supportive statements such as "I understand." Social workers may be operationally defined as those holding BSW or MSW degrees or as all persons who work in a certain program regardless of their educational background (e.g., a child protection investigation unit or foster care program).

As one begins to operationally define the key concepts for a proposed evaluation or study, often the vagueness disappears. In the case of the vague statement, "This evaluation will determine if specialized in-service training on the use of empathy helps social workers perform their jobs better," operationally defining important concepts might change it to: "Do social workers with higher levels of empathy place more children in adoptive homes per year than social workers with lower levels of empathy?"

The effort to become more precise does not rule out the subjective experience in program evaluation. While a single "bad" subjective experience cannot constitute a program evaluation, it may lead to a formal evaluation as a program manager, agency director, or members of the board of directors become concerned about whether an incident or experience reflects what is "really going on" with the program. The program evaluator seeks to understand the "reality" or "truth" about a program. In the process, the evaluator may collect a large number of subjective opinions about the program. Objective evaluations seek not to rely upon the opinions of any one person (no matter how influential), but instead to gain a comprehensive view from the opinions of the aggregate or group.

Because the reality about a program's performance can sometimes be painful and have far-reaching implications (e.g., loss of funds and the corresponding laying off of a number of an agency's employees), program evaluators often seek the best possible objective evidence that they can obtain (given such pragmatic constraints as budget, time, access to clients or their records, and cooperation of the staff). Having objective or "hard data" to guide decisions about programs is superior to decision making without program evaluation data. By way of analogy, if you were on trial for an offense that you did not commit, you would want your lawyer to present as much objective evidence on your behalf as possible to assist the jury in realizing your innocence. You probably would not feel comfortable in allowing your attorney to hinge the entire case upon the subjective testimony of a single character witness who would testify that you were a "good" student or a "good" friend.

■ Chapter Recap

Whether you are a direct service worker, program director, or an agency administrator, you want the agency that employs you to be well managed and responsive to the needs of clients and community. How does an agency become a well-managed agency? One essential way is the evaluation of its efforts, where problems are identified and corrective action taken (Sugarman, 1988).

What is essential to learn about program evaluation? Besides understanding the purpose of program evaluations and some of the various reasons why they are conducted, you need to know the difference between a subjectively held opinion and one that is derived from objective data. This text will help you develop ways of identifying, collecting, and using data that will allow you to be as objective as possible when evaluating programs in the social and human services. Objective data is seen as having greater credibility and as providing better information for the decisions that face program managers. Operational definitions are used by evaluators to obtain objective data that can be replicated if necessary.

QUESTIONS FOR CLASS DISCUSSION

1. Make a list of five or six human service programs with which you or members of the class are familiar. In another column list what is known about how well each program does its job. For example, what is its success rate? Other than subjective feelings about these programs, what is known about how "good" these programs are? In a third column, make a list of questions that you would like to have answered about each program.
2. What are the characteristics of a poorly managed human service program? How would you recognize a program to which clients should not be referred? List characteristics of "good" or "poor" social and human service programs.
3. Discuss your experiences with program evaluation in your job or field practicum.
4. What are the characteristic of a "good" television program? Make a list of all the subjective opinions held by the class members about a "good" television program. How could you objectively determine if a television program is "good"?
5. Why is it necessary to develop operational definitions about such things as what constitutes recidivism or a successful client outcome? Use specific examples.

MINI-PROJECTS: EXPERIENCING
EVALUATION FIRSTHAND

1. In a page or two, outline an evaluation procedure that would demonstrate the effectiveness of a drug education program in your community aimed at seventh, eighth, and ninth graders. On another page address the strengths and weaknesses of your evaluation effort.
2. Choose a product (e.g., coffee-makers, tape recorders, VCRs, televisions, microwave ovens) and develop a set of objective standards that could help consumers select a product of superior performance and to avoid the inferior models. Once you have finished, consult back issues of *Consumer Reports* to see how the standards you used compare with those used by the Consumer Products Testing Union.
3. Try to find another article similar to the *Newsweek* piece cited in this chapter that discusses a social problem and the need for evaluation. Read the article and share it with your class.

- **4.** What would you request in the way of an evaluation if you were in a position to require evaluation of a national program? Select a national program and identify what information would be needed in order for an unbiased panel of experts to conclude that the program was successful.

REFERENCES AND RESOURCES

American Psychological Association. (1981). *Specialty guidelines for counseling psychologists.*

Austin M. & Associates. (1982). *Evaluating your agency's programs.* Beverly Hills, CA.: Sage.

Chelimsky, E. (1989). Evaluating public programs, in James L. Perry (Ed.), *Handbook of public administration.* San Francisco, CA.: Jossey-Bass.

National Association of Social Workers. (1979). Code of Ethics.

Rossi, P.H., & Freeman, H.E. (1985). *Evaluation: A systematic approach.* Beverly Hills, CA.: Sage.

Royse, D., Keller, S., & Schwartz, J.L. (1982). Lessons learned: The evaluation of a drug education program. *Journal of Drug Education,* 12 (2), 181–190.

Schalock, R.L., & Thornton, C.V.D. (1988). *Program evaluation: A Field guide for administrators.* New York: Plenum Press.

Sugarman, B. (1988). The well-managed human service organization: Criteria for a management audit. *Administration in Social Work,* 12 (4), 12–27.

Teaching kids to say no: How effective are drug-awareness classes? *Newsweek* (June 5, 1989), 77.

CHAPTER 2

The Evaluation of Need: Needs Assessment

Ideally, planning should precede the development of programs. Long before programs begin serving clients, **needs assessments** ought to have been conducted to determine or verify that there is sufficient need to justify the funding of a new human service program. In fact, Hornick and Burrows (1988) define needs assessment as the first type of program evaluation—using the logic that one needs to *evaluate* whether the proposed program is needed before it is begun. Needs assessments are also known as feasibility studies or even "front-end analyses" (Evaluation Research Society, 1980). Despite the various names that they may be called, needs assessments not only provide information about whether a program is needed but also provide guidance once a program has started.

Needs assessment is the cornerstone of responsible planning for human service programs. It is the measure against which program implementation and outcome will be compared. Lewis and Lewis (1983) have described needs assessment as the first step of a generic planning process. Rossi and Freeman (1985) write, "A critical step in the design of an innovative program is to verify that a problem either currently ignored or being treated unsuccessfully exists in sufficient degree to warrant a new or additional intervention" (p. 107). After the first step of needs assessment has been conducted, subsequent steps in the program development process include: development of goals and objectives for the proposed program, consideration of alternative methods for meeting these goals and planning for the implementation of the program. The cycle of program development would be complete once the program has been implemented and evaluated. In identifying the gap between a community's needs and its services, needs assessment begins the process where resources can be mobilized toward meeting those needs.

Another way to think about needs assessment is in terms of external and environmental monitoring systems. While program evaluation is an "internal monitoring system," needs assessment "data provide a fundamental navigational system for program planning and modification based on continuous assessment of changing community needs" (Nguyen, Attkisson & Bottino, 1983, p. 107). While we, as social workers, may feel that we know the needs of our clients (or of certain neighborhoods and communities), this presumed knowledge is only subjective opinion until we can provide some documentation or hard evidence of these needs in our communities.

Numerous needs assessments appear in the literature. A few examples of these will illustrate their usage in quite diverse areas. Needs assessments have frequently been directed at discovering the training needs of various professionals. For instance, Pecora (1989) surveyed frontline and supervisory public child welfare staff members to assess staff training needs. Smith, Paskewicz, Evans, and Milan (1986) discussed an effort to identify the training needs of professionals in the field of corrections. Shayne and Kinney (1986) designed a needs assessment to identify the instructional needs of directors and coordinators of employee assistance programs. Flynn and Diaz (1988) reported on a study conducted in Madrid, Spain, to learn the management training needs of persons holding administrative positions in the social services. Long, Schutz, Kendall, and Hunt (1986) examined health risk predictors in a needs assessment of employees in a large metropolitan school district.

Other examples of needs assessments include examining what types of services are required for the chronically mentally ill to function in the community (Lynch & Kruzich, 1986), identifying the need for additional services among female patients in a psychiatric hospital for veterans (Rothman, 1984), determining the rates of psychiatric disorder among homeless people (Bean, Stefl & Howe, 1987) and psychiatric impairment rates in rural communities (Husaini, Neff & Stone, 1979), as well as identifying geographic locations with the highest concentrations of Hawaiian children with the most intensive education-related needs (Heath & Plett, 1988).

■ Planning Needs Assessments

How can one go about evaluating whether there is sufficient need to justify the start of a new program? To start with, we must either find or create the necessary information. But where do we get data about a program that hasn't even started? Let's quickly work through one example.

Suppose you feel that there is a need for a latchkey program in your community. You are particularly concerned about elementary school aged children who, because of working parents, are at home for several hours in the afternoon without adult supervision. You learn that a local foundation has expressed interest in funding a pilot latchkey program in your community the next school year.

Before beginning a needs assessment, ask yourself, "What information sources are available?" As you think about the information sources that would be helpful and obtainable, it occurs to you that among your friends are three elementary school principals. You contact them and find that two are convinced that a latchkey program is needed, while the third is undecided. You don't feel that this is sufficient information to take to the foundation. What more could you do? You could ask all of your friends and neighbors if they thought that this program was needed. Unfortunately, as another friend indicates to you, these opinions do not constitute objective information. Asking only people you know about their opinions will give you *biased information*—even if the number of people you have talked to is now up to twenty-five.

What else could you do? If there is a "true" need for the latchkey program, it would be evidenced by parents who are interested in having their children participate in the program. Their interest could be documented (with the principals' support) by sending home a brief questionnaire to every parent with elementary aged children explaining that a planning effort is being conducted to determine if there is sufficient interest in a latchkey program. When parents and guardians return the questionnaire, you will have objective information regarding the perceived need for a latchkey program. However, there is at least one other information source that could provide useful data. With the cooperation of the child protection agency, you could survey the child protection staff in your community in order to learn if they, too, perceive the need for a local latchkey program.

■ Types of Needs Assessments

In this latchkey program example, several informational sources immediately came to mind. And you may have thought of several others. More informational sources are available to us than we may suspect. (We'll discuss this in-depth later in this chapter.) This is a desirable situation, however. It is very likely that we will have to use different information sources with each needs assessment. When planning for certain programs in the community, it might be inappropriate to contact school principals or parents. At this point, it will be helpful to move away from thinking about specific information sources to understanding general categories or types of needs assessment data approaches. As we examine these approaches, other avenues of potential information will be suggested.

■ *Secondary Data Approaches*

Secondary data is existing information that comes from census data, public documents, and reports. Even data generated by other researchers or surveys can be re-examined for relevance to the new program. Census data, for instance, contains a wealth of information, and since it is readily available in most public libraries, it should be reviewed before collecting any other data. At a minimum, census data can provide you with estimates of the population likely to need or to benefit from the program you are proposing.

You could, for example, consult census data to learn the number of children five to nine years of age or the number of poverty level families with children in your community. Census data are available for geographical units known as census tracts and census blocks. (Note that the block data are available only for large metropolitan areas.) By referring to census data, it is possible to learn how many school aged children reside in a defined geographical area. You could learn the race and sex of these children and the number living in poverty. There is even a category that provides information on the number of females in the labor force with children under six and between six and seventeen years of age.

To switch examples for a moment, if we were planning a program for senior citizens, census data could be used to provide reliable estimates (providing the data were not too dated) of the number of persons fifty-five, sixty, or older, areas within the community where these older adults tend to reside, and the number of older adults living in poverty. Census data can also be used to provide such information as the general level of affluence in a community, the average level of educational attainment, the number of substandard dwellings, and the number of persons with work disabilities.

In order to protect the confidentiality of information supplied to it, the Census Bureau suppresses data which could be used to identify specific individuals or families. Census data *cannot* be used to gain personal information on a specific family or families. It *cannot* supply you with the addresses, names, or phone numbers of families having school aged children or living in poverty. You can, however, use census data to plot a map of those areas in the community that have the highest concentrations of older adults or children or families living in poverty.

In addition to census data, every state maintains a wealth of useful data for planners and evaluators. It is possible to learn from the state health department such information as the number of births, marriages, deaths, and suicides that occurred in a county in a given year. If you were developing a prenatal program for teen-age mothers, it would be possible to find both the number of babies born to teen-age mothers and the number of infant deaths in the years prior to the start of the program. Persons interested in starting an alcoholism prevention or treatment program may want to document the number of persons who have died as a result of cirrhosis of the liver. These and many other categories of information are available from the state health department. (These variables and others that help us to gauge the extent of social problems are known as **social indicators.**)

From the state department of education you can find such information as the number of school dropouts, the number of ninth graders reading at grade level, and school enrollments. Other state departments keep records of such social indicators as the number of children receiving food stamps, medically indigent children, free or reduced-cost school breakfast recipients, child abuse allegations, substantiated abuse allegations, delinquency cases, unemployment, psychiatric admissions to public hospitals, and so on.

Secondary data sources are generally convenient to access (if they are not in your public library, a phone call to the appropriate state department will often get you what you need free or at a very nominal cost) and are easy to understand and use. (Anyone can rank counties or census tracts in terms of those having the most or least of some characteristic. Anyone can identify the county with the highest unemployment rate or determine what the unemployment rate has been in a selected county for the past five years. In metropolitan areas, census tracts or blocks may be ranked in terms of percentage of families living in poverty or number of older adults.)

One source of already existing data that should not be overlooked for needs assessment purposes is called **patterns of use** or **client utilization data.** Most human services agencies report annually on the characteristics of those who have been clients in the past year. This data can be reviewed to see what groups within the community are being served (and underserved). Table 2.1 shows how the data from one counseling agency could be used for needs assessment purposes.

From this table, we can identify potentially underserved segments of the community based upon the numbers of clients who have received service. We can see that there has been greater demand for the adult program than the children's program and more usage of it than the older

Table 2.1   Client Utilization Data, Public Counseling Services, Inc.

	1989	1990	1991
Children served	363	383	407
Number on waiting list	16	19	21
Adults served	785	791	818
Number on waiting list	14	12	15
Older adults served	63	72	84
Number on waiting list	0	3	9
Drug abusers served	302	414	545
Number on waiting list	75	124	183
Total clients served	1513	1660	1854
Clients on waiting list	105	158	228

adult program. These figures could be used to understand **expressed need**—that is, official requests for service. We can also see that the drug abuse treatment program appears to need additional staff. In 1989, over 20 percent of their potential caseload was awaiting service. Clearly, this program is in need of additional staff or resources in order to reduce the number of clients waiting for service to an acceptable level. None of the other programs had so many clients awaiting service.

Client data can also be used for such purposes as locating neighborhoods or streets with the highest prevalence rates of certain problems (e.g., drug abuse). Sundel (1983) has described placing multicolored pins in maps to help staff focus their outreach and education activities. Using service utilization data for needs assessment is sometimes referred to as a rates-under-treatment approach.

■ *Impressionistic Approaches*

After you have consulted the census data or other secondary data and have a firm grasp on the extent of the problem (or of the population to be served), additional information can come from consulting with service providers and other **key informants.** Key informants are those persons who are informed about a given problem because of training or work experience—usually because they are involved in some sort of service with that population. In our latchkey example, key informants could be the principal, guidance counselor, social worker, and teachers in a school. One person conducting a key informant needs assessment for the latchkey program could easily contact all of these personnel in a single elementary school. Key informants could also include child protection workers and their supervisors, or area ministers.

Impressionistic approaches have a subjective quality to them. That is, these approaches are not as accurate or scientific as large scale community surveys. Why? For one thing, sample sizes are often too small to be representative of the larger population. Think about a situation wherein a needs assessment involved talking with three principals. Even if the needs assessment had been expanded to include three teachers, three area ministers, and three parents, we still would not have a sample necessarily representative of the opinions of all the principals, teachers, ministers, and parents in the community. Our data would not be scientific—especially if we chose these individuals because we knew them. (We'll discuss sample size and representativeness more fully in subsequent sections.) While their opinions may be well founded and based on a superb knowledge of the problem, they may also be based on nothing other than personal bias, beliefs, or values. Suppose, for example, that two of the principals you selected strongly believed that women should not be employed outside of the home. These principals may be less likely to acknowledge the need for a latchkey program than a principal with more egalitarian values. The problem of dealing with subjective opinions is also present (and perhaps more visible) in another type of impressionistic needs assessment.

Public hearings and community forums are a type of needs assessment that are "grass-roots" oriented. What is more democratic than acquiring a public meeting room and posting a notice or advertising that anyone concerned with the problem of (fill in the blank) is invited to attend and share their concerns? This approach has the advantage of being reasonably inexpensive, not requiring a lot of preplanning, and again, needing little research expertise to interpret or summarize the results.

But there are some serious drawbacks to public hearings. For one, the "public" seldom seems to attend. Unless the issue is a controversial one, few people attend the public hearings that are supposed to generate planning data. Often, the only attendees are the planning staff and a few service providers from other agencies who have an interest in working with that specific population.

A second problem with community forums and public hearings is that even when citizens from the community attend, there is no guarantee that they represent the larger community. Sometimes certain interest groups can "pack" the meeting so that the opinions of others are not represented. Numerically small but vocal groups can dominate meetings. And persons most in need of the proposed service (e.g., families in poverty, juvenile delinquents, teen-age parents) probably will not be in attendance at all.

Several other impressionistic techniques provide good information from small groups (Siegel, Attkisson, & Carson, 1978). The nominal group technique (Delbecq, Van de Ven & Gustafson, 1975) involves a group of six to nine persons who, in response to a common problem or question, work independently at first, and then share their ideas. The group leader asks each person to offer one idea in round-robin fashion. These ideas are recorded in front of the group on a chalk board or large sheet of paper. This process continues until all new ideas are exhausted. This is followed by a discussion period when participants can elaborate, eliminate, combine ideas, and add new ones to the list. This phase is followed by each participant privately ranking the five most important ideas from the remaining ideas on the list. Individual rankings are compiled for the group in order to arrive at the most popular ideas or solutions to the question posed. The group then discusses the anonymous rankings to resolve any misunderstandings. After the discussion, group members are asked to give a final independent rating.

The Delphi technique (Delbecq, Van de Ven & Gustafson, 1975) involves the use of a questionnaire that is distributed to a panel of key informants or experts. (They do not meet together in person, and may remain anonymous.) Their ideas are solicited, and their replies are compiled. If there are areas of disagreement, a second questionnaire is developed based on the responses. This new questionnaire is sent to the panel, and their opinions solicited once again. This process continues until consensus is reached in all areas.

While impressionistic approaches have much to recommend them (they can "involve" the community, are inexpensive, are relatively quick to implement, and no special knowledge of needs assessment is required), it is difficult to know the accuracy of the obtained data. Those who are invited or chosen, or who elect themselves to participate may not be truly representative of the larger community. Their views may be atypical or not reflect those of the majority. If this is a major concern, a community survey would provide less biased and more accurate information. Perhaps the best use of impressionistic approaches is to add the "personal angle" to those approaches that have relied heavily upon "hard data."

■ Community Household Surveys

Surveys are quite familiar to most of us. Businesses use surveys to learn why we choose the brand of toothpaste that we buy; politicians use them to identify for whom we are likely to vote in the next election. Social scientists use surveys to determine our attitudes about such topics as abortion, capital punishment, and race relations and to determine the prevalence of such social problems as elder abuse (Pillemer & Finkelhor, 1988). Surveys are also used for program development purposes. For example, Rutz and Shemberg (1985) surveyed fifth and sixth graders' beliefs, feelings, and behavioral intentions toward mental health issues prior to the development of mental health education programs.

Surveys are exceptionally valuable tools to use for needs assessment. Although they require more planning and resources than the impressionistic approaches, they provide information that is much more objective and scientific. When a probability sampling design has been used, it is possible to talk very precisely and confidently about the extent of a problem in a community. You could find, for instance, as I did (Royse, 1986) that 42 percent of the respondents had not heard or read anything about a mental health center in their community. Similarly, only 44 percent knew that counseling could be obtained in the community for children who were not doing well in school or getting along with their families. Because the sample of adults was derived from a probability sampling design, I was 95 percent confident that the results were accurate within plus or minus 5.5 percent. That is the type of accuracy that the other needs assessment approaches cannot provide.

In another example, Stefl (1985) reported that in a needs assessment of a five county region in south central Ohio, of those who were judged to have *no need* of mental health services, 11.8 percent did not know about the availability of mental health services. However, 21 percent of those judged to be *in need* of outpatient or inpatient mental health services did not know about the availability of services. The precise estimate of the community's needs, beliefs, values, or behavior can come about only when the survey methodology has been sound. This type of needs assessment requires knowledge of both research methodology and sampling procedure.

While it is possible to conduct surveys with persons who are near at hand and easy to access, those who are chosen merely because it is convenient may not adequately represent the community. For instance, one could choose to survey those in attendance at a meeting of the parents' organization regarding the need for a latchkey program in a specific elementary school. If the parents who attend this organization are representative of all the parents in the community, they would be a good source of information. If, however, the parents' organization meeting was attended only by parents from upper-middle-class and two-parent households, then the organization may not represent the opinions of all the parents with children attending the school.

Why might we assume that the parents who attend the parents' organization meetings may not be representative of the larger community? First of all, parents from impoverished households may lack transportation to get to these meetings—they may not own cars. In rural areas and smaller cities, public transportation may not always be available (especially for evening meetings); even if they do have transportation, impoverished households often have multiple problems associated with day-to-day existence. Attendance at a school meeting (which is not required) often has very low priority. Additionally, single parents have the inconvenience of having to arrange for babysitters—still another financial burden upon impoverished households.

So, even if you were successful in surveying those in attendance at the monthly parents' organization meeting, your findings may be representative only of middle- or upper-middle-class households. The majority of these relatively affluent parents may have sufficient resources so that they may have no need, or perceive no need, for a latchkey program. This would be especially true in those affluent households where only one parent was employed outside the home.

In order to be **representative** of the whole community, every person in the population must have an opportunity to provide input. With small populations it may be necessary to contact everyone, or at least a majority, to have a representative sample of the population. With large populations, random sampling can be employed so that perhaps less than 10 percent of the population is contacted (but every person in the population still had an equal chance of being selected to provide their opinions.) While the method used to select the sample is important, the size of the sample chosen to represent the population is just as important.

Although we are going to spend more time discussing sampling in chapter 6, you can understand the importance of sample size if you think about a large metropolitan community of about one million persons. Suppose a friend of yours from another country is interested in the quality of life as perceived by persons in this country who live in large cities. Your friend (who knows nothing about sampling) asks you to send her the address of one person from your metropolitan community so that she can mail this person a questionnaire. Can any one person adequately reflect the diversity of opinions, experiences, and lifestyles that are found in large cities? "Do you think it would be possible," your friend later asks, "for you to send me the addresses of two more people?" Could a large metropolitan area be represented by the opinions of three persons? What if you sent thirty addresses? How many addresses would you have to send in order for this sample to be representative of the opinions held by the majority of persons living in your metropolitan area? The return or response rate is also important. A low response rate is the equivalent of inviting a large number of people to a party and only one or two show up.

The purpose of the previous illustration is to show that one needs to have a good grasp of sampling before beginning a community survey. There is nothing wrong with conducting small convenience surveys of twenty, forty, or even fifty respondents as pilot studies to provide for some beginning estimates of need. However, remember that unless all the members of the population are contacted or have an opportunity to be selected, the results will not have scientific accuracy. In fact, the results are very likely to be bi-ased and more subjective than objective. Done properly, large-scale surveys are more expensive, more time consuming, and tend to require more re-search expertise than impressionistic approaches or secondary data analysis. But they are more scientific and offer a level of precision and confidence not found with the other two approaches.

■ Convergent Analysis

Prior to beginning a needs assessment, the evaluator or program planner must decide what information is required. Saying this another way, what information would supply the kind of evidence that the proposed pro-gram is really needed? As one brainstorms the kind of information that would convince a skeptical funding body or board of directors, various possibilities and sources of data will come to mind.

For the latchkey program several sources of opinion could be tapped. We talked first about going to the school principals, key informants, and parents. Then we discussed the use of census or secondary data, the use of public hearings, contacting the parents' organization, and doing a com-munity survey. Since any one approach may provide a somewhat incom-plete picture of the "true" need for a latchkey program, convergent anal-ysis should be the focus of the needs assessment effort (Siegel, Attkisson & Carson, 1978; Warheit, Bell & Schwab, 1977).

Convergent analysis involves using multiple sources of information and attempting to confirm the need for the program by means of differ-ent assessment strategies and perspectives. For instance, Sung (1979) has reported a needs assessment that converged the views of two hundred American residents living on a military base overseas and thirty profes-sional officers and civilians engaged in the human services. Sung initially found noticeable differences in the way the two groups ranked problems and needed services. However, Sung was able to converge the needs data by computing an average for the two groups in terms of the seriousness of problems and desired services.

When needs assessment data is obtained from more than one source, areas of agreement may not always be immediately identifiable. How-ever, averaging is an acceptable technique to use in attempting to con-verge the data. Convergence of data can be thought of as similar to a pro-cess in navigation and surveying called triangulation, where multiple reference points are used to locate an exact position. Information from various sources is integrated or synthesized to provide a "reasonably via-ble portrait" of the community's perceptions (Nguyen, Attkisson & Bot-tino, 1983, p. 104). What would this look like in our latchkey example?

■ Needs Assessment Illustration 1

Let's imagine that as a school social worker you first became convinced of the need for a latchkey program when you learn of an eight-year-old child who started a fire in his bedroom and barely escaped without serious injury. Because both parents were at work and the child had been regularly without adult supervision from 3:20 P.M. until 5:30 P.M., legal and child protection authorities had become involved.

As you talk about your idea of a latchkey program with several elementary school teachers during lunch hour, they become excited and each names about four children who could benefit from such a program. The school principal agrees that a latchkey program is needed and suggests that you talk with the parents' organization scheduled to meet the next evening. The parents' organization wholeheartedly endorses the concept and asks the principal if a questionnaire can be sent to every child's home. The principal agrees. A small planning committee meets with you and designs a questionnaire that looks something like the one in figure 2.1.

Figure 2.1: Glenover Parents' Organization After-School Care Questionnaire

Dear Parent:

Because of the recent fire in our Glenover community and the narrowly adverted tragedy, we believe that there is a need for an after-school program. Our children would be supervised at school by teachers. Tutoring, games, and special "fun" classes could be arranged—if there is sufficient interest from the parents. The school board may agree to pay several teachers for two hours each day after school if sufficient need can be documented. Please take five minutes to complete the following survey and have your child return it tomorrow to his or her homeroom teacher.

1. If an after-school program were available January 15 and there were no charge for enrolling your child, would you enroll one or more of your children (kindergarten through sixth grade)?
   _____ YES, I WOULD ENROLL _____ (number of children)
   _____ NO, I WOULD NOT ENROLL ANY OF MY CHILDREN
   _____ UNDECIDED, I NEED MORE INFORMATION ABOUT THE PROGRAM

2. If the school board does not have sufficient funds and there is a charge of $25.00 per week for each child, would you still make use of an after-school program?
   _____ YES, I WOULD ENROLL _____ (number of children)
   _____ NO, I WOULD NOT ENROLL ANY OF MY CHILDREN
   _____ UNDECIDED, I NEED MORE INFORMATION ABOUT THE PROGRAM

3. If you want to make sure that we reserve a place for your children, please write your name and address below. However, please return the questionnaire whether or not you want us to reserve a place at this time.
   _____ (Name)   _____ (Phone)
   _____ (Address)

Figure 2.2: Convergence of Data

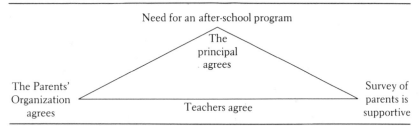

The needs assessment questionnaires are prepared and given to each child in the elementary school to take home. About 60 percent of the questionnaires are returned. The results are as follows:

Q1: Twelve percent of the parents would enroll their children in an after-school program if there were no charge. A total of 105 children would be expected to participate if there were no charge for the after-school program.

Q2: Five percent of the parents would enroll their children in an after-school program if there were a $25 a week charge per child. Approximately 40 children could be expected to participate if there were a $25 a week charge per child.

Q1 and 2: 8 percent of the parents were undecided about enrolling their children and wanted additional information.

Each of the informational sources explored in this fictitious example leads us to believe that there is a definite need for an after-school program. Visually, we might demonstrate this "convergence" of the data as shown in figure 2.2. The need for a latchkey program could be further supported by including secondary data such as the number of calls to police or rescue squads by unsupervised children. Such a needs assessment would make a strong and compelling argument for the proposed latchkey program. However, not every needs assessment could be expected to find such a high degree of convergence.

■ Pragmatic Issues

Given the assignment of conducting a needs assessment for a proposed new program, which approach or combination of approaches should you choose? Before quickly making such a decision, several pragmatic concerns ought to be reviewed.

First, the purpose for conducting the needs assessment must be well un-

derstood. Is the purpose of the needs assessment to satisfy some bureaucrat in the state capital, or will the data really be used by the agency? Is your supervisor or the board of directors anxious to see the needs assessment, or are your instructions to just put "something" on paper? Is it likely that your needs assessment will be used by others in the community, or will it simply be typed, submitted to some government office, and promptly forgotten? Depending upon the anticipated use of the needs assessment, it may be either "busy work" as far as the staff are concerned, or it could be viewed as a useful and valued project.

Second, how much time do you have to conduct the needs assessment? Planning a community survey obviously takes more time than contacting a handful of key informants. If you are working against a rapidly approaching deadline, your choice of a needs assessment approach may justifiably be influenced by what can be realistically accomplished in a short period of time.

Third, what kind of resources can you draw upon for the needs assessment? How much can be spent on the needs assessment? Can you afford consultants and paid interviewers for your community survey? What kind of technical expertise or staff resources will be available from your agency or cooperating agencies? If one is creative, low-budget approaches to needs assessment can be found. Stefl (1984), for instance, has reported on a community survey that was conducted by volunteers. However, the way some of these volunteers were recruited is interesting. One of the agency's board members was a probation officer. He was able to offer community service to a select group of offenders as an alternative to incarceration. These persons were screened very closely, trained as interviewers, and were said to have performed very well. Eight hundred and twenty-two telephone interviews were obtained in twenty-one days. The overall refusal rate was comparable to those reported by professional survey organizations.

Another counseling agency without a large budget for conducting a needs assessment was able to use information obtained from surrounding counties which had completed needs assessments. How can needs assessment information from one county be applicable to another? Let's consider the following example.

■ Needs Assessment Illustration 2

Warbler County (population 99,570) hired a consultant to conduct a community survey using a standardized instrument derived from earlier studies. This instrument contained scales from which could be inferred the extent of the population having either a possible or a probable need for mental health services. Various scales made up the instrument, but for the purposes of illustration, the relevant data from the needs assessment effort have been simplified in table 2.2.

Table 2.2   Warbler County Needs Assessment Data

Scale	Need for Counseling	Percent
Anxiety	Possible	6.2
	Probable	5.3
	Total	11.5
Depression	Possible	8.5
	Probable	4.5
	Total	13.0
Psychosocial	Possible	3.6
dysfunctioning	Probable	5.5
	Total	9.1

A short time later, Thrush County (population 90,831) also retained the consultant to conduct a needs assessment of their county. Once again, a probability sample was obtained, and the same instrument used. The agency executive in adjoining Franklin County wanted very much to have a needs assessment conducted in his county, but a severely limited budget could not be stretched to encompass a community survey. However, he contacted the agency directors in the neighboring counties, and both were cooperative and shared the data produced from their needs assessments. With this information, it was possible to estimate needs that a similar study might have found in Franklin County (table 2.3).

Note how similar the percentages are between Warbler and Thrush Counties. While there are some minor variations, the percentages of persons in need of mental health services in both counties are almost equal. We can arrive at the estimated number of persons in Franklin County in need of services by averaging the Warbler and Thrush County data. Thus, Franklin County would expect a slightly larger proportion of depressed persons than Warbler County, but less than Thrush County.

This approach uses survey data, but in its methodology it is most akin to the use of secondary data. Of course, the problem with this approach is that the data did not come from Franklin County. In actuality, 17 percent of the population of Franklin County might be depressed and 20 percent might score above normal levels of anxiety. We would not know the "true" level of these dimensions without conducting a probability survey in Franklin County. However, if a convincing case of the similarities among these three counties can be built, then this type of estimation is as good as any of the other indirect approaches. How would we know if the counties were similar? We would begin by making comparisons on such variables as the average age of the population, average income per capita,

Table 2.3   Estimated Needs in Franklin County

Scale	Need	Warbler Co.	Thrush Co.	Franklin Co.
Population		99,570	90,831	85,422
Anxiety	Possible	6.2%	6.9%	6.5%
	Probable	5.3%	5.1%	5.2%
	Total	11.5%	12.0%	11.7%
Depression	Possible	8.5%	9.6%	9.0%
	Probable	4.5%	5.1%	4.8%
	Total	13.0%	14.7%	13.8%
Psychosocial	Possible	3.6%	4.5%	4.0%
dysfunction	Probable	5.5%	6.0%	5.8%
	Total	9.1%	10.5%	9.8%

the percentage of families in poverty, and the percentage of divorced and separated persons, and by looking at the racial and religious mix of the counties. Sometimes it is relatively easy to know if two counties are similar or dissimilar. If one county borders a large metropolitan area and the other is rural and remote from any large city, then they probably should not be compared. If two counties are primarily rural, in close proximity to each other, and compare well on demographic variables, then it is reasonable to use them to estimate needs in a third, similar county.

Needs assessments do not have to be financially burdensome to a human service agency. Some surveys (e.g., key informant studies) can be conducted without major expenditures of monetary or personnel resources. On occasions when a needs assessment will cost several thousand dollars, cooperative efforts among social service providers or funders (e.g., United Way) should be explored. Partial funding may also be possible with creative planning. For instance, in seeking to learn what was known about mental health services in one community (Royse, 1986), I incorporated additional questions that asked respondents about their favorite radio stations (during day, evening, and "drive" time). Because advertising is based on the number of listeners, radio stations were interested in purchasing this data (percentage of area listeners by age, education, and township). Several radio stations purchased that portion of the results dealing with their listening audiences and thus underwrote part of the total cost for the community awareness study.

If you are given the assignment of designing a needs assessment, think creatively. Shifman, Scott, and Fawcett (1986), for example, reported on the use of a game called "Family Few," modeled after the television program "Family Feud," to assess attitudes, beliefs, and knowledge about sexuality among female adolescents. In the process of obtaining a needs assessment profile on these adolescents, they were also able to provide didactic instruction!

Given the assignment of conducting a needs assessment, spend some time brainstorming all of the various ways one *could* go about examining the needs of the clientele. Make a list of these—whether they are feasible or not. When you run out of ideas, then review the list and choose the best approach. Following is a list of several different types of needs assessments that one mental health agency conducted during a six year period. This will give you some idea of the variety of ways in which needs assessment information can be obtained.

- **Community survey.** Over three hundred questionnaires were mailed to elected officials, school principals, attorneys, and other "key informants." In addition, over five hundred questionnaires were mailed to randomly selected community respondents.
- **Clergy survey.** Over one hundred questionnaires were mailed to clergy in two counties to ascertain their knowledge and perceptions of the community mental health system.
- **Client utilization study.** The characteristics of present and past clients of the mental health system were examined. Potential groups who were not being served (e.g., minorities, low-income families, etc.) were of special interest. This client utilization data was felt to be so useful that it was subsequently prepared in an annual report for several successive years.
- **Key informant study.** Representatives from thirty-five human service organizations were contacted by phone and letter about their perceptions of the community mental health system.
- **Community awareness survey.** Over three hundred respondents were contacted by telephone to discover the extent of their knowledge about the availability of local mental health services.

■ Final Thoughts

Before you begin any needs assessment activity, you and your agency would be well served to review the following list of questions. This list is a condensed version of one first suggested by Warheit, Bell, and Schwab (1974). For the sake of clarity, I have superimposed the two categorical headings.

Objectives of the Needs Assessment
1. What do we want/need to know?
2. Why do we want to know it?
3. How will the information be used once it is obtained?

Data Collection Concerns

4. Where can we find the necessary data?
5. What useful data sources already exist?
6. How much can we spend?
7. How much time do we have?

Needs assessments do not have to be terribly complex. Sometimes the simplest of documentation procedures provides useful data for establishing that there is a need for a new program or facility. Once, after lecturing to a class about needs assessment, a student who believed that she didn't know enough about needs assessment to do an assignment came to my office to talk to me. As she told me about where she worked (a diversion program for juveniles who had been arrested) and the kinds of problems she experienced in her work, she mentioned a desperate need that she encountered every day. There simply was not enough temporary shelter for status offenders (young people who were picked up by the police for running away, being out too late, or being in possession of alcohol). Because of the lack of suitable shelter, young people were placed in jail until beds became available elsewhere.

I asked her how many times a month the jail was used inappropriately. She said about eighteen to twenty times. I asked if she could document this, and she indicated that it would be easy to do since a special form had to be completed each time. In a few minutes, we outlined an approach she could use to show county and state officials that there was an on-going need for additional shelter care for juveniles. She not only met the requirements for a class project but also used a methodology that could produce documentation for local officials and the community to help them understand the need for additional temporary shelter for status offenders.

QUESTIONS FOR CLASS DISCUSSION

1. On the hypothetical questionnaire designed by the parents' organization, would better information have been obtained if either of the following questions were substituted? Why or why not?
   a. Do you ever leave your elementary school age children alone after school without adult supervision? If yes, how often?
   b. In an average week, how many days per week do you leave your children alone after school without adult supervision?
2. List on the board several social agencies familiar to most of those in the class. What information are these agencies likely to collect on a routine basis, and how could this information be used for needs assessment purposes?

3. Bring in census data for your community. Choose a social service program that has recently been in the news, and brainstorm ways the census data could be used to assess the need for that program.
4. Have the class identify some social service need in the community, and then discuss various ways in which this need could be documented.
5. Discuss why surveying only people you know is likely to generate biased information. Discuss what shared events or characteristics people who know each other are likely to have in common.
6. Discuss how opinions may not reflect "true" need. For instance, is the social problem of homelessness best attacked by constructing more overnight shelters? Would there be a difference in what the homeless say their needs are and what the average citizen might say are their needs? Which is the most important need of the homeless: vocational training, job opportunities, medical care, or shelter?

MINI-PROJECTS: EXPERIENCING EVALUATION FIRSTHAND

1. For some human service program with which you are familiar, design a needs assessment using exclusively secondary data. Be sure to describe:
   a. the program.
   b. the objectives of the needs assessment.
   c. the data collection procedure.
   d. estimates of the amount of time and money that will be required.
   e. the advantages and disadvantages of the approach you will be using.
2. For some human service program with which you are familiar, design a needs assessment using some impressionistic approach. Be sure to describe:
   a. the program.
   b. the objectives of the needs assessment.
   c. the data collection procedure.
   d. estimates of the amount of time and money that will be required.
   e. the advantages and disadvantages of the approach you will be using.
3. For some human service program with which you are familiar, design a needs assessment using community surveys. Be sure to describe:
   a. the program.
   b. the objectives of the needs assessment.
   c. the data collection procedure.
   d. estimates of the amount of time and money that will be required.
   e. the advantages and disadvantages of the approach you will be using.

4. For some human service program with which you are familiar, design a needs assessment that combines secondary data, impressionistic, and community survey approaches. Be sure to describe:
   a. the program.
   b. the objectives of the needs assessment.
   c. the data collection procedure.
   d. estimates of the amount of time and money that will be required.
   e. the advantages and disadvantages of the approach you will be using.

REFERENCES AND RESOURCES

American Psychological Association. (1981). *Specialty guidelines for the delivery of services by counseling psychologists.*

Bean, G. J., Steftl, M. E., & Howe, S. (1987). Mental health and homelessness: Issues and findings. *Social Work, 32*(5), 411–416.

Delbecq, A. L., Van de Ven, A. H., & Gustafson, H. (1975). *Group techniques for program planning: A guide to nominal group and delphi processes.* Glenview, IL: Scott, Foresman.

Evaluation Research Society Standards Committee. (1982). Evaluation Research Society Standards for Program Evaluation. In P. H. Rossi (ed.), *Standards for evaluation practice.* New Directions for Program Evaluation, no. 15. San Francisco, CA: Jossey-Bass.

Flynn, J. P., & Diaz, A. A. (1988). Identifying management training needs for social service workers in Madrid, Spain. *International Social Work, 31* (2), 145–56.

Hall, O., & Royse, D. (1987). Mental health needs assessment with social indicators: An empirical case study. *Journal of Mental Health Administration, 15* (1), 36–46.

Heath, R. W., & Plett, J. D. (1988). The identification of priority sites for parent-child services. *Journal of Social Service Research, 11* (4), 45–60.

Hornick, J. P., & Burrows, B. (1988). Program evaluation. In R. M. Grinnell, Jr. (Ed.), *Social work research and evaluation.* Itasca, IL: Peacock.

Humm-Delgado, D., & Delgado, M. (1986). Gaining community entree to assess service needs of Hispanics. *Social Casework, 67* (2), 80–89.

Husaini, B. A., Neff, J. A., & Stone, R. H. (1979). Psychiatric impairment in rural communities. *Journal of Community Psychology, 7,* 137–146.

Lewis, J. A., & Lewis, M. D. (1983). *Management of human service programs.* Monterey, CA: Brooks/Cole.

Long, B. C., Schutz, R. W., Kendall, P. R., & Hunt, C. G. (1986). Employee health service for teaching and nonteaching staff: A needs assessment. *Evaluation and Program Planning, 9* (4), 355–366.

Lynch, M. M., & Kruzich, J. M. (1986). Needs assessment of the chronically mentally ill: Practitioner and client perspectives. *Administration in Mental Health, 13* (4), 237–248.

McKillip, J. (1987). *Need analysis: Tools for the human services and education.* Beverly Hills, CA: Sage.

Nguyen, T. D., Attkisson, C. C., & Bottino, M. J. (1983). The definition and identification of human service needs in a community. In Roger A. Bell, Martin Sundel, Joseph F. Aponte, Stanley A. Murrell, & Elizabeth Lin (Eds.), *Assessing health and human service needs: Concepts, methods, and applications.* New York: Human Sciences Press.

Pecora, P. J. (1989). Improving the quality of child welfare services: Needs assessment for staff training. *Child Welfare,* 68 (4), 403–420.

Pillemer, K., & Finkelhor, D. (1988). The prevalence of elder abuse: A random sample survey. *The Gerontologist,* 28 (1), 51–57.

Rossi, P. H., & Freeman, H. E. (1985). *Evaluation: A Systematic approach.* Beverly Hills, CA: Sage.

Rothman, G. H. (1984). Needs of female patients in a veterans psychiatric hospital. *Social Work,* 29 (4), 380–385.

Royse, D. (1986). Community perceptions of quality of care and knowledge of specific CMHC services. *Journal of Marketing for Mental Health,* 1 (1), 151–166.

Royse, D., & Drude, K. (1982). Mental health needs assessment: Beware of false promises. *Community Mental Health Journal,* 18 (2), 97–106.

Rutz, M., & Shemberg, K. M. (1985). Fifth and sixth graders' attitudes toward mental health issues. *Journal of Community Psychology,* 13, 393–401.

Shayne, V. T., & Kinney, T. J. (1986). An employee assistance program needs assessment. *Journal of Continuing Social Work Education,* 3 (4), 40–51.

Shifman, L., Scott, C. S., & Fawcett, N. (1986). Utilizing a game for both needs assessment and learning in adolescent sexuality education. *Social Work with Groups,* 9(2), 41–56.

Siegel, L. M., Attkisson, C. C., & Carson, L. G. (1978). Need identification and program planning in the community context. In C. C. Attkisson, W. A. Hargreaves, & M. J. Horowitz (Eds.), *Evaluation of Human Service Programs.* New York: Academic Press.

Smith, R. R., Paskewicz, C. W., Evans, J. H., & Milan, M. A. (1986). Development, implementation, and results of a correctional mental health professional training needs assessment. *Journal of Offender Counseling, Services, & Rehabilitation,* 11 (1), 95–106.

Stefl, M. E. (1984). Community surveys in local needs assessment projects: Lessons from a case study. *Administration in Mental Health,* 12 (2), 110–122.

Stefl, M., & Prosperi, D. C. (1985). Barriers to mental health services. *Community Mental Health Journal,* 21 (3), 167–177.

Sundel, M. (1983). Conducting needs assessment in a community mental health center. In Roger A. Bell, Martin Sundel, Joseph F. Aponte, Stanley A. Murrell, and Elizabeth Lin (Eds.), *Assessing health and human service needs: Concepts, methods, and applications.* New York: Human Sciences Press.

Sung, Kyu-taik. (1989). Converging perspectives of consumers and providers in assessing needs of families. *Journal of Social Service Research,* 12 (3/4), 1–29.

Warheit, G. J., Bell, R. A., & Schwab, J. J. (1974). *Planning for change: Needs assessment approaches.* Rockville, MD: National Institute of Mental Health.

CHAPTER 3

Formative Evaluation, Program Monitoring, and Quality Assurance

Let's assume that the needs assessment and planning for the new program you wanted to start have been completed. The program has been implemented and has now been in operation about three months. If we were to talk to the staff, they probably would acknowledge that there are still some "rough edges" to the program due to its newness. Perhaps a few disgruntled clients have made complaints, and the agency director wants to initiate some sort of program review or evaluation. You are called into the director's office to design a process for obtaining some constructive feedback on the program. The agency director is committed to making the program successful and wants a program that the community will be proud of. Since the concern is not whether to continue or discontinue the program, but how to improve the program, what type of evaluation will you recommend to the agency director? How would you go about designing an evaluation that is concerned solely with program improvement?

■ Formative Evaluation ────────────────────────

Formative evaluation ought to be your recommendation to the agency director. Formative evaluations are employed to adjust and enhance interventions. They are not used to prove whether a program is worth the funding it receives but serve more to guide and direct programs— particularly new programs. For this reason, formative evaluations are not as threatening and are often better received by agency staff than other forms of evaluation.

A good analogy for formative evaluation would be an experienced driving instructor sitting beside a beginning driver. If you have taught anyone to drive recently (or can objectively remember your own initial experiences), you may recall the beginning driver's jerky steering movements and sudden accelerations and decelerations. The driving instructor helps the beginner become a more skillful driver by observing the process of driving and making constructive suggestions. The instructor is more concerned with the process than with any particular destination. Once driving skills have been acquired, it is assumed that the driver will be more likely to reach his or her destination.

Correspondingly, the purpose of the formative evaluation is to provide a smooth running program. This is done by looking at the management strategies and philosophies, the costs associated with a program, and the kinds of interactions among clients and practitioners (Chelimsky, 1989). This type of evaluation can be used to determine if a new or pilot program has been implemented as planned. Formative evaluations present data on what the program looks like at some point in time. Sometimes known as process evaluations, formative evaluations address how the program was implemented, including "what services were provided, to whom, when, how often, and in what settings" (Moskowitz, 1989). Formative evaluations are often considered "internal" agency business. Both strengths and weaknesses of a program may be identified.

Formative evaluations, however, are not limited to new programs. Managers of well-established programs may request formative evaluations in an effort to "fine-tune" their programs. For instance, Velasquez, Kuechler, and White (1986) described a formative program evaluation system that operated for a number of years for 180 mental health and social service programs provided directly or purchased by a county Community Human Services Department in Minnesota. Among the purposes of the evaluation system were these:

—to improve program performance by providing information on strengths and weaknesses to those who manage these programs;

—to inform the planning and funding decisions which had been delegated to the local level. (P. 69)

Formative evaluation does not rely upon a specific methodology or set of procedures. Instead, it is distinguished by its "continuous description and monitoring of the program as it develops" (Morris & Fitz–Gibbon, 1978a, p. 30) and its focus on program improvement. "The formative evaluator will be primarily concerned about tracking changes in a program's implementation, keeping a record of the program's developmental history, and giving feedback to the program staff about bugs, flaws, and successes in the process of program installation" (Morris & Fitz–Gibbon, 1978b, p. 49).

Formative evaluators are, in a sense, program historians who record the development of a new program. They can include personal observations as well as interviews with staff and clients for their observations and comments. However, formative evaluations can also be somewhat more dynamic. Let's take a partly true and partly fictionalized account as an example.

Assume that you are the manager of a new residential program that is funded to teach independent living skills to adults with chronic mental health problems. The house has been open about six months and accommodates fourteen people—seven men and seven women. The halfway house's board of directors has discussed conducting an evaluation of the residential program. However, no definite plans ever developed because of disagreement over what kind of "success" they should expect. While one goal could be to have 100 percent of the residents learn the necessary skills to enable them to live independently, this is unrealistic given the residents' chronic mental illness. Most residents can be expected to be rehospitalized several times within any thirty-six month period.

Last month there was a tragedy. One of the male residents was killed in an accident with a freight train. The engineer said that when the train came around a bend he saw the resident sitting on the track. The engineer blew a warning whistle and braked the train but was unable to stop in time. He also indicated that the resident seemed to make no effort to get up. Later it was found that the resident had been drinking. It is not clear whether the resident was drunk and disoriented or whether this was a suicide.

The community's perception was that the resident had not been supervised closely enough and that the program was at fault. However, the staff were not aware of any suicidal tendencies the resident may have had. Prior communications between the residential program staff and the local community mental health center seem to have been rather limited. The board of directors now wants to examine this program in-depth in order to improve it and to prevent any other unfortunate occurrences.

Knowing that the goal of formative evaluation is not to provide any sort of "final" or summative evaluation but to organize information needed for program improvement, where would you start a formation evaluation of this program?

■ Conducting a Formative Evaluation _____

At least three different ways to approach this formative evaluation come to mind. Faced with such a scenario, an evaluator could recommend any one or a combination of approaches. The logic for the approaches that come first to mind are based in part on what might be attributed to Malcolm Provus (1971), the originator of the Discrepancy Model of evaluation.

■ *Approach 1: Locate Model Standards*

If standards for similar programs have been developed or proposed by national accrediting or advocacy groups, then the local program could be compared against these standards and any discrepancies identified. This approach is frequently used by governmental units that fund, license, or oversee human services. When there are written standards, these are often put into the form of a checklist, and evaluators can monitor compliance with the standards and identify any areas of deficiency. This approach appears to work best when the expectations are easily defined (a window in each bedroom, a fire-escape from the second floor, and fire extinguishers every fifty feet). Standards are not so helpful when they are vague or difficult to operationalize (as when they state that a program should provide "adequate recreational opportunities").

I wish I could tell you that standards exist for every type of human service program that you might need to evaluate. Unfortunately, it is more likely that you will find the situation is somewhat "hit or miss." In some human service fields there are well-developed and substantive standards. In other areas, there are no or only minimal standards. However, you may find that standards developed for one human service program can be utilized for a similar but different program. For instance, the Child Welfare League of America has prepared standards for various programs. In the example of a residential program for the severely mentally ill, one set of standards that might prove useful to review (in the absence of more applicable standards) is entitled *Standards for Residential Care Centers for Children*. Every residential program faces some of the same issues. For instance, facilities must have safe and effective heating systems, and they must safely store flammable and potentially dangerous materials. Residents must have their own beds and storage space, nutritional meals need to be provided, and so on. With a little bit of luck, an evaluator may be able to find a set of standards that can be adopted or slightly modified to fit the local program of interest.

Even if several phone calls to state or national organizations fail to produce worthwhile standards, do not overlook university libraries as resources of information. You might come upon a program evaluation in a review of professional journals that would provide useful "standards" that you can use to gauge a local program. For instance, an article reviewing the literature on inpatient alcoholism treatment may have found that the average relapse rate in five separate programs across the country was 48 percent during the first six months after discharge. If your local inpatient program was experiencing a 78 percent relapse rate within the first six months, this may be a strong indication of the need for a more in-depth formative evaluation.

Professional literature is always a source of potentially useful standards or benchmarks. Even if no "standards" are directly mentioned, a journal article might discuss how one agency dealt with the problem of suicide among halfway house residents. Even marginally relevant articles may contain the name of an agency or an "expert" who could be contacted to provide consultation to your program.

■ Approach 2: Get Expert Consultation

With this approach you might seek out consultation from a recognized expert or from a program with a solid reputation. A person of some authority—the director or program director—from the program could be asked to conduct a site visit of your program. The consultant could review operating policies and procedures, interview residents, staff, and board members, and make suggestions for improvement by making comparisons with his or her own program or some other "model" program. (The standards in this instance may be more informal than formal if they are drawn from the consultant's experience.) If money to pay the consultant is problematic, a low-cost alternative would be free consultation from the appropriate state officials who have an interest in the success of your program (e.g., the state department for mental health). It is not unusual for small agencies to have virtually no money for expert consultation. Since the perceived quality of the free consultation may be expected to vary considerably from community to community, and with no funds for consultation, some evaluators may be interested in still a third approach.

■ Approach 3: Form an Ad Hoc Evaluation Committee

This committee could be composed of halfway house staff, board members, professionals from the community, and other concerned persons. The committee might begin by interviewing staff and then move to residents and their family members, staff at the community mental health center, and other professionals in the community. Some or all of the committee members could visit other residential programs. If this is not economically feasible, the committee could write to other programs asking for copies of their policies and operating procedures. From reviewing these, new policies or procedures may be developed as the evaluation committee devise their own set of standards for the residential program. The committee may identify a number of areas or discrepancies that, in their opinion, need to be addressed so that the program can conform to local expectations.

It is impossible to predict what might come from a formative evaluation using one of these three approaches. The ad hoc evaluation committee may find that the program needs additional staff on weekends and recommend procedures for more closely monitoring residents. The same committee might find that the program lacks vocational and recreational activities and recommend increased activities in these areas. Some formative evaluation recommendations may come from examining the operation of different programs, while others may be based upon the opinions of a single "expert."

Even a not very astute consultant may be able to diagnose poor communication between the residential program and the community mental health center. Such perceptions may be admittedly subjective, but accurate. Because the staff who work day-to-day on a program are so close to it, it is not unusual for staff to be blind to certain areas where their programs could benefit from improvement. (This may be particularly true in those environments where staff are tremendously overworked.) Formative evaluations often bring in experts or outsiders in order to obtain fresh perspectives so that the existing program can be seen in a new or different light.

It is not always necessary to bring in expensive experts to provide formative evaluation. Sometimes, other concerned professionals in the community can provide useful insights. Occasionally students have told me what I regard as "horror stories" of program administration. Two instances where common sense should have prevailed come readily to mind. One former student was interning at a shelter for battered women. They had a telephone, but because of concern that expensive long-distance phone calls would be charged to it, the phone was programmed to make only local calls. Whenever a long-distance call had to be placed, these victims of domestic violence had to go to a pay phone at a gas station down the block. This procedure placed in jeopardy those women who were attempting to avoid men who had assaulted them. It does not take a nationally prominent domestic violence expert to recognize that any procedures which place sheltered women in jeopardy need revision.

In a second example, another graduate student told me of a residential program for children that had such an intricate and detailed admissions process that three to four weeks were often required to complete it.

This certainly worked to the agency's disadvantage when, one summer, the agency had about 20 percent of its beds vacant at one time. Meanwhile, children in need of admission remained at risk in dangerous settings and without treatment because of the bottleneck in the admissions process. Again, it doesn't take a very high-powered expert to realize that the admissions process needed to be streamlined. Where cost is a major concern, it may be possible to ask friends who are social workers or other human service professionals to spend a day or two with your program in order to get some inexpensive, but potentially sound, common sense feedback that could be called a formative evaluation.

■ Program Monitoring

Like formative evaluation, program monitoring is a very basic or elementary form of program evaluation. Rossi and Freeman (1985) define program monitoring as a systematic attempt to measure the extent that a program is reaching its intended population and the extent to which the service being provided matches what was intended to be delivered. Program monitoring does not require elaborate research designs nor does it usually require an advanced understanding of statistics. Instead, program monitoring can start developing specific objectives and collecting the kind of data that most human service programs routinely produce—what we previously discussed as patterns of use or client utilization data. Practically all human service agencies keep records on the numbers and characteristics of clients served during the year. This data can be "monitored" to insure that the program is serving those for whom the program was designed.

It is entirely possible that with the passage of time a program may somehow be diverted and not be serving the population initially targeted. Changes occur in practically all programs. Once the initial excitement of starting a new program has worn away, staff and agency resources may be siphoned off or redirected as newer, more urgent problems come along. As the original staff take other jobs, retire, become promoted, or move to other programs, incoming staff may have different notions as to what the program should accomplish or to whom it should be directed. Subtle, almost imperceptible changes in staff, the program philosophy, the composition of the clientele, or the orientation of new employees can result in programs departing significantly from what was first proposed.

It is crucial that conscientious program managers, administrators, and agency boards of directors continuously monitor the progress of programs. Only poor management would benevolently ignore a new program for ten or eleven months, and then at the end of the funding period attempt to hold the program staff and its manager accountable. To insure that a program serves the target population in the manner expected by the funding source, regular program monitoring is required. Unlike formative evaluations which tend to be single-episode evaluations and others that we'll discuss later, program monitoring ought to be ongoing. Program monitoring should be thought of as a regular or routine activity where a program director reviews patterns of use data on a weekly, bi-weekly, monthly, or quarterly basis. As Chelimsky (1985) has noted, "Its function is to inform on problem characteristics, or to track program or problem progress (long-term or short-term) in several areas (for example, size of or change in the problem addressed by the program, program compliance with policy, changing spread or characteristics of service delivery, etc.)" (p. 11).

■ Beginning to Become Program Monitors _____

Human service programs exist to provide either goods or services to clientele. Some programs provide tangible goods: food (e.g., soup kitchens), beds (emergency shelter), or clothing. Other programs provide services where the products are more intangible (counseling, mental health education or prevention services, self-esteem groups).

Regardless of whether the client/consumer receives a tangible or intangible product, there is always something that can be counted. For instance, a child protection agency may provide homemaker services to 189 families during the course of a year. This same agency may complete 42 adoptions, approve 64 foster homes and provide 1,195 hours of individual or group therapy. Each of these program products can be used to provide some measure of accountability. The agency director may be unhappy with the provision of homemaker services to only 189 families, because she had hoped that 200 families would receive homemaker services. On the other hand, the director may be pleased (since there had been major staff turnover in the program) that 64 foster homes were approved. (At one point it looked as if only 50 foster homes might be inspected and approved.)

The first step in program monitoring consists of deciding what program products, events, or activities are important enough to count. Not every activity associated with a program is important enough to monitor. For example, I've never seen an annual report that listed the number of times that the stapler was used. It may not be important to count the number of times that calls are placed. However, if you are the manager of a telephone crisis hotline or a telephone information and referral service, it may be important to keep records on the number of telephone contacts categorized by problem (e.g., suicidal ideation, drug use, or unexpected pregnancies).

Just because something can be counted does not mean that it ought to be counted. Once I came across a report of a telephone counseling service that recorded daily (by shift) the number of telephone calls received by problem area. Even though they used twenty or so categories to log the type of call, about 15 percent of the calls fell into the miscellaneous category. I found this strange since, in my opinion, they already had too many categories. As I investigated a little more, I learned that they were counting incoming phone calls that might be best described as "personal." A mechanic might call to report that a staff member's car had been repaired, or a child would call a parent at work upon arriving home from school. While these calls may have been important to the person receiving them, counting them in the monthly service report gave the appearance that the telephone hotline was actually a lot busier than it was. Counting these calls could not tell us anything important about whether the program was providing the type of service originally planned. So, while there was accountability, counting for the sake of counting led to some inane results.

■ Mission Statements, Goals, and Objectives

In deciding what is important to count or monitor, it is helpful to go to the agency's mission statement. **Mission statements** are statements of purpose—they explain what the agency is all about. Mission statements provide a common vision for the organization, a point of reference for all major planning decisions; they answer the question, "Why do we exist?" Mission statements not only provide clarity of purpose to persons within an organization, but also help gain understanding and support from those people outside the organization who are important to its success (Below, Morrisey, & Acomb, 1987). If you are in an agency that does not have a formal mission statement, or if you find it necessary to draft one, start by looking at the agency's charter, constitution, or by-laws. These documents describe the purpose behind the creation of an agency. Four examples of agency mission statements follow.

> The mission of the Northern County Victims' Assistance Program is to provide assistance to individuals who have been victims of felony crimes in Northern County. This assistance will be directed at the devastating emotional and psychological consequences that victims of crime and their families experience.

> [Excerpt from the Mission Statement of a Catholic Social Service Bureau:] Our mission calls us to live out the interdependent values of love and justice to lift oppression and heal brokenness of individuals and families, of groups and of society itself.

The mission of the Western County Mental Health Board is to improve the quality of life in our community by promoting mental health, by preventing and reducing mental and emotional problems, substance abuse problems, and by minimizing their residual effects.

It is the purpose of KET, a unique communications resource linking all Kentuckians by television, to be an institution of learning for children and adults of every age and need, a statewide town hall through which interested citizens can together explore issues of mutual significance, a performance stage for the outstanding talent of Kentucky and the great artists of the world, and a catalyst for uniting the citizens of the Commonwealth in common purpose to solve common problems and to stimulate growth and progress for all.

As can be seen from these examples, mission statements are not going to tell you exactly how they will go about their business or when they expect to complete their missions. But, they do inform as to the nature of the organization. One can readily deduce the religious orientation of the agency in the second example. Mission statements are useful in that they communicate the agency's purpose and they express values, suggesting what is important for the agency to address with its resources. Mission statements are usually stated in somewhat vague terms. They are not specific as to what types of services will be provided or how the client will get those services. How important are mission statements? Sugarman (1988), in listing six major criteria that define a well-managed human service organization, noted that the first characteristic is "a clearly defined mission or purpose, well-understood by its members, and it has goals and plans based thereon" (p. 19).

Occasionally it becomes necessary for an agency to change its mission. Perhaps the best example of this is the March of Dimes. This agency was created because of the problem of polio (an infantile paralysis caused by a virus). With advances in research, vaccines were discovered and the disease has now been virtually eliminated. The March of Dimes continues to exist, however, but its mission is now to fight birth defects. Whenever there is a change of mission, there must be a corresponding change of program goals and objectives.

Goals follow from mission statements and also tend to be general and global with regard to activities and products. Patton (1982) noted that a goal statement should specify a program direction based on values, ideals, political mandates, and program purpose. Goals are not specific as to when or how something will be accomplished but speak instead to aspirations. Many people make the mistake of thinking that goals have to be accomplished within a short period of time (perhaps even within one's lifetime). However, there is no such requirement. Many human service agencies have goals that will likely never be accomplished because they represent continuing needs. How many of the following goals do you feel it will be possible to attain?

1. The agency will eliminate all poverty.
2. The program will prevent child abuse and neglect.
3. The hospital will rehabilitate persons having problems with alcohol.
4. The university will strengthen its commitment to scholarship and academic excellence.

It is perfectly acceptable for an agency or institution to have broad goals that they may never reach. Goals provide a sense of direction by means of which an agency's activities can be understood and organized. An agency (or a program for that matter) is not a failure when a goal is not achieved; the reason is that the goals that human service agencies typically set are not easy to achieve.

Unlike mission statements and goals, **objectives** are specific and precise. Objectives allow us to measure progress being made toward the achievement of a goal. They declare what will be accomplished by a certain date. Objectives should have a single aim and an end-product or result that is easily verifiable. Drucker (1980), in an article entitled "The Deadly Sins of Public Administration," notes that program objectives such as "to aid the disadvantaged" or "to provide health care" are sentiments (and vague ones at that) explaining why a program was initiated rather than what it was meant to accomplish. He continues:

> To have a chance at performance, a program needs clear targets, the attainment of which can be measured, appraised, or at least judged. . . . Even "the best medical care for the sick," the objective of many hospitals in the British National Health Service, is not operational. Rather, it is meaningful to say: "It is our aim to make sure that no patient coming into emergency will go for more than three minutes without being seen by a qualified triage nurse." (P. 231)

Patton (1982) makes the distinction of separating the concept (the goal) from the measurement of it (the objective). I find this a useful way to think about the differences between the two. If you are still unclear, look carefully at the examples that follow.

1. To increase admissions from minority clients by 15 percent by March 1, 1993.
2. To reduce the number of recidivists by 20 percent by June 30, 1995.

3. To have 50 percent of all clients attending weekly AA meetings six months after the end of treatment.
4. To provide two thousand individual counseling sessions to clientele by the end of the calendar year.

When objectives are properly developed, they leave little doubt about what will be done and the date when its accomplishment can be expected. To be useful, objectives must specify events or activities that can be independently determined. In the fourth example above, for instance, it should be relatively easy to establish whether the program came close to providing the two thousand individual counseling sessions.

■ How to Write Specific Program Objectives

To write an objective that provides some measure of accountability (so that it can be determined whether or not the objective was met), think in terms of activities that can be counted or observed. The objective should state what will be accomplished and when it can be expected. A model for writing specific objectives is as follows:

To	*increase*	*admissions 10 percent*	by *June 30, 1993.*
	(verb)	(specific target)	(date)

Several examples of useful verbs for writing objectives are:

> to increase, add, develop, expand, enlarge
> to decrease, reduce, lessen, diminish
> to promote, advertise, publicize
> to start, create, initiate, begin, establish

However, the choice of the verb may not be as critical as insuring that the reader can visualize a measurable result. The use of vague terms can make it difficult to determine if the results were obtained. Avoid such language as is contained in the following objectives:

> To help clients discover healthier relationships with others.
> To help clients develop an appreciation of etiquette.
> To help students become better citizens.
> To assist clients in getting their lives back together.
> To increase the community's support of _____.
> To improve clients' understanding of themselves.
> To help families learn about alcohol and alcoholism.

All of the above objectives share the same problem—they lack specificity. They do not inform as to how much has to be learned, developed, or understood. (How would we know if clients had improved their understanding of themselves?) Also, they do not provide any indication of dates when these events will be accomplished. There is also no way of knowing exactly when the objective should be accomplished—the target event that should allow independent verification is too vague or absent.

Sometimes agency directors and program managers, in an effort to make their programs look good, write objectives that will be too easily achieved. Monitoring bodies can contribute to this situation. I once saw an evaluation form that contained these two questions: "Did the project achieve its objectives?" and "How many of the project's objectives were realized?" Every program manager would like to say that he or she accomplished 100 percent of the program's objectives. If there is no assessment of the quality of these objectives, program managers may write only objectives that they know they can meet. Setting objectives too low results only in pointless "busywork." If a program provided 2,200 units of individual counseling one year, then it should be expected to exceed that number in the next year. (The exception to this rule is when the program expects to lose a significant amount of staff, funding, or other resources.) Objectives should be set high enough to challenge the staff. They should not be impossible to obtain, but they ought to cause the staff to stretch a bit, to work a little harder, or to find more creative ways of solving their problems.

Once program objectives have been developed, monitoring for managerial purposes is possible. When objectives are being developed for new programs, there may be a natural tendency to make conservative estimates of what can be accomplished. Rather than over-estimate the number of clients who can be served in a year, program managers may be more likely to underestimate what can be done. These objectives can be tempered by reality if data exist for the start-up phase of other formerly "new" programs. In the absence of such data, educated guesses are appropriate.

However, program monitoring really comes into play when programs have begun to generate service data. In the example from a counseling agency given in table 3.1, it is possible to identify groups that are not getting their "fair share" of the agency's resources.

As can be seen from the table, widowed persons, those over the age of 60, and minorities are not represented in the agency clientele to the extent that would be expected from their proportions in the population. With just this much information, a program manager could develop the following objectives:

Table 3.1   Client Utilization Data, Acceptall Counseling Services, Inc.

Variable	1988	1989	1990	1991	1990 Census
Widowed	3%	3.6%	2.5%	2.3%	4.95%
Over 60 yrs.	4%	4.5%	5.5%	5.2%	14.75%
Minority	5%	5.5%	6.3%	6.5%	13.25%

- **Objective 1:** To increase the percentage of widowed persons served by the program to 5 percent of the total clientele by December 31, 1993.
- **Objective 2:** Through special outreach efforts, to increase the number of older adults served by the program until 15 percent of the program's clients are sixty or older. This objective to be reached by July 1, 1993.
- **Objective 3:** By January 1, 1995, to double the number of minority clients served by the program in 1993.

With these objectives in place, the program manager and the program's staff now have a clear set of expectations for their future efforts. Once these objectives are met, new ones can be developed. If they are not met, corrective actions may be needed (providing there were no extenuating factors to explain the nonperformance.) The setting of objectives provides a basis against which the program's accomplishment can be examined.

Because they are concerned with the logistical problems associated with getting programs started, program managers and agency administrators often write such program objectives as:

To hire a new receptionist for the XYZ program by July 10.
To write position descriptions for the six new program staff by
August 1.
To secure another 4,000 square feet of office space downtown.

While these objectives may be viewed as being crucial to the success of a program, they are poor program objectives because they do not address the *performance* of the program. All of us understand that programs must have staff, office space, office furniture, and telephones. Having all of these things, however, does not necessarily make a quality program. Having a receptionist is not directly related to improving services provided to clients. Staff might, for instance, take advantage of the fact that a receptionist can intercept phone calls and extend their sixty minute lunch period to an hour and a half or longer each day. With the addition of a receptionist, clients could get less, rather than more, of a therapist's attention.

While it is permissible to have administrative objectives (e.g., to hire a new receptionist by July 10), this type of objective does not help a neutral observer determine whether a program is performing as it was designed. Program objectives should address the products of the program—not what it takes to implement a program. Here's an illustration of this point:

Last year I went to an "open house" at the school where my son was a 7th grade student. I was eager to meet his music appreciation teacher since my son had brought home several assignments (e.g., finding musical terms in scrambled word puzzles) that were very difficult (even for his parents, who were trying to assist). His teacher, after introducing himself, said that all his students were "good students" and that they would all be getting A's or B's. He went on to say that he wanted students to "come alive" and interact with him. "One day," he said, "I brought a tennis ball to class, and we spent the entire period just bouncing the ball around." My wife and I both left the open house with the strong impression that having a music teacher present in the classroom was no guarantee that the seventh graders would learn anything at all about music. (However, better results are usually obtained with such personnel as teachers and receptionists than without them.)

■ What Kinds of Things Are Important to Monitor? _____

Program monitoring is properly used to check for program progress in meeting certain objectives (e.g., increasing the number of minority admissions). In this sense, it is analogous to being told by your physician what kinds of things to monitor to maintain health. For instance, persons with a diagnosis of diabetes must monitor the amount of sugars and carbohydrates they consume. Persons with hypertension are told to monitor their salt intake. However, managers need not wait for their programs to become "ill" before employing program monitoring.

Program monitoring can be used most effectively in a diagnostic sense. Managers can use program monitoring to look for "symptoms" that would help them diagnose potential problems. What kinds of problems is difficult to state succinctly because of the enormous diversity in human service programs. They range from small, one-person programs to programs that employ hundreds of staff. Programs administered by the same agency in different locations may bear only a faint resemblance to one another. Every program can be expected to have a somewhat unique set of problems. Even similar programs are likely to have different problems. This is due to differences in staff composition, local (and often informal) policies and procedures, relationships with other professionals and agencies within the community, the guidance and leadership of the agency administrator, the amount of financial support, and such factors as the interest and involvement of the board of directors.

Veney and Kaluzny (1984) summarized the data appropriate for monitoring as inputs, process, and outputs. They described inputs as consisting of the resources by which the program is carried out. Resources include such categories as project staff, office space, and office equipment and supplies. With regard to inputs, the important thing to monitor is the amount budgeted for a program against what is actually used or allocated. For process, it is important to monitor the activities that were intended to be carried out during program implementation. Outputs are the results of the program—what the program actually produces.

Using this scheme, a manager might check to make sure that a program is not overspending its budget (or that it is getting all that it is entitled to); that planned activities are being conducted on a timely basis; and that regular accounting is being made of the number of service units produced (such as meals provided or other quantifiable products). Thus, a manager would know there were problems if the agency spent 75 percent of its budget by the half-year mark, if scheduled program activities were not being performed, or if the program started off providing 300 service units during the first month but fell off to only 125 service units during the second month.

Monitoring inputs, process, and outputs gives the program manager basic information needed to manage programs. However, this information may not be complete enough to allow a manager to "fine-tune" a program. A program could be meeting expectations in terms of its budget expenditures, its activities, and the number of products that were expected and still not be doing the job it was designed to do in terms of serving all facets of the population or community. This could come about because too little time was devoted to planning prior to program implementation, because of lack of management, or because of other reasons.

What other informational items might be helpful to monitor? For one, referral sources. The conscientious manager should monitor where referrals are coming from and in what proportion. It may be perfectly acceptable for a private counseling agency to have 92 percent of its clients self-referred. On the other hand, public agencies may want to see referrals coming from a broad spectrum of the community. The program manager in a public agency who notes that over a three month period of time no referrals have come from the criminal justice system may want to undertake some special efforts to insure that professionals in that system, who are in a position to refer, know whom to contact and how to make a referral. Similarly, there might be concern if physicians, clergy, or other human service agencies are not referring to the program—or are not referring in the proportion that one might expect.

A more refined level of program monitoring would examine the number of clients who drop out of the program. How many clients complete only one or two sessions? What proportion drop out by the third session? How many clients notify the program staff that they will not be returning? It is also important to know such things as how long it takes for clients to receive service from the time of their initial contact or application. Managers should know how many clients are on their waiting lists so that scheduling and programming can be planned accordingly.

Besides using program monitoring to determine if the obvious segments of the population are being served (older adults, low-income persons, minorities), program managers can determine if clients from remote geographical areas and those with special needs (e.g., persons who are mentally retarded or have physical handicaps) are being served. Additionally, program monitoring can inform as to whether there is an increase of clients with certain types of problems or diagnoses. If, for example, there is a significant increase in the number of clients reporting sexual abuse, this may necessitate training for the staff or require some other modification in the program. (Perhaps a support group for victims of sexual trauma should be started.) The discovery of a substantial number of clients addicted to crack cocaine may require either program modification or at least closer working ties with other agencies in the community. Examining client data by area of residence may indicate the need for a new satellite office.

Sorensen et al. (1987) have developed a set of twenty-five key performance indicators in four major areas (revenue, client, staff, and service mix) to assist managers and policymakers in assessing the performance of their programs relative to others. A sampling of these indicators includes: revenue per client, revenue collected as a percent of total charges, percent of severely mentally ill, average number of service units per F.T.E. (full-time equivalency), average caseload by program, total cost per unit of service, and total client turnover.

As management's use of program information increases, additional items, such as productivity of individual members of the staff, can be added to the items being monitored. As program managers make greater use of program information, often times it becomes necessary to develop (or purchase) more sophisticated ways of managing data. Although the term **management information systems** can be applied to simple manual tabulations of service data, it has generally come to be associated with computerized systems. (For a good overview on how computers can benefit the social services, see Pardeck and Murphy, *Computers in Human Services*.)

Figure 3.1: Example of a Service Ticket

McDowell Counseling Center

Service Ticket 10456   Today's Date _____
Therapist # _____   Client #_____
Time spent with client _____ hrs./_____ minutes
Program:_____
   01 Individual and Family Counseling
   02 Group Counseling
   03 Crisis Counseling (hotline only)
   04 Diagnostic Assessment
   05 Case Management
   06 Case Consultation
   07 Community Education
   08 Psychiatric Consultation
   09 Client Cancellation/No-Show

Next appointment date: Fee paid today $_____ . _____

Management information systems depend upon source documents (sometimes called service tickets) that record transactions such as the service a client received, the number of hours of service received or service units provided, the staff member involved, the location, the date, and so on (see figure 3.1). This information is useful for billing purposes as well as for understanding staff and program productivity.

Service tickets can be linked to a client's file containing the initial application data (sometimes called a "face sheet") or other forms containing the diagnosis and other pertinent information. Computerized information systems allow for the most sophisticated monitoring of service utilization because of the ease with which the computer can process large quantities of data. Examples of program monitoring questions that a management information system could answer are:

1. How many service units, on average, did clients with the diagnosis of bipolar disorder receive? (Or, what was the average length of stay for patients with bipolar disorder?)
2. Which worker produced the most counseling units during the last quarter? (Alternatively, which worker was the least productive last pay period?)
3. What percent of the clients were able to pay the full fee?
4. Of those clients referred for services last month, how many were referred by the criminal justice system?
5. How many cancellations (or no-shows) were there last month? What were the characteristics of those who canceled and gave no notifica-

tion? (Were they single mothers with small children or unemployed persons with no transportation?)

It should be noted that program monitoring data, while useful for some management purposes, does not necessarily inform as to the *quality* of care provided to the various groups of clients using the agency's services. While you may be pleased with a program because poor or minority clients were well represented in the clientele, this does not guarantee that the services they received actually helped them. Your program could be serving a large number of persons inadequately or inappropriately. By examining only the characteristics of those clients being served, you still have very little idea about how "good" the program is. When you want to know if the clients are better off as a result of being served by the program, then you need to shift from program monitoring to program evaluation models. These are discussed in the next chapter.

■ Quality Assurance

Another type of program monitoring is known as **quality assurance**. This term is usually applied to the ongoing review of medical or clinical care records. As such, quality assurance has as its aim the identification and correction of deficiencies occurring in the process of providing care to consumers of services. Quality assurance is more concerned with compliance (e.g., the percent of these records that meet standards, such as having correctly completed treatment plans and progress notes) than with client outcomes. This can be seen in a sampling of items taken from a booklet on quality assurance prepared by the Joint Commission on Accreditation of Hospitals (1987).

- diagnostic procedures are appropriate
- treatment is consistent with clinical impression
- services provided are relevant
- treatment frequency is appropriate
- medical record entries are accurate
- medical record entries are complete
- least expensive alternative resources are used
- evidence exists of continuity of care
- reasonable treatment follow-up

Unfortunately, many social and human service organizations have considered this "medical model" of quality assurance to be synonymous with program evaluation. All too often, quality assurance has been conceptualized as and limited to a checklist that would indicate whether the case contained documentation for services that were planned and rendered. This can be seen in figure 3.2, an example of a quality assurance form used by a state agency to monitor the performance of its social service employees.

Neither medical nor nonmedical quality assurance efforts necessarily indicate the extent to which a program is successful with its clients—whether clients improve as a result of intervention or whether a program is worth funding again next year. This is due to the strong tendency for quality assurance efforts to focus almost exclusively on the process of treatment rather than on the outcome.

Because of the confusion that exists, it is necessary to briefly highlight the differences between quality assurance and program evaluation activities. First of all, quality assurance efforts often stem from legislative mandate. In 1972, amendments to the Social Security Act (P.L. 92–603) established Professional Standards Review Organizations (PSROs). The intent of this legislation was to establish peer review systems to assure that federal and state expenditures of Medicare, Medicaid, and the Maternal and Child Health Programs were spent on "medically necessary and high quality care" (Tash & Stahler, 1984). Second, other distinctions have been noted by Tash, Stahler and Rappaport (1982): clinicians tend to be involved in quality assurance efforts (i.e., peer reviews), whereas program evaluators are usually not a provider of the care that is being evaluated. Third, in quality assurance, recommendations are customarily relayed back to clinicians in order to improve the record-keeping process, whereas evaluation findings may or may not be given as feedback to the clinical staff and are more often used at the administrative level. Fourth, quality assurance often relies upon the expert opinion of peer reviewers and consensus that a sample of records met expected standards. Program evaluation methodologies tend to rely much less on peer review and more on quantitative data, research designs, the formal testing of hypotheses, and statistical analysis.

If quality assurance is not required of a program, the conscientious manager may want to implement these activities in some form. Coulton (1987) has noted, "A successful organization continually looks for, finds, and solves problems. In this context, quality assurance—with its cycle of monitoring, in-depth problem analysis, and corrective action—serves as a self-correcting function within an organization" (p. 443). It is important for every agency providing direct intervention to clients to be able to identify such problems as: a large percentage of cases without treatment plans; initial assessments not providing enough information to substantiate diagnoses; inappropriate referrals or discharges; or an increase in discharges against clinical advice.

Some human service professionals resent the amount of time it takes

Figure 3.2: Casework Evaluation Form

	YES	NO
1. Was a thorough, family-based assessment completed that reflects the family's needs for on-going services?	___	___
2. Is a current, family-based treatment plan in the case record that is specific enough to be utilized in providing services?	___	___
3. Does service delivery follow the treatment plan?	___	___
4. Are types, frequency, and location of professional/family contacts appropriate?	___	___
5. Are problem-solving strategies used during family contacts that indicate good casework skills and knowledge?	___	___
6. Does the professional use identified resources through collateral contacts with service providers?	___	___
7. Does the running record clearly document casework activity and case progress?	___	___
8. Is the case being managed according to present policies and procedures?	___	___
9. Has the professional assured the safety of the adults/child(ren) in their current living arrangement?	___	___
10. Are the family's perceptions and preferences included in the provision of social services when possible?	___	___
11. Are services directed toward strengthening the family and preventing out-of-home placements?	___	___

(This form is scored as follows: 1 point is awarded for each "Yes" and a 0 is given for each "No." The quality of the casework is rated "Excellent" if there are 11 points; "Good" if there are 7 to 10 points; "Fair" if there are 3-6 points; and "Poor" if there are only 1-2 points.)

to document what they have already done. Especially when caseloads are large, paperwork is an anathema. Workers may feel that time spent on paperwork is time taken away from needy clients. However, viewed from a manager's perspective, this "paperwork" is needed for a variety of reasons:

1. To protect clients from unethical or inappropriate treatment. (I have heard of two consulting physicians in two different states whose contracts were canceled by mental health agencies. At one center, the staff felt that the physician was overmedicating clients. Staff at the other center believed that the consulting physician was misdiagnosing an inordinate number of clients as multiple personalities.) In a more positive sense, quality assurance activities help to demonstrate that the organization does care about the services provided.

2. To protect staff from charges of inappropriate treatment or incompetence. (In this litigious society, the documentation of services ren-

dered is some protection against unfair or untruthful claims.) Quality assurance data also can be used to identify reasons for patient dissatisfaction with services. Satisfied clients always help to improve the marketability of programs and services.

3. To recover reimbursements from insurance companies and other third parties. (As noted earlier, quality assurance activities are required by Medicare, Medicaid, and other third party payors.)

4. To better plan for effective and efficient utilization of staff and agency resources. (Having such information as the average length of stay or the numbers of patients with certain diagnoses can help program managers evaluate special and unmet needs as well as better supervise staff whose cases exceed the average length of stay.)

Green and Attkisson (1984) have noted that, while program evaluation and quality assurance are distinctly different approaches to evaluating the delivery of human services, there are changes within each approach moving them toward convergence. They note that quality assurance now embraces the criteria of efficiency or cost-effectiveness of services (in the medical field, this is referred to as cost-containment), and adequacy of services relative to the needs present in the population. At the same time, they feel that program evaluators are more comfortable with incorporating qualitative methods into their evaluations, with the result that former boundaries between the two approaches have been obscured.

Any movement toward convergence may be so subtle or slow that it would be imperceptible to the novice evaluator. It is much more likely that evaluators will feel the frustration identified by Sherman (1987): "One of the largest problems in devising useful indicators for quality assurance continues to be a lack of conceptual clarity about how to operationalize what quality assurance should focus on" (p. 227). In his article, Sherman presents an example of criteria developed to help with the decision of appropriateness for admission to an adult outpatient counseling program. For instance, an inappropriate admission to such a program would include suicidal or homicidal clients, those whose primary problem was child management, those with a history of or hospitalization within the past thirty days, and so on.

It is beyond the scope of this evaluation text to teach how to develop or improve upon quality assurance plans. Fortunately, there are several publications along this line available from the Joint Commission on the Accreditation of Hospitals and others (Meisenheimer, 1985; Coulton, 1979). The purpose of this discussion is to help you develop an understanding of how quality assurance could be used for program improvement (for instance, to identify employees who tend to make inappropriate diagnoses or treatment plans, or whose interventions are not consistent with expectations or accepted practice; to identify the need for inservice or continuing education; and to provide other useful data for management decisions). Additionally, quality assurance systems have the capacity to contribute to our knowledge base and should be used to improve social work practice (Coulton, 1979).

■ Chapter Recap

This chapter introduced formative evaluation for those occasions when the chief concern is with improving programs. Program monitoring was discussed as a tool for the conscientious manager—one who wants to know who the program is reaching and what they are receiving in the way of services. Program managers ought to know such things as the composition of their clientele, the average length of time clients are actively involved with a program, and the percent of clients terminating prematurely. For an example in the literature of a special program (a mental health program for persons with developmental disabilities) that examined its client utilization data, see Reiss and Trenn (1984).

Depending upon the age, complexity, and sophistication of the agency whose program you have been asked to evaluate, you may find either the absence or presence of mission statements and corresponding statements of program goals and objectives. In fact, your first act as an evaluator may be to assist the agency to develop or adopt mission statements and program goals. You may find yourself writing goals and objectives simply because they've never been done and no one else has any experience writing them.

Also, keep in mind that a program can have more than one goal, and each goal can have multiple objectives. For instance, I once heard of a mental health agency that had purchased a fast food restaurant. This purchase enabled the agency to employ their clients with chronic mental illness while providing them with necessary training and income to become employable in a competitive job market. The restaurant also brought in needed operational income to the agency. Each of these goals would be evaluated independently (with different criteria).

Patton (1982) has made several astute observations about management information systems. He noted that "if there is nothing you are trying to find out, there is nothing you will find out" (p. 229). He suggested that a management information system is not an "endpoint" but a beginning point for raising issues for additional study. Management information systems only provide data—they do not make decisions. An evaluation doesn't occur until someone actually does something with the data.

Quality assurance was presented as another variation of program monitoring. Quality assurance, as usually practiced, is distinctly different from the type of program evaluation designs that we will explore in the next two chapters. In program evaluation, the emphasis is often on what the clients achieve, become, or obtain—the number of days they successfully stay in the community and out of the hospital or the cost of a unit of service, for example. Quality assurance procedures are client-specific and note inappropriate or missing services with a focus on correction of deficiencies at the individual case level. Quality assurance efforts often are concerned with the percentage of records in compliance. Program evaluators tend to have a broader interest in a program (e.g., its impact in the community or upon a sample of clients).

Despite different areas of concern and differing emphases, a trend toward the convergence of program evaluation and quality assurance has been observed. As computerized information systems become even more common and greater reliance is made upon them, the distinction between quality assurance and program evaluation activities will grow less pronounced (Woy, Lund, & Attkisson, 1978).

QUESTIONS FOR CLASS DISCUSSION

1. What is wrong with the following objectives?
   a. To improve statewide planning capacity and capability.
   b. To maximize collections from first and third party payors.
   c. To improve the skills of current staff through appropriate in-service training.
   d. To improve staff/patient ratios in state psychiatric hospitals.
   e. To participate more actively in economic development activities.
2. Rewrite the following objectives to improve them.
   a. The Free Clinic will facilitate early initiation of prenatal care by maintaining relations with local physicians and other agencies to facilitate referrals to the clinic.
   b. The Free Clinic will distribute brochures and posters describing the need for early prenatal care and the location of these services.
   c. For high risk patients, the Free Clinic will perform follow-up counseling as needed.
3. Discuss how a board of directors would know when a program is in need of a formative evaluation.
4. Tell what you know about the various ways in which social and human service agencies in your community conduct quality assurance and program monitoring activities.
5. Discuss the extent that social and human service agencies with which your class is familiar utilize computerized management information systems. What are their advantages and disadvantages?

6. Briefly describe a local social or human service program to your class and then engage in a discussion of information that would be useful for program monitoring.
7. Referring to table 3.1, what possible explanations could there be for certain populations utilizing services less than might be expected? Could it be argued that some populations have a greater need for services than their proportion in a community's population?
8. Discuss your experience with quality assurance programs. Viewed from a management perspective, what do you believe to be the benefits of quality assurance?

MINI-PROJECTS: EXPERIENCING EVALUATION FIRSTHAND

1. Choose a human service program with which you are familiar and then do the following:
   a. briefly describe it
   b. write at least one program goal
   c. write three specific program objectives
2. Write a mission statement for a fictitious agency of your choosing.
3. Imagine that a friend asks you to conduct a formative evaluation of the agency where you now work or intern as a practicum student. What sort of recommendations would you expect? List at least six realistic recommendations that could apply to this agency.
4. Briefly describe the quality assurance procedures of a social or human service agency with which you are familiar. Draft a short paper outlining how these procedures could be improved.
5. Obtain a monthly, quarterly, or yearly report from a social or human services agency. What additional information would be useful if you were a program monitor for that program? What information is missing and should be incorporated in future reports? Draft a set of recommendations based upon your reading of the reports.

REFERENCES AND RESOURCES

Below, P.J., Morrisey, G.L., & Acomb, B.L. (1987). *The executive guide to strategic planning.* San Francisco, CA: Jossey–Bass.

Chelimsky, E. (1985). *Program evaluation: Patterns and directions.* Washington, DC: American Society for Public Administration.

Commission on Accreditation of Rehabilitation Facilities. (1990). *Standards manual for organizations serving people with disabilities.* Tucson, AZ.

Coulton, C.J. (1987). Quality assurance. In S.M. Rosen, D. Fanshel, and M.E. Lutz (Eds.), *Encyclopedia of social work.* Silver Spring, MD: National Association of Social Workers.

Coulton, C.J. (1979). *Social work quality assurance programs: A comparative analysis*. Washington, DC: National Association of Social Workers.

Dhooper, S.S., Royse, D., & Wolfe, L.C. (1990). Does social work education make a difference? *Social Work*, 35 (1), 57–61.

Drude, K.P., & Nelson, R.A. (1982). Quality assurance: A challenge for community mental health centers. *Professional Psychology*, 13 (1), 85–90.

Drucker, Peter. (1980). The deadly sins in public administration. *Public Administration Review*, 40 (2), 103–106.

Garrison, J.E., & Raynes, A.E. (1980). Results of a pilot management-by-objectives program for a community mental health outpatient service. *Community Mental Health Journal*, 16 (2), 121–129.

Green, R.S., & Attkisson, C.C. (1984). Quality assurance and program evaluation: Similarities and differences. *American Behavioral Scientist*, 27 (5), 552–582.

Joint Commission on Accreditation of Healthcare Organizations. (1990). *Accreditation manual for hospitals*. Chicago, IL.

Joint Commission on Accreditation of Healthcare Organizations. (1988). *The Joint Commission guide to quality assurance*. Chicago, IL.

Joint Commission on Accreditation of Hospitals. (1987). *Quality assurance in ambulatory care*. Chicago, IL.

Joyce, L. (1989). Giving feedback in formative evaluation: A nondirective strategy. In R.F. Conner and M. Hendricks (Eds.), *International innovations in evaluation methodology*. New Directions for Program Evaluation, no. 42, 111–118. San Francisco, CA: Jossey–Bass.

Kuechler, C.F., Velasquez, J.S., & White, M.S. (1988). An assessment of human services program outcome measures: Are they credible, feasible, useful? *Administration in Social Work*, 12 (3), 71–89.

Landsberg, G. (1985). Quality assurance activities in community mental health centers: Changes over time. *Community Mental Health Journal*, 21 (3), 189–197.

Meisenheimer, C.G. (1985). *Quality assurance: A complete guide to effective programs*. Rockville, MD: Aspen Systems.

Morris, L.L., & Fitz–Gibbon, C.T. (1978a). *Evaluator's handbook*. Beverly Hills, CA: Sage.

Morris, L.L., & Fitz–Gibbon, C.T. (1978b). *How to measure program implementation*. Beverly Hills, CA: Sage.

Moskowitz, J.M. (1989). Preliminary guidelines for reporting outcome evaluation studies of health promotion and disease prevention programs. *Evaluating health prevention programs*. New Directions for Program Evaluation, no. 43. San Francisco, CA: Jossey–Bass.

Nevo, D. (1989). Expert opinion in program evaluation. In R.F. Conner and M. Hendricks (Eds.), *International Innovations in Evaluation Methodology*. New Directions for Program Evaluation, no. 42, 85–93. San Francisco, CA: Jossey–Bass.

Pardeck, J.T., & Murphy, J.W. (1989). *Computers in human services: An overview for clinical and welfare services*. New York: Harwood Academic Publishers.

Patton, M.Q. (1982). *Practical evaluation*. Beverly Hills, CA: Sage.

Provus, M. (1971). Discrepancy evaluation for educational program improvement and assessment. Berkeley, CA: McCutchen.

Reiss, S., & Trenn, E. (1984). Consumer demand for outpatient mental health services for people with mental retardation. *Mental Retardation*, 22 (3), 112–116.

Rossi, P.H., & Freeman, H.E. (1985). *Evaluation: A systematic approach.* Beverly Hills, CA: Sage.

Sherman, P.S. (1987). Simple quality assurance measures. *Evaluation and Program Planning*, 10 (3), 227–229.

Smith, M.E. (1987). A guide to the use of simple process measures. *Evaluation and Program Planning*, 10 (3), 219–225.

Sorensen, J.E., Zelman, W., Hanbery, G.W., & Kucic, A.R. (1987). Managing mental health organizations with 25 key performance indicators. *Evaluation and Program Planning*, 10 (3), 239–247.

Spano, R.M., & Lund, S.H. (1986). Productivity and performance: Keys to survival for a hospital-based social work department. *Social Work in Health Care*, 11 (3), 25–39.

Sugarman, B. (1988). The well-managed human service organization: Criteria for a management audit. *Administration in Social Work*, 12 (4), 17–27.

Tash, W.R., & Stahler, G.J. (1984). Current status of quality assurance in mental health. *American Behavioral Scientist*, 27 (5), 608–630.

Tash, W.R., Stahler, G.J., & Rappaport, H. (1982). Evaluating quality assurance programs. In G.J. Stahler and W.R. Tash (Eds.), *Innovative approaches to mental health evaluation*. New York: Academic Press.

Velasquez, J.S., Kuechler, C.F., & White, M.S. (1986). Use of formative evaluation in a human services department. *Administration in Social Work*, 10 (2), 67–77.

Veney, J.E., & Kaluzny, A.D. (1984). *Evaluation and decision making for health services programs*. Englewood Cliffs, NJ: Prentice-Hall.

Woy, J.R., Lund, D.A., & Attkisson, C.C. (1978). Quality assurance in human service program evaluation. In C.C. Attkisson, W.A. Hargreaves, M.J. Horowitz, & J.E. Sorensen (Eds.), *Evaluation of human service programs*. New York: Academic Press.

CHAPTER 4

Preparing an Outcome Evaluation

Formative evaluations, program monitoring, and quality assurance procedures will meet the evaluation needs of some but certainly not all agencies. While program monitoring can tell you whether the program is serving those for whom the program was originally designed, it cannot demonstrate the quality of the program. Program monitoring cannot tell you if the consumers are happy with the program, if clients tend to improve, or if the program has made a difference in the community. Quality assurance procedures can tell you if the patient's treatment was appropriate, timely, and well documented. Quality assurance procedures typically are not concerned with whether the patient actually improved after he or she was discharged. To learn more about the impact of our programs, it is necessary to think in terms of whether they have successful outcomes.

■ Outcome Evaluation

Outcome evaluations (sometimes called impact, effectiveness, or summative evaluations) are another whole category of designs. Outcomes of service have been described as the "ultimate criteria of program effectiveness" (Speer & Tapp, 1976, p. 220). These designs are used when we want to know the success of a program over a period of years or in comparison with other programs. Outcome evaluations are often characterized as using "hard" or quantifiable evidence to document the success of a program—that is, what it has achieved or accomplished. Applying the driving instructor analogy from the last chapter, we can understand outcome evaluation in terms of wanting to know: (1) What percent of pupils pass the examination for their driver's license on the first try? and (2) What is the average number of lessons that are required for pupils to pass the examination? If you were looking for a driving instructor and found one who claimed that 65 percent of his driving pupils passed their test after ten lessons, but a friend tells you of another instructor who claims an 85 percent passing rate after eight lessons, which instructor would you choose? Outcome studies are intended to provide decision makers with information needed to make informed (not subjective) decisions.

■ Starting an Outcome Evaluation

Your agency director wants you to conduct an evaluation for the agency. The agency currently does some program monitoring and has made use of consultants for formative evaluations in previous years. Now, however, the agency director wants an outcome evaluation and wants you to coordinate this effort. Where do you begin? Although the director may strongly urge you to do an evaluation of the whole agency (or examine all of the agency's programs simultaneously), it is not recommended that the novice evaluator attempt a multi-program evaluation. Instead, a single program should be chosen as the object or target of the evaluation. The wisdom of this recommendation can be seen if we look at the programs contained in a single "yellow pages" phone listing for one moderate-sized mental health center, shown in figure 4.1.

It is hard not to notice the rich variety of programs that are provided in this agency. This assortment of programs prevents an evaluator from using any one tool or instrument to measure the same outcome for every program. One would expect the Day Treatment Unit to have a different set of outcomes than the Employee Assistance Program or the Chemical Dependency Outpatient Counseling Center. Thus, the evaluator starts an evaluation effort by selecting a single program to be the focus of the evaluation. (Later on, as you know more about evaluation, you may find the same evaluation procedure or the same instrument can be used with several programs simultaneously, but for now keep in mind that we are to evaluate one program at a time.)

Once a single program has been selected, it is possible to begin to

Figure 4.1: Yellow Pages Phone Book Listing for the Comprehensive Mental Health Services Agency

Main Office:	
234 W. Burton Street	885-4000
Adult Counseling Clinic	885-4001
Chemical Dependency Services	885-4911
Detoxification Center	885-4999
Inpatient Treatment Center	885-4949
Outpatient Counseling Center	885-4989
Child Guidance Program	885-4363
Community Support Services	885-4888
West Side Personal Care Home	885-4212
Campbell House	885-4175
Employee Assistance Program	885-4222
Forensic Services	885-4333
Lifestyles	885-4545
Parent's Place	885-4721
Partial Hospitalization Services	885-4110
Our Place	885-4166
Day Treatment Unit	885-4699
Passages	885-4677
Teen Help	885-4444

think about criteria that would help differentiate a "good" program from a poor program. Start by thinking in terms of single indicators. For instance, with programs designed to employ the "hard-core" unemployed, success could be measured by the percentage who actually become employed. A program designed to help agoraphobics could be evaluated based upon the percentage who, after treatment, are able to leave their homes without symptoms in order to shop, work, volunteer, or play. Bereavement counseling programs should help participants become less depressed. Treatment programs for impotence should determine the percent who are still impotent after intervention.

These examples provide illustrations of the kind of indicators needed for outcome evaluation. Evaluators do not always have to come up with these indicators on their own. If the agency already has developed goal statements and objectives for the program, outcome indicators can often be obtained from reviewing these.

Once the evaluator has a firm notion of an outcome indicator (sometimes called a dependent variable), he or she can formulate a research question or hypothesis to further focus the program evaluation. For example, the evaluator might ask of a job training program, "What percentage of clients completing the program secure full-time employment within six months of graduation from the program?" or, "What percent of persons completing the Impotency Treatment Program remain impotent?" Sometimes a program director or the evaluator might propose a hypothesis instead of a research question. An example of a hypothesis might be: "The Teen Help outpatient counseling program is more effective in combating adolescent chemical dependency than the Life Adventure program." Or, "A greater percentage of the clients of Chrysalis House will be drug-free one year after completion of the program than those who complete residential treatment at Pilot House." No matter whether you tend to think in terms of hypotheses or of questions, either will provide the necessary focal point with which to begin planning an evaluation. Once a question or hypothesis has been selected to guide the outcome study, the next step is to choose an evaluation design.

■ Understanding Outcome Evaluation Designs

When we conceptualize various strategies or ways in which we might evaluate the success of our programs, convention points to the use of evaluation designs. Fitz-Gibbon and Morris (1987) have defined an **evaluation design** as "a plan which dictates when and from whom measurements will be gathered during the course of an evaluation" (p. 9).

Evaluation designs are roughly analogous to blueprints in that they suggest a plan or model to be followed. Even though you may know nothing about building a new house, you can appreciate the carpenters' frustration if the only instructions they were given were, "Build a house." Without more elaboration, the carpenters will not know whether to begin framing for a six room house or a house with eight bedrooms. Should there be one bath or a bath adjacent to each bedroom? Will the house be brick or frame? Beyond even the basic features, there are still important details that must be worked out, such as the number of windows to be used, and their placement. To guide the carpenters as they work on the house, detailed sketches or blueprints are used. These diagrams provide guidance and direction to the carpenters in their construction.

Evaluation designs describe the key features and procedures to be followed in conducting an evaluation. They make it possible to estimate the cost of the evaluation, the length of time that will be required, and the rigorousness of the evaluation. Just as a carpenter could take a set of blueprints to another site and build a house identical to the one that had just been constructed, an evaluation design contains the necessary information to allow other evaluators to replicate or reproduce the original evaluation.

There are plenty of designs and evaluative criteria to choose from. More than twenty years ago, Suchman (1967) discussed the focus of evaluation in terms of effort, performance, adequacy, efficiency, and process. Attkisson and Broskowski (1978) defined program evaluations as having a special focus on accessibility, acceptability, comprehensiveness, integration of services, awareness, availability, continuity, and cost of services. Shipman (1989), an employee of the U.S. General Accounting Agency, described general criteria that were developed to ensure fair comparisons and comprehensive reviews of federal programs for children. Three criteria assess the need for the program: problem magnitude, problem seriousness, and duplication of services. Three criteria relate to program implementation: program fidelity, administrative efficiency, and interrelationships between the program and other programs. The last set of criteria relate to the effects of the program: achievement of intended objectives, targeting success in reaching intended clients, achievement of intended objectives, cost-effectiveness, and other effects (e.g., unforeseen or unintended effects).

Michael Patton, the author of several books on evaluation, demonstrated his creativeness by listing one hundred different types of evaluation in his 1981 text. However, unless you are particularly interested in the absolute number of variations that can be made of a small set of evaluation designs, there is little reason to contemplate, name, or enumerate all of the evaluation designs available to us. You will find it more useful to learn how to conceptualize ways of evaluating programs. Any program can be viewed from numerous perspectives and can be evaluated for various purposes.

How do you go about selecting a program evaluation design? The design follows from the research question or hypothesis and purpose of the evaluation. Evaluation designs are selected based upon what information is needed about the program. What do you want to know about the program? Often times it is useful to make a list of all the relevant questions. (If this list becomes too long, it will have to be pared down to those questions that are crucial and that realistically can be addressed.)

Once it is clear what information is needed from the evaluation, the evaluator must consider the resources available and the constraints in the agency. It has been my experience that the selection of an evaluation design is made a great deal easier if some of the realistic constraints under which the evaluation must operate are considered. I often hear from students and agency personnel such complaints as: "We can't evaluate our services. We don't have any money." Sometimes this is expressed another way: "The director is very supportive, but we don't have a computer and can't afford a consultant." Besides the problem of the cost of the evaluation, there occasionally are constraints on the type of data that the evaluator can access: "I don't know what kind of evaluation to do—the director says that we cannot recontact any of our former clients."

The amount of time allowed or available for completion of the evaluation can be another constraint. Because of the press of other concerns, an evaluation may need to be conducted and a final report prepared within three or four weeks. This constraint has a way of ruling out a number of evaluation designs.

Another consideration is the evaluation audience. On some occasions, the evaluator anticipates that the findings will be warmly received. There will be no hostility or attacks upon the evaluation methodology. Given that situation, it may not be necessary to use a very rigorous evaluation design. On other occasions, the evaluator may expect a hostile reaction to the evaluation results. Where the evaluation is expected to be attacked, the evaluator will want to provide the best possible information from the most rigorous methodology that can be applied in that setting. Fitz-Gibbon and Morris (1987) have noted, "Your task as an evaluator is to find the design that provides the most credible information in the situation you have at hand" (p. 10).

When these and other constraints have been identified, the evaluator can effectively eliminate some evaluation designs from consideration and begin to develop a plan for selection of the sample, the timing of the evaluation, and the data collection procedures. The evaluation design will dictate when and from whom measurements will be gathered during the course of an evaluation. Your task as an evaluator is to find the design that provides the most objective and convincing information that can be produced in that particular setting.

In order to reduce the confusion associated with choosing among the plethora of evaluation designs available, the designs in this chapter have been arranged in terms of the simplest (pre-experimental) designs, followed by the quasi-experimental, and then the more rigorous (experimental). Generally, the simpler designs tend to require less effort and are therefore the least expensive. Although this is not a perfect categorization scheme, thinking about designs in this way may be of benefit to beginning evaluators. Since these designs are generally covered in introductory research methods courses, they will not be presented here in great detail.

■ Low-cost, Minimal Effort Evaluation Designs

The evaluation designs in this group will appeal to those of you who have any of the following constraints:

- very little budget or staff support
- very little time in which to conduct the evaluation
- very little research expertise

The designs in this section are not very rigorous and are best suited for those occasions where an evaluation is needed but those who are requiring it are not expected to be terribly fussy. In short, the evaluation will be used not so much as a fact-finding mission as to confirm or "rubber stamp" a decision that is likely to be made (e.g., to continue funding a program).

■ One-Group Posttest Only Design

Although it may sound impressive, this evaluation design is one of the most elementary. This design involves providing an intervention or program to a group of clients and then determining if they have changed for the better. For example, suppose you are running a smoking cessation program. The goal of the program is for participants to be completely free of all smoking by the end of the intervention. Assuming this intervention ran over a number of weeks, the evaluator could determine how many of the workshop participants had stopped smoking by the time of the last session. If you started the group with eighteen participants and nine stopped smoking by the time of the last session, then your program would have experienced a 50 percent success rate. Schematically, we can represent this design:

$$X \quad O$$

where X is the intervention for some smokers, and O represents the observation or measurement of the effect of the intervention.

Note that cost, staff support, research expertise, and the amount of time required to complete the evaluation would be minimal. Since so little is involved here, the evaluator could even get the results from prior workshops and compute an average success rate for the past year (or even the past three years). This evaluative data could be displayed rather handily in a single table, as shown in table 4.1.

Table 4.1   Number of Participants Not Smoking by Last Session

| | Calendar Year 1991 | | | | Average Success Rate |
	Feb.	April	July	Oct.	
Number of Participants	24	21	25	18	
Number Not Smoking	9	9	12	9	
Success Rate	38%	43%	48%	50%	43%

Of course, the problem with this design (as any smoker would know) is that "success" could be better determined if the participants were surveyed six months or a year after completion of the intervention. Often times smokers quit for a brief period of time, only to start up again. However, tracking down former participants to learn if they are free of their smoking habit would involve some expenditure of possibly scarce funds. Postage would not be a large expense unless hundreds of questionnaires are to be mailed. Phone calls are not usually expensive (unless they involve long-distance tolls), but they do require staff time to place the calls. (However, these might be made by clerical staff in between other assignments.)

A problem with this design is that it is not rigorous. It will tell us very little about the differential effectiveness of the intervention. We would not know if just as many smokers were successful by quitting on their own. This is also a weak evaluation design because the workshop participants were not randomly selected from the population of all smokers. Without that random assignment, there is the possibility that your sample of participants does not represent all smokers in the community. Perhaps those who have enrolled in this program were encouraged to participate by their physicians because of smoking-related health problems. These smokers may be more willing to quit smoking than other (healthier) smokers because further smoking will be injurious. Your program may show better results with such "motivated" smokers than with those who do not currently have health problems related to smoking. Similarly, your program might be more effective with those who have quit previously than with those who have never been able to quit on their own. Since there was no control group, there is little "hard" evidence that it was your program and not some other influence that was responsible for the participants' success. (Perhaps physicians' stern warnings played a greater role than your program in any smoking cessation.)

■ Posttest-Only Design with Nonequivalent Groups

This design is a slight improvement over the prior design because it uses a control group. A control group is simply a comparison group. In the example of a smoking cessation program, the group of program participants is known as the experimental or treatment group. With this design, another group of smokers must be located for comparison. Ideally, this should be a similar group of smokers who are different only because they are trying to quit on their own. The evaluator compares the success rate of the workshop participants against the success rate of those smokers in the control group who were trying to quit on their own. This design might be diagrammed:

$$X \quad O_1$$
$$O_2$$

where X is the intervention, O_1 is the observation or measurement made of the group who received the intervention and O_2 is the measurement or observation made of the comparison group.

The weaknesses of this design can be seen. For one, it may or may not be easy to identify a group of smokers trying to quit on their own, and, even if you learn that those attending the smoking cessation program have a much higher success rate than the control group, you do not know that the control group was a fair comparison. There may have been great differences between the two groups in the average number of cigarettes smoked daily. Perhaps the majority of those in your smoking cessation program were young employees of a factory in town where they expected a cash bonus at the end of the year if they could quit smoking. Although you had not intended the control group to be dissimilar from the intervention group, you discover later that the control group is much older and that they have been smoking, on the average, for thirty-seven years. It could have been more difficult for this group to stop smoking than it was for young adults who had been smoking for five years or less. Since the control and treatment groups were not equivalent, an "apple and orange" type of comparison is being made. While it may be possible for you to find a control group that is more like the intervention group than the one mentioned here, the burden of trying to demonstrate the rough equivalence of the two groups is still yours.

■ *One-Group Pretest-Posttest Design*

Sometimes it is not convenient to gather a control group. We'll examine this problem later, but for now let's assume that there is not enough time prior to the starting of the intervention to coordinate a control group. However, you have been successful in locating what you consider to be a wonderful instrument to monitor the success of those participating in your program. In the situation where you can get a measurement before the intervention (this is called the **pretest**) and also get a measurement after the intervention (the **posttest**), you have the One-Group Pretest-Posttest Design. This design can be diagrammed:

$$O_1 \quad X \quad O_2$$

where the first observation (the pretest) is represented by the O_1 while the second observation (posttest) is O_2.

You could use this design when starting most new programs.

Let's say that you are going to begin a support group for women who have recently gone through a divorce. Knowing that such women are often depressed, you decide upon an intervention that is designed to reduce depression. In theory, these women should be less depressed after the ten week support group than they were when they started. After some library work, you decide to use the twenty-item depression scale (the CES-D) developed by the National Institute of Mental Health's Center for Epidemiologic Studies (Radloff, 1977) for both the pre- and post-test measures of depression.

When the group comes in for their first meeting, you explain the purpose of the pretest, respond to any questions, and then distribute the instrument. At the final meeting of the group, you administer the same depression scale a second time. Having both the pretest and posttest data, it is possible to determine what percentage of the support group showed an improvement by the end of the tenth week.

Since two measurements were obtained with a standardized instrument, success could be measured in terms of (1) any decrease in the percentage of support group members who were no longer depressed or (2) improvements in the group's average score from pretest to posttest. This information would be valuable in terms of helping future consumers or policymakers decide whether the support group is effective. This evaluation design would meet many agencies' needs for evaluation.

However, this design is inadequate on those occasions when it becomes important to establish that it was the intervention—and the intervention only—that produced the improvement. For instance, perhaps you have observed that most persons who are depressed immediately after a divorce tend to improve with the passage of time—whether or not they get professional help. In other words, this design does not eliminate other explanations that might actually be responsible for the improvement. In many situations, it may not be necessary to rule out these alternative explanations. One therapist might say, "So what if it really was the passage of time and not the intervention? The vast majority of my clients improved in the past ten weeks and that, after all, is the reason they came here."

Because this evaluation design is not very rigorous, it cannot rule out alternative explanations, such as changes due to greater maturity (a potential explanation to be especially considered when children are involved), or the effect of repeated use of the instrument (testing), or several others. On those occasions when there is a need to rule out alternative explanations (for instance, you may want to market the intervention), you can employ more rigorous (experimental) evaluation designs. Weiss (1972) advocated the use of experimental evaluation designs in those situations where

> it is for purposes outside the immediate program that experimental design is best suited. Decisions on the order of continuation or abandonment of the program, decisions on whether to advocate nation-wide use of the program model—these require great confidence in the validity of the research, and therefore experimental design. Other types of decisions may not need such rigor, at least initially. (Pp. 66–67)

■ Quasi-Experimental and Experimental Evaluation Designs

The evaluation designs described so far can be thought of as elementary or beginning designs. Campbell and Stanley (1963) call them pre-experimental designs. Methodologically, they are weak, because they cannot rule out alternative explanations for any observed changes. While the pre-experimental designs may provide information that satisfies friendly supporters of programs, they cannot provide conclusive evidence that it was the intervention alone that was responsible for changes. Fortunately, there are other, more rigorous evaluation designs available. Since the next group of designs tend to require more planning, and more extensive involvement with control groups, and may result in more data to analyze, they are more expensive and require more resources than the pre-experimental designs.

Envision program evaluation efforts as a series of steps with formative evaluation, program monitoring, and quality assurance representing the first step and pre-experimental evaluation designs the second step. Quasi-experimental designs would be the third step, and experimental designs would be the top step. Quasi-experimental designs are better than the pre-experimental designs but not so good as the experimental designs for providing "hard evidence" that the intervention was responsible for the observed changes. Because they do not use randomization and may not always involve a control group, **quasi-experimental designs** draw their name from not quite being experiments.

■ *Nonequivalent Control Group Design*

The Nonequivalent Control Group Design is one of the most commonly used evaluation designs. In this design a group of persons who are similar in composition to the group receiving the intervention is used as the control in both pretest and posttest observations. This design can be diagrammed:

where O_1 and O_3 are pretests for the intervention and control groups, respectively; O_2 and O_4 are posttests for the intervention and control groups.

Suppose you are an evaluation consultant to a school principal who wants to implement a drug education program with all seventh, eighth, and ninth graders. If the principal, the parents, or the school board has determined that all of the students will receive the intervention, then it may not be possible to develop a control group from within the same school. It may be necessary to locate a control group in a different school or community.

With this design, the control group can be used to help eliminate alternative explanations. It is quite possible, for instance, that any increase in the intervention group's knowledge about drugs at the time of posttest could have occurred merely from interaction with older students or their own firsthand experience with drugs. Perhaps as seventh, eighth, and ninth graders mature, they read the newspapers to a greater extent and thus "educate" themselves about the dangers of drugs. These explanations and the effectiveness of the intervention can be understood by making comparisons to the control group. If those receiving the intervention are more knowledgeable at the time of the posttest than those in the control group, then the intervention appears to have been a success. If, however, the control group shows the same gains in knowledge about drugs as the experimental group, then you would know that it was not the intervention that was responsible but some other factor or combination of factors.

The problem with this design is that while you could establish that the seventh, eighth, and ninth graders in the control group were equivalent to those receiving the intervention in terms of knowledge about drugs at the time of pretest, students receiving the drug awareness program could simultaneously be exposed to other influences or have access to resources that were not available in the comparison school. For example, suppose that the principal in the intervention school has been especially active in getting local businesses to contribute computers to the school. Let's further suppose that while the great availability of computers in this school has nothing directly to do with the drug awareness program, use of the computers by a large majority of the student body serves to increase their reading skills. Even though you were concerned only about their scores on the instrument that measured their drug awareness, as the children in the intervention school learned to read better, they learned more on their own about the dangers of drugs. So, it may not have been the intervention program alone that was responsible for the improvement in test scores, but the double whammy of greater access to computers in addition to the drug awareness program. Conversely, if the control group showed greater improvement, it may have been the influence of factors not known to the evaluator (such as pairing every student with a volunteer reading tutor) that had the effect (as students began reading more on their own, they learned about the dangers of experimenting with illicit drugs).

It is easy to see the importance of obtaining groups that are similar not only in the skill, behavior, or characteristic being observed, but also in other major variables. What kinds of variables are important? (This question becomes especially critical if we have to go to another school to obtain a control group.) Would it be fair to compare a suburban school with an inner city school? If one school was situated in a low income, high-dropout area, would both schools need to be? How essential is it for the teachers to be similar with respect to commitment to teaching or years of experience?

Although finding a comparison group that is as alike as possible to the intervention group may be a problem at times, in other situations it presents no problem at all. For instance, the military attempts to produce companies of soldiers that are pretty similar to one another. There is a presumed equivalence in the comparison of one company of soldiers to another company. An example of this has been reported by Majchrzak (1986). Evaluating a program designed to reduce unauthorized absenteeism in the Marine Corps, she used the Nonequivalent Control Group Design because complete random assignment could not be employed. Majchrzak first matched available infantry and artillery battalions on the variables of deployment schedule, mission, regiment, and tenure of commander and then randomly assigned battalions either to a control condition or to participation in the unauthorized absenteeism prevention program. All subordinate companies were then asked to participate in the experiment. This procedure yielded twenty treatment companies and twenty control companies of Marines.

■ Time Series Design

Another quasi-experimental design is called the Time Series or sometimes the Interrupted Time Series Design. The advantage of this design over some of the others is that it allows the evaluator to detect trends. If there is a trend in the data (maybe children in remedial math classes begin to do better simply as a result of growing older), this gradual process would become apparent. It could be observed prior to the start of an intervention and monitored afterwards. We can use the following notation to represent this design:

$$O_1 \quad O_2 \quad O_3 \quad X \quad O_4 \quad O_5 \quad O_6$$

where O_1 is the first measurement, O_2 is the second measurement, and O_6 is the sixth measurement

Usually this design is depicted as having three equally spaced observations before the intervention and three (separated by the same time intervals) afterwards. However, as with other designs, this may be modified according to the needs of the evaluator. There would be nothing wrong with having four or more observations prior to the intervention and the same number (or perhaps fewer) after the intervention. The time intervals between measurements might be days, weeks, or even months. The lengths of these intervals are determined by the evaluator. This type of design relies upon **longitudinal data**. Longitudinal data are collected at several different times during the course of the study.

The time series designs are especially useful when finding nonequivalent control groups is a problem. These designs are often the design of choice when evaluating the impact of new legislation or policies. For instance, Shore and Maguin (1988) used a time series design to determine that the passage of a new law in Kansas that prohibited plea bargaining in Driving Under the Influence (DUI) arrests resulted in a decrease of eight fatal accidents per month during the eighteen month postintervention period. This translated to a 20 percent reduction in the number of fatal accidents. Of course, the revision of the law alone was not responsible for the decrease. Accompanying the change in the law was widespread publicity, media coverage, and an increase in DUI arrests. Still, the authors concluded that:

The Kansas experience supports deterrence theory in that the increase in certainty and severity of punishment provided by the change in the state's Driving Under the Influence law was associated with a reduction in those accidents which are more frequently linked with the combination of drinking and driving. (P. 253)

Another interesting use of a time series design was reported by Ross and White (1987), who explored the effect that seeing one's name in the newspaper had on persons convicted of shoplifting, impaired driving, or failing to take the breathalyzer test. They concluded that publishing the court results of persons arrested for shoplifting in the newspaper resulted in a decrease in the number of shoplifting incidents. However, publishing the names of impaired drivers and persons refusing the breathalyzer did not reduce their numbers.

■ Multiple Time Series Design

While the Time Series Design seemed to work well tracing the benefits of legislation within Kansas, there is at least one alternative explanation that cannot be ruled out. The number of DUI arrests may be decreasing across the nation not as a result of local legislation but due to such factors as increased awareness of health risks and decreased drinking among Americans. One might argue that the Time Series design suffers from tunnel vision—its scope does not encompass what may be going on in the larger world. The problems with this design are eliminated by adding a control group:

$$O_1 \quad O_3 \quad O_5 \quad X \quad O_7 \quad O_9 \quad O_{11}$$
$$O_2 \quad O_4 \quad O_6 \quad \quad O_8 \quad O_{10} \quad O_{12}$$

where O_1 is the first measurement of the intervention group; O_2 is the first measurement of the control group; O_{11} is the third measurement for the intervention group following the treatment; O_{12} is the sixth measurement of the control group.

With this design, an evaluator could identify a control state (in terms of rural-urban mixture, the rate of DUIs per 100,000 population, etc.) or use several states as controls. If there were national trends (such as for a decreased number of arrests for drinking while driving), this should be picked up among the control state(s), and the evaluator would not be so quick to conclude that it was the new legislation that brought about fewer DUIs.

■ Eliminating Alternative Explanations _____

The designs that have been presented to this point are subject to problems with internal validity. That is, these designs cannot conclude that it was the intervention alone that accounted for any observed changes. The pre-experimental and quasi-experimental designs cannot rule out many (or most) of the alternative explanations that skeptics of a program's success might be quick to identify. The strongest and most credible information about the effectiveness of an intervention comes from experimental designs. Efforts to eliminate the alternative explanations result in the most rigorous designs but also tend to increase the costs of evaluation.

Before we begin discussing experimental designs, let's look at alternative explanations that sometimes make researchers (or critics) question evaluation results.

■ *Threats to the Internal Validity of an Evaluation*

History

The role of history can be understood if we consider significant events occurring at the local, state, or national level. For instance, in August of 1987, twenty-seven children were killed outside of Cincinnati when a drunk driver crashed into a bus returning from a weekend outing. Assume that prior to this you had been asked to evaluate a public education program designed to reduce the number of DUIs and planned on using a relatively weak evaluation design (for instance, the One-Group Time Series Design) to monitor the number of arrests for driving under the influence. Some months after the accident, you conclude that the decrease in DUI arrests was due to the intervention, when it probably was the tragedy that resulted in fewer drivers driving while intoxicated.

Without a control group, you might not detect the influence this tragedy had on drivers' attitudes and behavior. Such an event could also be responsible for a greater number of DUI arrests as a consequence of the public becoming less tolerant and more often reporting drunk drivers to law enforcement officials. Law enforcement officials themselves might decide to be more vigilant and to make more arrests for DUI. The comparison between the intervention and the control communities (or states) would help the evaluator to understand any national trends in DUIs.

Maturation

Sometimes problems improve as a result of the passage of time. An evaluator might conclude that an intervention was effective when actually the subjects receiving the intervention matured or the passing of time served to make the problem less acute. For instance, persons suffering from the loss of a loved one normally grieve less and are less depressed as time passes. While the program staff may wish to think that it was the support group that made all of the difference, unless there is a control group it is difficult to rule out the role that the passage of time alone may have played.

Testing

If you are using a design (e.g., the Times Series Design) where the same test is administered sequentially a number of times, the persons receiving the intervention may show improvement in their scores as a result of figuring out "correct" responses on the test. On the other hand, their scores could also decrease as a result of becoming careless and bored with repeated use of the same test. Without a comparison group, it is difficult to rule out possible testing effects.

Instrumentation

Just as those enrolled in a program can become bored by taking the same test on numerous occasions, the evaluator or other persons making observations might subtly or unconsciously modify the procedures. Instead of counting every time a hyperactive child got out of his seat in the classroom, the weary observer by the end of the study may be counting only the incidents when the child got out of his seat and was corrected by the teacher. Observations ought to be made in the same way throughout the course of the evaluation. Tests should be administered the same way (e.g., in the same setting, at the same time of day, using the same rules or set of instructions) each time. The effect of this threat to the internal validity of a study can be quickly understood in a situation where, for example, a teacher gave more than the allowed time to a class to finish the posttest and less to the control group. Merely because they had more time, the intervention group might score higher than the control group.

Selection

This alternative explanation plays a potential role whenever control groups are used without random assignment. Suppose you were to start a new intervention and invite former clients (who may still be having problems) to attend. If there is improvement among these clients, will it be due to the recent intervention? Or did the improvement come about because it built upon their prior involvement? Taking another example, suppose you want to start a new support group, and you want to open it up to anyone in the community. To announce the beginning of the support group, you run an invitation in the local newspaper. If this group later shows improvement, it may have been due to the fact that the individuals who participated were unlike others in the community with the same problem. Maybe those who answered the newspaper article were more literate (they read the ad in the newspaper), better educated, more assertive, or more intelligent. One would be left with the nagging thought that maybe the intervention was effective only with the kind of people who would answer an ad. This group may not be representative of the rest of the people in the community with the same problem who failed to respond to the invitation.

Mortality

Mortality refers to the loss of subjects from the evaluation. This threat to the internal validity is a problem for those evaluations that stretch over a long period of time. Professionals in the human services frequently find that their clients move (sometimes without leaving forwarding addresses), drop out of treatment, get locked up, become sick, and sometimes become rehospitalized. For various reasons, it is not at all uncommon to have fewer participants in a program at its conclusion than when it started. A problem exists when too many of the participants drop out. Any commonality among those who drop out could bias the study. For instance, suppose you were running a program for parents of adolescents. Twelve parents sign up to learn how to better communicate with their adolescents. A few parents drop out during the nine week program, but this doesn't concern you because you can objectively show that the program is working—that communication is improving among those parents who remain. However, as you begin to examine your data, you realize that the parents who remained in the program were all college graduates. The parents who dropped out were high school graduates. While the intervention may have worked, it did so only for parents who were college graduates.

■ Protection Against Alternative Explanations

The best protection against alternative explanations for the results you note in an evaluation is to control them. Control is made possible by anticipating the kinds of problems that may be encountered. For example, if you expect that you may have mortality problems, build in an incentive. With children, there could be some sort of a party on the last session or after the posttest data have been obtained. With adults, money is an incentive that works reasonably well. But when funds are not available, the evaluator can be creative in other ways, perhaps by issuing "Certificates of Completion" for the intervention group and "Certificates of Appreciation" for the control group. If you expect that repeated testing may present some problems, explore whether there are different or alternate forms of the same test.

If you suspect that critics of the evaluation may say things like, "Well, no wonder! The comparison groups weren't even similar!" then you need to insure that the groups in the study are as similar as possible. Where random assignment isn't possible, you can gain credibility by matching group participants with their controls on important variables (e.g., years of education, income, sex) and then using a statistical test to determine that the groups are comparable. (See chapter 8 for information on the appropriate statistical test to use). If a standardized scale is being used, the evaluator might compare the average pretest scores of the control group and the intervention group (Nonequivalent Control Group Design) using the t-test (explained in chapter 8). The t-test will tell you whether differences between the two groups are statistically significant. If there are no significant differences between the control and intervention groups on important variables, then the groups are very similar.

Another way to produce a credible evaluation is to use a rigorous evaluation design known as an experimental design. These designs eliminate alternative explanations through the use of random selection and assignment; persons are assigned to either the intervention or control groups without any form of bias. Unexpected improvement within a control group developed with randomized procedures allows you to suspect that some alternative explanation (such as history, maturation, or testing) was having an influence.

Before we leave our discussion of alternative explanations, it would be well to note that there are many more threats to the internal validity of a study than have been identified in this brief explanation. As an evaluator, you need to develop a sensitivity or an appreciation for factors that can influence the results of the evaluation. For instance, those involved in an evaluation may be keenly aware that they are being tested and may work harder than they normally would to make a good impression. Any "over-cooperation" will confound the evaluator's data and make it more difficult to understand the true impact of any intervention. If you would like to read more about additional threats to the internal validity of a study, consult Campbell and Stanley (1963), Cook and Campbell (1979), or Mitchell and Jolley (1988).

■ Experimental Designs

The "classic" experimental design is the standard against which other designs are compared. Experimental research designs are the most rigorous and represent the "ideal" for inferring that an intervention either did or did not have an effect. In an **experimental design**, participants are randomly selected and randomly assigned to either the intervention group or to the control group. The notation for the basic experiment is:

$$R \quad O_1 \quad X \quad O_2$$
$$R \quad O_3 \quad \quad O_4$$

where R stands for subjects who have been randomly selected and assigned to either the intervention or control groups; where O_1 is a pretest or first observation of the intervention group; where O_4 is the posttest or second observation of the control group.

Since the groups are equivalent at the start of the study (this is guaranteed by the random assignment), this design is inoculated against most threats to its internal validity. (Can you see how the evaluator would be able to determine if there were selection bias or effects from maturation or history?)

As an example of this design, let's consider the program evaluation of a forty-bed residential treatment program that provides milieu therapy. Velasques and McCubbin (1980) evaluated such a program using an experimental design where applicants were randomly assigned to either the residential program or informed that they would not be able to enter the program for six months; for the latter group, alternative forms of health services were available (inpatient hospitalization in a different program, day treatment, or another residential facility not providing milieu therapy).

Nine different instruments were used to collect data about potential applicants. There were ratings by the program director for such dimensions as degree of psychiatric impairment and social adjustment. Other measures (the Tennessee Self-Concept Scale and the Problem Solving Scale) were completed by the applicants. Analysis revealed strong evidence that the residential treatment program increased the participants' responsibility for self, social participation, and continuation in employment, improved their self-concept, and reduced the probability of hospitalization six months later. The authors concluded, "The consistency of findings from this experimental investigation present a clear and fairly convincing picture of the effectiveness of this residential program" (p. 357).

■ Posttest-Only Control Group Design

Another experimental design, the Posttest-Only Control Group Design, is an elegant modification of the basic experimental design. Even without the initial pretests, it is a useful experimental design, ideal for those situations where it was not or is not possible to conduct a pretest or where a pretest could conceivably affect the posttest results. This design is also advantageous on those occasions when matching pretests with posttests is not possible or desired.

Random selection and assignment of subjects establish equivalence between the control and experimental groups. Measurement of the control group (O_2) serves as a pretest measure for comparison with the experimental group's posttest (O_1). This design can be diagrammed:

$$R \quad X \quad O_1$$
$$R \quad \quad O_2$$

where R represents subjects who have been randomly selected and assigned to either the control or intervention groups; O_1 is the first measurement (a posttest because it occurs after the intervention); O_2 is the first measurement of the control group.

As an example of this design, imagine that you are a social worker in a forensic program. Your boss, who is the county's prosecuting attorney, asked you to start an intervention program for persons who have been arrested for shoplifting. Careful screening will eliminate any persons who have ever been arrested so that all of your clientele will be first-time offenders. If these first-time offenders complete a four week intervention program on consecutive Saturday mornings, the record of their arrest will be erased. Because the prosecuting attorney will be running for reelection in about two years, she asks that you design a sound evaluation component so that she can point to the program's success in her election campaign.

Assume that there will be more first-time offenders eligible for participation in the intervention program than can be initially served. Given this situation, the only fair procedure would be a random selection where some first-time offenders are chosen to participate in the program and others either are not invited to participate or are informed that they can participate at a later date.

In this example, there is no need to conduct a pretest because all of the persons eligible for participation in the program have already been arrested for shoplifting, and it has been determined that they are first-time offenders. Vitally important is the measure that will be used to gauge the success of the intervention program. Let's say that you and the prosecuting attorney agree that the best indicator of success would be whether the first-time offenders are arrested again for shoplifting. For simplicity's sake, let's suppose that the posttest data consists of the number of arrests of those who received the intervention during the period beginning one month following their arrest and concluding six months later. The longest wait for the start of the intervention group would be one month; this means that if the intervention is effective, there should be no shoplifting arrests among these program participants in the five month period following the intervention. Similarly, arrest data will be examined for the control group beginning one month from the time of their arrest and will conclude six months later. During this time, they will receive no intervention.

If the shoplifters cannot be randomly assigned to the treatment or to the control conditions, or if the intervention cannot be postponed for those selected to be in the control group, the evaluator could not use this design. The evaluator must rely upon a less rigorous design such as the Nonequivalent Control Group Design. With the quasi-experimental design, there is more flexibility and several options present themselves.

Since not all shoplifters will agree to participating in an intervention program (some will refuse to attend, some will attend once and never return, some would rather pay a fine), those who choose not to participate constitute a "natural" comparison group for the Nonequivalent Control Group Design. If the intervention is successful, fewer of those receiving the intervention should be rearrested than those who were in the comparison group.

Another option would be to use historical or archival data for the comparison. In this instance, the control group would be those first-time shoplifting offenders who received no intervention (simply because it was not available). The evaluator could select a sample of shoplifters who were arrested during some interval of time (e.g., the year prior to the start of the intervention program) and then examine arrest data for each of these first-time offenders for a period of time comparable to that of the intervention group. If the intervention is effective, the intervention group should have fewer repeat shoplifters during a twelve month (or similar) time interval.

■ Solomon Four-Group Design

The Solomon Four-Group Design is another elaboration of the basic experimental design. As can be seen from the diagram below, this design requires that two groups receive the intervention and that two groups do not. Only two groups are given a pretest, but all four groups are administered the posttest.

This design is very rigorous because it allows the evaluator to maximally control for alternative explanations and thus increases the confidence that can be placed in the findings. However, this design also requires more planning and coordination, and as a result, not many evaluators will have the opportunity to utilize it.

$$R \quad O_1 \quad X \quad O_2$$
$$R \quad O_3 \quad \quad O_4$$
$$R \quad \quad X \quad O_5$$
$$R \quad \quad \quad O_6$$

where R represents random selection and assignment to one of the four conditions (two with treatment); O_1 and O_3 are the only pretests; O_2, O_4, O_5, and O_6 are posttests.

As an example of this design, imagine you are the director of a summer camp for children who have come from economically deprived homes. Many of the children have been victims of abuse or neglect. You feel that the summer camp experience significantly increases their self-esteem and improves their outlook on life. You know that if you demonstrate such results to funding sources, they will be interested in helping with the expense of the summer camp. You are anxious to conduct an evaluation that is as strong and rigorous as possible. In this example, you would randomly select and assign eligible children to one of the four conditions specified in the design: two groups would attend summer camp and two groups would not.

While a simple experimental design could be used, you are concerned that the children, being anxious to please and to show that camp was meaningful to them, might infer the nature of the self-esteem instrument and by their responses indicate improved self-esteem, when this may not reflect reality. The more times a test is given to a group, the greater the likelihood that the subjects can understand or anticipate the purpose of the test. One of the advantages of the Solomon Four-Group Design is that any influence of testing can be identified since two of the four groups are tested only once.

A major problem with this design may come from the fact that you may not believe that some children should be denied the experience of summer camp. Depending upon the length of the camp experience and the timing of the posttest, it may be possible for all of the children in the control groups to also participate in summer camp—they attend after they have finished serving in control groups. This would be possible in those situations where the duration of summer camp is only one or two weeks for each group of campers. The issue here is whether a one or two week camp experience increases self-esteem—not whether any improvements to self-esteem are maintained throughout the summer or the subsequent years. If you were concerned about whether the gains in self-esteem were maintained, the posttests would be planned for six months or a year after the completion of the intervention—which would prevent the control group from attending camp in the same summer as those in the intervention group.

■ Chapter Recap

The aim of this chapter has been to present the traditional approaches used in evaluating human service programs. By providing a range of designs, from the not very rigorous to the experimental designs, it is hoped that one can be found for every situation. While the "standard" may be the experimental design, it is not always feasible to implement it. This can be seen in the way authors discuss their choice of an evaluation design. Velasquez and Lyle (1985), for instance, wrote, "Although random assignment . . . was technically achievable, strong opposition to this approach from some officials resulted in the selection of a less rigorous design" (p. 148). In another example, Toseland, Kabat, and Kemp (1983) noted, in writing about a smoking-cessation program designed by a clinical social worker,

> The authors used a quasi-experimental, nonequivalent control-group design to evaluate the Breathe Free program. Because of ethical considerations, the American Lung Association of New York State thought it was not appropriate to randomly assign those who wanted to stop smoking to a true experimental treatment-control group design. A control group of persons on a waiting list was also rejected because it was believed that subjects should not have to wait for treatment, that they might lose their motivation to attend a program, and that they might decide to attend other programs if they were placed on a waiting list. (P. 14)

The choice of an evaluation design is often the evaluator's alone, although this is clearly not always the case. The design should follow logically from the questions or hypotheses that need to be explored. However, there are circumstances that do not warrant evaluation. Carol Weiss (1972), in her now classic book, noted that evaluation is not worth doing in four kinds of circumstances:

1. When there are no questions about the program. . . . Decisions about its future either do not come up or have already been made.
2. When the program has no clear orientation. . . . The program shifts and changes, wanders around and seeks direction.

3. When people who should know cannot agree on what the program is try-ing to achieve. If there are vast discrepancies in perceived goals, evalua-tion has no ground to stand on.
4. When there is not enough money or staff sufficiently qualified to conduct the evaluation. Evaluation is a demanding business, calling for time, money, imagination, tenacity, and skill. (Pp. 10–11)

It should also be noted that in any evaluation you may use more than one design. You may use multiple approaches (remember the triangula-tion discussion in the chapter on needs assessment?), you may use several different instruments, or you may even employ a different design with each instrument.

Suchman (1967) made some important observations regarding the choice of evaluation design. He observed that ultimately the best design is the one most suitable for the purpose of the study, and since designs often reflect compromises dictated by practical considerations, there is no such thing as a single correct design. Questions and hypotheses can be explored using different methods or approaches. This thought was re-cently expressed by the Ann Hartman (1990), editor-in-chief of *Social Work*: "This editor takes the position that there are many truths and there are many ways of knowing. Each discovery contributes to our knowledge, and each way of knowing deepens our understanding and adds another dimension to our view of the world" (p. 3).

QUESTIONS FOR CLASS DISCUSSION

1. Discuss conducting program evaluations in various community agencies. Do some of the designs in this chapter seem to "fit" some programs better than others? Why?
2. Discuss the advantages and disadvantages of an evaluator monitor-ing similar programs in different agencies using these four questions:
   a. Did this program have objectives derived from the goals for the program?
   __ Yes __ No __ Cannot be determined
   b. Did the program serve as many clients as projected?
   __ Yes __ No __ Cannot be determined
   c. Did the agency conduct an outcome evaluation of this program?
   __ Yes __ No __ Cannot be determined
   d. Did the agency staff seem committed to evaluating the outcome of their program?
   __ Yes __ No __ Cannot be determined
3. Discuss the problems of using a self-report questionnaire with smok-ers in a smoking cessation clinic. What percent might be motivated to

indicate that they had stopped when in fact they were still smoking? What would constitute "hard evidence"?

4. Have the class identify a local program that would be interesting to evaluate using one of the designs in this chapter. What evaluation design would be used? What would be the primary outcome variable? What would be the threats to the internal validity? How would you control for these? What would be the data collection procedures? Who would need to assist with the evaluation? Who would be the subjects?

5. Discuss for any specific program the various outcome indicators that might be chosen in a program evaluation. Are some more valuable than others for showing an impact the program is having upon the lives of clients?

MINI-PROJECTS: EXPERIENCING EVALUATION FIRSTHAND

1. Browse through professional journals in a field of your choice to find the report of an evaluation using a nonequivalent control group design. Read the article and critique it. If you don't wish to take the time to find one on your own, either of the following can be used:

> Bennett, S.F. and Lavrakas, P.J. (1989). Community-based crime prevention: An assessment of the Eisenhower Foundation's Neighborhood Program. *Crime and Delinquency*, 35 (3), 345–364.

> Pennell, S., Curtis, C., Henderson, J. and Tayman, J. (1989). Guardian Angels: A unique approach to crime prevention. *Crime and Delinquency*, 35 (3), 378–400.

2. A program has recently been funded to provide intensive services to the homeless. The mission of the program is to identify those who, with the necessary supportive services, can realistically be expected to be employed and self-sustaining within three years. Design a program evaluation for this project. Be sure to identify your evaluation design and other necessary details.

REFERENCES AND RESOURCES

Attkisson, C.C., & Broskowski, A. (1978). Evaluation and the emerging human service concept. In C.C. Attkisson, W.A. Hargreaves, M.J. Horowitz, and J.E. Sorensen (Eds.), *Evaluation of human service programs*. New York: Academic Press.

Campbell, D.T., & Stanley, J.C. (1963). *Experimental and quasi-experimental designs for research*. Chicago, IL: Rand McNally.

Cook, T.D., & Campbell, D.T. (1979). *Quasi-experimentation: Design & analysis issues for field settings*. Chicago, IL: Rand McNally.

Fitz-Gibbon, C.T., & Morris, L.L. (1987) *How to design a program evaluation*. Beverly Hills, CA: Sage.

Hartman, A. (1990). Many ways of knowing. *Social Work*, 35 (1), 3–4.

Majchrzak, A. (1986). Keeping marines in the field: Results of a field experiment. *Evaluation and Program Planning*, 9 (3), 253–265.

Mitchell, M., & Jolley, J. (1988) *Research design explained*. New York: Holt, Rinehart and Winston.

Radloff, L.S. (1977). The CES-D Scale: A self-report depression scale for research in the general population. *Applied Psychological Measurement*, 3 (1), 385–401.

Ross, A.S., & White, S. (1987). Shoplifting, impaired driving, and refusing the breathalyzer. *Evaluation Review*, 11 (2), 254–269.

Shipman, S. (1989). General criteria for evaluating social programs. *Evaluation Practice*, 10 (1), 20–26.

Shore, E.R., & Maguin, E. (1988). Deterrence of drinking-driving: The effect of changes in the Kansas driving under the influence law. *Evaluation and Program Planning*, 11, (3), 245–254.

Speer, D.C., & Tapp, J.C. (1976). Evaluation of mental health service effectiveness: A "start up" model for established programs. *American Journal of Orthopsychiatry*, 46 (2), 217–228.

Suchman, E.A. (1967). *Evaluating research: Principles and practice in public service and social action programs*. New York: Russell Sage Foundation.

Toseland, R.W., Kabat, D. & Kemp, K. (1983). Evaluation of a smoking–cessation group treatment program. *Social Work Research and Abstracts*, 19 (1), 12–19.

Velasquez, J.S., & Lyle, C.G. (1985). Day versus residential treatment for juvenile offenders: The impact of program evaluation. *Child Welfare*, 64 (2), 145–156.

Velasquez, J.S., & McCubbin, H.I. (1980). Toward establishing the effectiveness of community–based residential treatment: Program evaluation by experimental research. *Journal of Social Service Research*, 3 (4), 337–359.

Weiss, C.H. (1972) *Evaluation Research: Methods of assessing program effectiveness*. Englewood Cliffs, NJ: Prentice–Hall.

CHAPTER 5

Additional Evaluation Designs

There is no single model, design, or "recipe" to follow in planning the best way to evaluate a social or human service program. While we, as evaluators, might have a preference for a particular approach, each program and evaluative situation brings a unique set of considerations which influence the choice of an evaluation design. In addition to the agency constraints associated with recruiting the assistance of staff and clients and the amount of time and monetary resources available, the very nature of the questions asked about the program have an effect upon the evaluation design. Just as there will be occasions when randomization cannot be employed or when suitable control groups cannot be located, there will be occasions when some of the questions being asked will be determined by the cost of operating the program relative to other programs or in terms of cost-effectiveness. The evaluator may feel that the more traditional designs explained in chapter 4 are not particularly well-suited. In an attempt to anticipate evaluative situations where additional designs could be useful, several more approaches are offered in this chapter. They can be used individually or conjointly with other designs (remember the concept of triangulation explained earlier?).

■ Cost-Effectiveness Designs

Cronbach (1982) noted that practically all of the literature on evaluation speaks of it in terms of serving decision makers. Besides wanting to know if a program is effective, decision makers may also be concerned with the cost of this effectiveness. They want evidence that programs operate efficiently and are cost-effective. To illustrate this point somewhat ludicrously, purchasing each member of a self-esteem group a new Mercedes might wondrously increase their self-esteem—but at what cost? Could the same results be achieved with less expense? Because of limited funds, policymakers are increasingly requesting program evaluations that look at the cost relative to a program's accomplishment.

While the popular conception may be that "efficiency" is synonymous with "least costly," Mayer (1985) asserts that efficiency should be understood in terms of "trying to achieve the most of a desired benefit in relation to a given level of expenditure. Efficiency is a way of choosing among alternative means for achieving a standard end" (p. 10). Since the least costly approaches may not always be the most effective, it is important to recognize that choices must be comparable. For each alternative program, clients must receive about the same quality of care. Once this assumption can be made, the question becomes: "Which means of delivering such care will serve the most number of people at the lowest cost?" (p. 10).

As an example, one group of evaluators interested in increasing safety belt use examined the effectiveness of four different evaluation approaches and the corresponding cost of each approach. They found that the approach which combined persuasive communications and incentives resulted in a 20 percent point increase in safety belt use. The total cost of this approach was $770. The cost-effectiveness of this approach could be viewed as $38.50 per percentage point increase ($770/20). Or, it could be computed in terms of the cost it took to convert each driver to a safety belt wearer. Twenty-one drivers began wearing safety belts at a cost of $37 each ($770/21).

Another approach that proved to be effective was a more intensive campaign which combined persuasive communications, monitoring, prompts, and incentives. While this approach was actually more effective (a 28 percentage point increase in safety belt use), the costs for this approach were also greater ($5,360). In terms of cost-effectiveness, this was a cost of $191 per percentage point increase or $97 dollars for each new driver who started wearing a safety belt (Simons-Morton, Brink & Bates,

1987). Which of these two programs would you choose, the slightly less effective but cheaper program or the more effective and more expensive program?

Another set of evaluators were interested in comparing the cost-effectiveness of alcohol treatment in a partial hospital program and extended inpatient treatment. It was found that the partial hospitalization program (1) cost almost $1,700 less per client and (2) produced more abstinent days per $100 of treatment costs, and that (3) estimates of total treatment costs per abstinent client also favored the partial hospitalization program over the extended inpatient treatment ($18,935 versus $21,637) (McCrady, Lonabaugh, Fink, Stout, Beattie, & Ruggieri-Authelet, 1986).

Cost-effectiveness studies have also been used to show that foster family care for frail elderly persons would result in major savings to hospitals (by reducing the wait for nursing home beds to become available) and in savings to Medicaid (by providing less expensive care than nursing home care). One study showed that foster family care provided not only cheaper care than hospitals or nursing homes but also better quality care. Vandivort, Kurren, and Braun (1984) reported that a greater percentage of foster family care clients than nursing home residents showed improved functioning in activities required for independent living (e.g., bathing, dressing, self-feeding).

In another example, Weinrott, Jones, and Howard (1982) explored whether community-based group homes for youths using a Teaching Family Model (TFM) were cost-effective in the treatment of delinquency when these homes were compared to other group homes and facilities. (In TFM group homes five to eight youths are supervised by a young married couple.) A quasi-experimental design was used to estimate the program costs and results, and to translate these into monetary values. While the TFM homes were less expensive to operate on a per diem basis and in terms of average length of stay, TFM and comparison group homes were found to be equally successful in terms of reduced deviant behavior, occupational status, and social/personality adjustment. In other words, the authors could not show superiority of the TFM homes over the comparison programs when "global measures" of effectiveness were considered.

Other examples of the use of a cost-effectiveness evaluation include: determining if the cost of voluntary surgical contraceptions in Guatemala are more expensive in fixed clinics than when mobile teams are used (McBride, Bertrand, Santiso, & Fernandez, 1987) and if community follow-up services reduce rehospitalization and the overall cost of mental health care of persons discharged from an acute psychiatric unit (Solberg, 1983).

Cost-effectiveness evaluations have also been used to compare computer-assisted instruction with alternatives—cross-age tutoring, reduction in class size, and increases in daily instructional time. Levin, Glass, and Meister (1987) found that peer tutoring and combined peer and adult tutoring had the best cost-effectiveness ratios, followed by computer-assisted instruction. For the same cost outlay, peer tutoring produced almost four times as large an effect on reading and mathematic achievement as reducing class size or increasing instructional time.

Our final example is one reported by Armstrong (1983). A Family Support Center was designed for families considered to be at risk for mal-treating their preschool-age children. The cost of running the program for one year was approximately $180,000. By relying upon previous re-search studies for similar at-risk populations, Armstrong estimated the probability and associated costs of outpatient, inpatient, foster care, and special education that could be expected to occur had there been no Family Support Center. With these projections, the net savings were $278,000.

Economic factors often are the catalysts or influences for adopting large-scale innovative programs. Mor (1987), for example, attributed eco-nomic factors as providing the necessary incentive allowing hospice ser-vices to become routinely reimbursed by Medicare.

■ An Example of a Cost-Effectiveness Evaluation _____

Let's compare two programs with the same mission—to assist the "hard-core" unemployed to obtain employment. The first program is called JOB PREP (for Job Preparedness) and the second, JOBS NOW. Both are located within large metropolitan areas and were developed to help adults who have never experienced full-time employment. The clientele is composed of about equal proportions of persons who dropped out of school and who are functionally illiterate. Many are recovering drug ad-dicts and persons with criminal records. Both programs begin with teach-ing work preparedness skills (being prompt, proper attitude, appropriate dress) and progress to teaching marketable job skills. As a final step, "in-terns" are placed with potential employers for actual on-the-job experi-ence. Table 5.1 presents evaluative information on the two programs.

Table 5.1   Cost-Effectiveness Comparison of Two Job Training Programs

	WORK NOW, Inc.	JOB PREP, Inc.
Total Program Costs	$275,000	$345,000
Graduation Rate	64%	40%
Persons Employed Full-Time		
One Year	48	73
Cost Per Employed Client	$5,729	$4,726

We can tell at a glance that JOB PREP is a more expensive program than WORK NOW. In fact, JOB PREP requires 20 percent more budget than WORK NOW. We also note that the less expensive program has a higher graduation rate than JOB PREP. This is partly explained by the fact that WORK NOW is a less intense program and can be completed a month quicker than JOB PREP. However, JOB PREP is known for doing more screening and more carefully selecting from among its applicants.

If we were to stop at just this point in comparing these two programs, WORK NOW would appear to be the better program. However, if we consider that the mission of the two programs is to help the hard-core unemployed to become *employed,* then we need to go a bit further. Contacting the employers with whom the "interns" of both programs were placed and locating former trainees who were no longer with those employers allows us to establish the number of trainees who are employed in a full-time capacity one year after completion of the program.

By dividing the total program cost by the number of employed graduates of the program, we can develop a cost-effectiveness comparison. We learn that it cost an average of $5,729 to produce an employed graduate of WORK NOW, but only $4,726 to produce a graduate from the JOB PREP program. Even though JOB PREP is a somewhat more expensive program overall, it is more successful than the less expensive program in doing what it was designed to do. The sophisticated comparison looks not only at the budgets and graduation rates, but also at the programs' outcomes in relation to their expenditures.

■ How to Do a Cost-Effectiveness Study

Five basic steps have been identified as being necessary for a cost-effectiveness analysis (Shepard & Thompson, 1979).

■ Step 1: Define the Program

It is vitally important that the evaluator fully understand the program—especially what it was designed to produce and the target population. If the program is to be compared to alternative approaches, it is critical that the programs were designed to reach similar populations.

■ Step 2: Compute Costs

The evaluator must compute the total costs for operating the program. Levine (1983) suggests that every intervention uses ingredients that have a cost—the job for the evaluator is to identify these ingredients and their cost. The most common ingredients are:

a. **Personnel.** Includes the salaries and fringe benefits for all employees. It is suggested that the value of efforts contributed by volunteers also be included.

b. **Facilities.** This includes rent for physical space and related costs for insurance, electricity, heating, air conditioning, and so on. Where the building is owned, estimate the cost for similar space by talking with a local real estate agent or by following a set of procedures Levin (1983) has recommended for determining the annual value of an owned facility. This involves such steps as determining the replacement value of the facility, the life of the facility, the cost of depreciation, and the interest on its undepreciated value.

c. **Equipment and materials.** Includes furnishings, computers, instructional materials, office equipment and supplies, commercial tests, and maintenance of the facility.

d. **Other inputs.** Includes all ingredients that do not fit any other category, such as pro-rated administrative overhead when an agency director oversees more than one program.

e. **Client inputs.** Includes any contributions required of the clients or their families, such as books and uniforms.

■ Step 3: Compute Program Outcomes

In this step, the evaluator must document the program's successes. Examples of indicators of success for various programs are: the number of clients who have not relapsed after twelve months, the number of clients employed, the number of children adopted, the number of months of sobriety, or the number of months or years clients have lived independently in the community. Keep in mind that a program may have more than one indicator. (In the example immediately preceding this section, graduation rate and number of persons employed after one year were both program indicators.)

■ Step 4: Compute Cost-Effectiveness Ratio and Apply Decision Rule

The cost-effectiveness ratio is computed by dividing the total cost of the program by the effectiveness outcome indicator. This allows the evaluator to see the relationship between costs and outcomes. Decision rules have been developed to assist decision-makers. Shepard and Thompson (1979) distinguish four possible situations. In the first, there are desirable benefits of a program but real costs. In such a situation, decision-makers should choose those programs that have the best cost-effectiveness ratio. A second situation would be one in which the costs are negligible or nil and yet good benefits are produced. These inexpensive programs (such as fluoridation of drinking water) should generally be implemented. A third situation is one where there are no positive effects and substantial costs. These programs should not be continued. In the fourth case, a program has no positive effects, but a cost savings is realized. For example, closing a mobile health unit may save close to $80,000 a year, making this option a more efficient method of containing costs than eliminating the program of inservice training at $2,500 per year. Shepard and Thompson (1979) point out that "programs that save resources but result in worse health should not be excluded automatically; by shifting those resources to more effective programs, overall improvements in health could be realized for the same total level of expenditure" (pp. 538–39).

■ Step 5: Perform Sensitivity Analysis

The last step in a cost-effectiveness study is to conduct a sensitivity analysis. This means that recommendations based on the cost-effectiveness data are tested. This step is more important when extensive use of estimation was used in the cost-effectiveness study than when all costs and effects were "real." When estimation was used liberally, the evaluator could go back and make high and low estimates in order to see if a different decision about the program would be justified. If the final decision is not affected by slightly different assumptions, then the evaluator would be more confident in the decision than if the decision were affected by lower or higher estimates.

■ Other Methods of Cost Analysis

Cost analysis is not limited to cost-effectiveness studies. Levine (1983), for instance, discusses cost-benefit analyses, cost-utility analyses, and cost-feasibility analyses. Of these, cost-feasibility is the simplest and entails estimating expected expenses associated with a program. This is done in order to determine if a given program is affordable. Cost-utility analyses are a little more esoteric and are described as having a major disadvantage—"the results cannot be reproduced on the basis of a standard methodology among different evaluators, since most of the assessments are highly subjective ones that take place in the head of the persons doing the evaluation" (p. 29).

In cost-benefit analysis, effort is made to measure both costs and benefits in monetary units. While it is theoretically possible to enumerate all of the benefits of a given social service program, it is usually difficult to determine a monetary value for these benefits. For example, let's say that you work for an agency that has started a respite program for senior citizens. The program serves people sixty years old and older who live at home and who require constant care. The respite care program provides family members relief from the daily care of a disabled family member. Volunteers are recruited from within the community to provide primary caregivers with time off to take care of personal business, to go shopping, or just to have an afternoon to go to a movie or visit with friends.

The cost of the program can be computed easily enough. (There are the salary and fringe benefits associated with the volunteer coordinator's position, prorated expenses for the volunteer coordinator's share of the receptionist, as well as the prorated facility expenses—rent, insurance, utilities.) However, how do we measure the benefits of this program? What are the benefits of having time away from twenty-four-hour custodial responsibilities? What dollar figure do we place on the pleasure that the caregiver got from enjoying a movie or visiting with some friends? If the disabled senior enjoyed having a volunteer read the newspaper, what was that worth in terms of measuring benefits? Cost-benefit studies require that monetary value of these benefits be estimated or measured. Because of the difficulty in arriving at monetary values of intangible benefits, it may not always make sense to do a cost-benefit analysis. (How does one appraise the value of a new playground for children located within the inner city? How does one value the increase in self-esteem of a fifty-five-year-old migrant laborer who learns to read?) You are probably much more likely to conduct a cost-effectiveness study.

The terminology is not standardized with regard to cost analysis terms. For instance, some prefer the term "benefit-cost analysis," while others will use "cost-benefit analysis." And, there are other variations that are beyond the scope of this text.

■ Acceptability, Client Satisfaction, and Consumer Feedback Designs

Lebow (1987) stated that "indices of acceptability number among the simplest and most widely used measures in mental health program evaluation" (p. 191). Most professionals in the human services, if told to design a program evaluation, would immediately begin to consider some procedure whereby clients would be surveyed about whether they "liked" the services they received. Such approaches may be variously known as soliciting client feedback, conducting a client satisfaction study, or exploring service acceptability.

Program evaluations where client acceptability measures have been the chief focus are frequently found in the literature (see, for example, the references cited by Lebow, 1982; Heath, Hultberg, Ramey, & Ries, 1984; and Royse, 1985). And, there is much to commend the use of client satisfaction as a form of evaluation. Such approaches tend to be relatively inexpensive and easy to interpret, and they can be implemented on short notice without a great deal of planning. Furthermore, they may indicate to clients that their experiences and observations are important—further indication that someone cares about them. Whether we inquire about the accessibility of our services or the acceptability of our services, these approaches are a "client-oriented" form of evaluation. They stem from the assumption that clients provide the most valuable and accurate information available on how our program impacts their lives.

There is just one major problem with client satisfaction approaches. In practically every instance, the majority of respondents indicate satisfaction with services received. This positive response bias occurs so often that Lebow (1982), in a review of twenty-six studies, found that three-quarters had satisfaction rates higher than 70 percent—even though the surveys were conducted of totally different programs, in diverse settings, using various counseling approaches and assessment methods. As Lebow (1982) noted, these high satisfaction rates came from clients who "have little choice of facility, type of treatment, or practitioner" (p. 250). Studies have shown that there are no significant differences in satisfaction between voluntary and involuntary clients (Spensley, Edwards, & White, 1980). Another study concluded that clients were more pleased with treatment and less displeased with commitment than one would expect them to be (Kalman, 1983).

Positive client evaluations are not proof of a "good" program; in fact, Rocheleau and Mackesy (1980) suggest that a problem may be indicated if a program receives satisfaction rates of less than 70 to 75 percent. If only two-thirds of your clients are pleased with your services, then your program may warrant closer inspection.

There can be many reasons why consumer satisfaction studies tend to reveal positive findings. First of all, client feedback instruments are often "homemade" and nothing is known about their reliability or validity. (More detail on what to look for in an instrument is provided in chapter 6.) Even strongly positive client satisfaction data obtained from an instrument that lacks reliability and validity is not convincing information to evaluators and informed professionals.

A second reason that client satisfaction surveys tend to have a strong positive bias is that they usually seek feedback from clients who have remained with an agency or program. Clients who are dissatisfied with services tend to drop out early—perhaps after the first visit. Those clients who stay with a program are more likely to have had a positive experience with a therapist or with the agency's services than those who drop out. Biased samples result when only those clients having a positive experience choose to respond to a survey.

Third, not enough consideration is given to the problems associated with getting back a representative sample of questionnaires. As a rule, only about 25 to 30 percent of all those surveys mailed out can be expected to be completed and returned. Sometimes, response rates are 10 to 15 percent. How are the results to be interpreted when 85 percent of a sample do not respond? Results based upon a 15 percent response rate are virtually meaningless because we would be hearing from a minority instead of a majority of the clients. It is very likely that those who respond to the client satisfaction survey might not be representative of the rest of the clients (those who didn't respond). Clients who return mailed surveys tend to have higher levels of educational attainment than those who don't return surveys. As we think about our clients, we realize that a sizable proportion are functionally illiterate. Impoverished clients who are battling every day for survival probably have more important concerns than filling out a client satisfaction questionnaire. Also, clients may move frequently and not leave forwarding addresses. In order to keep the response rate high, it may be necessary to offer a *small* incentive. If the incentive is too large, the results could be viewed as biased because of a perception that the respondents were "bought."

In order to avoid the problems associated with mailing survey instruments to clients, agencies sometimes distribute them in person and ask clients to complete the service satisfaction surveys while they are in the agency. While a higher response rate is usually guaranteed, this procedure may also threaten some clients. Feeling that their anonymity is threatened, clients may have concerns about losing benefits or not receiving future services if they say anything negative. Bias can easily creep into those procedures designed to elicit client feedback data. Consulting with client groups and involving some representatives in the planning process is advised.

Even given these problems, it is possible that the advantages associated with client satisfaction surveys will always make them attractive to managers in the social and human services. Instead of considering a client satisfaction survey as the sole source of information about a program's performance, the trained evaluator will consider this form of evaluation as part of a more comprehensive effort. Consumer satisfaction studies often offer valuable insight into a program from a client's perspective. If you decide to conduct a client satisfaction survey, I recommend the following:

1. Use a scale that has good reliability and that has been used successfully in other studies. (See the example and references included in the next chapter.) Avoid the use of hastily designed questionnaires for which there is no psychometric information. When you use instruments that have been employed in other research or evaluation activities, often times data can be found in the literature for compari-

Figure 5.1: Client Satisfaction Ratings

Onestop Counseling, Inc.			
100%			
95%			
90%	●		
85%			
80%		●	
75%			
70%			●
65%			
	March	June	September

son with your study. Greenfield and Attkisson (1989), for instance, present the means for a fifteen item Service Satisfaction Scale administered to patients of a university student health service and a mental health clinic, and patients in four clinics within a private non-profit health system.

2. Use the same instrument on repeated occasions and develop a local baseline of data so that departures from the norm can be observed. Conduct client satisfaction studies regularly and routinely (for example, twice or three times a year), then compare the data with the results from prior efforts. The advantage of doing this as opposed to a one-time client satisfaction study can be seen in figure 5.1.

   In this example it can be seen that the actual level of client satisfaction with services is dropping. Such a trend could be discovered only by doing more than one study. Had the evaluator conducted one study in the month of March, this decreasing satisfaction with services would not have been detected.

3. Employ at least one and possibly two open-ended questions so that the consumers of your services can alert you to any problems that you didn't suspect and couldn't anticipate. (For instance, "If you could make any improvements to this program, what one thing would you change?" Or, "What about this program do you like best and least?")

4. Use a "ballot box" approach where one week is set aside when every client (old and new) entering the agency is given a brief questionnaire and asked to complete it while waiting for the scheduled appointment. Often times, client satisfaction studies have focused not on active clients but on those who have completed the program or who are no longer receiving services. It is necessary to learn about clients' experiences in every phase of the program. (If a significant proportion of the agency's clients are illiterate, written questionnaires should be

accompanied by procedures that will insure that a clerical person, friend, or family member reads the questions to the client.

■ The Judicial Model

Another evaluation model has been described by Wolf (1975), Levine et al. (1978), Smith (1985), and others. What we might call the judicial or adversarial model relies upon human testimony and a "judge" or "jury" to weigh the evidence for and against a program. Ours being a litigious society, there is a wide understanding of the judicial process as well as a certain appeal associated with being able to present your best arguments and evidence as to why a program should be considered "good" and its funding continued.

Several strengths are associated with the use of a judicial model. You could, for instance, involve board members, clients, or representatives from the community or from the majority funding source to comprise the hearing panel or jury. This would be less expensive than bringing in an expert or experts to serve as the judge or jury. Another advantage of this model is that the hearing officer or the jury panel can request additional information if they do not understand the evidence. This flexibility allows for more evaluation data to be presented when it is needed. Perhaps the greatest strength, however, is that the judicial model encourages a wide variety of perspectives and alternative interpretations of the evidence, thus providing a more balanced evaluation than may sometimes result from a single perspective.

One of the major drawbacks of this model is that considerable preplanning is required before it can be implemented. Wolfe reports that six months of planning took place before a two-day hearing was scheduled. Hearing rules and procedures were developed for such items as cross-examination, criteria for determining the admissibility of evidence, instructions to the hearing panel, and so on. However, I believe it would be possible to use a judicial model without all of the rules and procedures that tend to make our current judicial system so cumbersome. The attractiveness of this model is in the point and counterpoint that comes from intelligent debate. The best application of this model would be with complex programs with multiple goals that may not easily lend themselves to quantitative measurement. The model would not be attractive to agencies if each evaluation would require six months of planning.

■ The Hammond Model

It is probably becoming clear to you that there are numerous ways to think about and conceptualize a program evaluation. Another model that

Figure 5.2: Schematic of the Hammond Model

Population	Environment	Behavior
Clients	Intents	Performance
Staff	Methods	Opinion
Administration	Resources	

is useful in planning and structuring evaluations was proposed by Robert Hammond (1975). The Hammond Model (figure 5.2) is a systematic approach for identifying foci for an evaluation.

Hammond identified several major elements that can be helpful in thinking about who and what to evaluate. His model starts with the identification of a **population** (those individuals who are involved in or influenced by the program). Note that the population is not limited just to *clients* served by the program. The broad definition employed here suggests to the evaluator that *staff* also constitute a population of persons involved with the program who could be the source of pertinent information about a program. The *administration* also is an appropriate foci of some evaluation efforts.

A program operates in an **environment**. This environment is defined by the program's *intents* (the purposes, goals, or objectives established for it); by the *methods* (or interventions) used; and by the *resources* (people, money, space, materials, and equipment) available to the program.

Once these program elements have been defined, the evaluator can begin to consider questions that can be grouped as to whether they relate to areas of *opinion* (judgments and beliefs) or behavioral *performance*.

With this model the evaluator can decide to be very comprehensive and to cover all of the population and environmental elements with regard to both opinions and performance. Or, more realistically, the evaluator may decide upon a more narrow evaluation. Using this approach the evaluator could, for example, survey *clients* regarding their *opinions* of the *methods* used by the program staff. Or, the evaluator might examine the *clients' performance* (outcomes) within a selected program (*method*).

The Hammond Model can help evaluators get an overview of the essential elements comprising a program so that a variety of ways to approach an evaluation can be seen. An evaluator should attempt to conduct as comprehensive an evaluation as is feasible. While it is possible to conduct a program evaluation involving only the staff and not the clients, the value of the Hammond Model is that it suggests that clients as well as administrators have important information or perspectives on the program. When the evaluator selects a narrow perspective, there is always some information about the program that is lost or not examined—

potentially valuable information. Perhaps there are times when the evaluator ought to expand Hammond's list and ask volunteers for their opinions or suggestions. The argument for doing as comprehensive an evaluation as can be afforded is seen in the following example (which is mostly true and has been only slightly embellished).

A new program manager wanted to make an emergency mental health program a superlative program—one of which all the citizens in the community could be proud. The first week she examined the client utilization data and made a number of recommendations that would provide better information for monitoring purposes. She trained her staff to keep timely and accurate records of the amount of services provided.

After a couple of months, she began an outcome evaluation of the program. Whenever sessions of emergency counseling were completed, the staff were instructed to ask consumers if they would talk with the director as part of a program evaluation. The director picked up the calls or met individually with the clients and asked a series of questions about whether the counseling had been beneficial. Although she wasn't able to talk with every client, the director began the process of gathering data to help her understand the clients' experiences with her program.

Even with these measures in place, the director was not entirely satisfied that the program was as good as it could be. As she thought about what might make the program a better one, it occurred to her that it relied too heavily upon volunteers. The paid staff generally worked the "day" hours and were not on-site after 6:00 P.M., unless they were called in to handle an emergency. Approximately thirty-five volunteers augmented the paid staff, volunteering between four to eight hours a week (usually in the evening).

The program director was successful in obtaining additional funding that allowed her to reassign full-time staff so that a qualified mental health professional was on-site twenty-four hours a day. Evening coverage was no longer the prime responsibility of volunteers. This change of policy would help, she reasoned, to insure that clients got "quality service" during the evening as well as during the day hours.

One night shortly after the new policy was implemented, the full-time staff person on duty was surprised to see a man walk into the emergency unit with a bag of groceries. There was a loaf of french bread extending out of the sack, and she could see a bottle of wine, some cheese, and a radio. The man informed the staff person that he was the Thursday night volunteer scheduled to be "on duty" and that she could go home. He became very animated when he found out that a full-time staff person would be on duty all evening. A few minutes later a woman drove up in the parking lot and he ran out to meet her. After some discussion with her friend, she marched inside and demanded to know why a paid staff person was needed on "their night." The two volunteers insisted that they had not been notified of the new policy and informed the staff, as they picked up the groceries and radio, that they would *not* be volunteering anymore!

The program director learned that the two individuals had driven from distant locations to "volunteer" and had been "volunteering" for several years—always on the same evening and with each other. Were they volunteering to be of service to humankind or to provide themselves with an opportunity to get away from their spouses? During their romantic interludes would they answer the crisis phone? Were clients getting the volunteers' undivided attention?

Many evaluation efforts probably would not have discovered this problem. It was only because of the program director's dogged pursuit of "quality" service that the staffing assignments were rearranged to rely less heavily upon volunteers during evening hours.

As a general rule, the more people the evaluator can talk with (including volunteers or the volunteer coordinator), the greater the likelihood that discoveries will be made about areas where the program can be improved. Get input from a variety of sources and be as comprehensive as possible when planning a program evaluation. Program evaluation should not be considered a "one-shot" episode. It should be an on-going process that continually provides useful information from an assortment of sources to program managers.

■ **Chapter Recap**

This chapter has introduced several different evaluation designs that do not rely upon the traditional experimental and quasi-experimental models. These designs should be thought of as additional tools that are available to you as a program evaluator. Your choice of an evaluation design will depend upon the resources you have, the constraints within the agency, as well as what is pragmatically possible. For instance, it may not be possible to use the classic experimental design because the program was implemented before you were asked to provide consultation. (This actually happened to a colleague of mine. While the experimental design would have been his choice, it requires that random assignment occur *prior* to the start of an intervention. He was contacted *after* the program began, and it was not possible to randomly assign to the control or intervention group. Since random assignment was not possible, he had to fall back on the Nonequivalent Control Group Design.)

Evaluation designs are tailored to a specific situation or program. For pedagogic reasons, the choice of a design has been presented here as being selected after an evaluation question has been formulated. But the choice of design and of the evaluation question may not be separate and distinct steps. Cronbach et al. (1980) noted, "We reject the view that 'design' begins *after* a research question is chosen, as a mere technical process to sharpen the inquiry. Choice of questions and choice of investigative tactics are inseparable" (pp. 213–14). Cronbach also referred to the choice of design as a "spiral process" where the evaluator lays out a rough plan and considers what will be left unsettled. The process may not be straightforward as concerns about information yield, costs, and political importance are considered and balanced (p. 261).

Beginning evaluators are sometimes too critical of their own efforts when they are prevented from using an experimental design. They may think that any design short of the "ideal" experiment will yield worthless data. This simply is not true. Something can be learned from just about any evaluation. Even highly competent evaluators often have to settle for designs much less stringent than the Solomon Four Group Design. Depending upon your audience, nonexperimental designs may, in some instances, be desired as they are less complex and more understandable.

For example, I know of a county prosecutor who was extremely pleased with the results of an evaluation that used the One Group Pretest/Posttest Design. He had been instrumental in getting a drug treatment program started for felons that combined systematic urine sampling and a structured counseling program. At the end of the first nine months, only 12 percent of over 4,500 urine samples from 176 felons indicated alcohol or drug use. Among those with "clean" urine samples, only 22 percent had been rearrested, while 66 percent of those with three or more "dirty" urine samples had been rearrested. Even though 48 percent of those in the program had been rearrested for some offense and there was no randomization or control group, the county attorney was making plans to speak to the state legislature about additional funding so that similar programs could be started in other communities in the state. In this example, the results of the study were perceived as being so powerful that even the relatively weak evaluation design seemed to be inconsequential.

Does the choice of a design make a difference? Yes, it does. It is not often that one can expect the same degree of success as reported in the previous example. I often see frustration and disenchantment with program evaluation when practitioners in the field and students realize much too late how any observed changes in clients after intervention could have been due to alternative explanations.

The difference between the competent and incompetent evaluator is that the competent evaluator knows what data will be produced, has plans for the analytical or statistical procedures that will be used, and understands the limitations of the chosen evaluation design. The incompetent evaluator is not sure what data will be produced, how it can be interpreted, or what can be done to make up for limitations in the data. The incompetent evaluator is not able to plan ahead and anticipate what might happen with the use of a given procedure or instrument.

When planning an evaluation, ask yourself such questions as:

1. What could go wrong with this data collection procedure? (Then strengthen or improve the procedure; collect data from more than one source.)
2. If the intervention is successful, how might the critics of the program explain it away? Conversely, if the intervention does not appear to be successful, how would I explain that?
3. What is the weakest aspect of this evaluation design?
4. What would make the evaluation more convincing?

As you answer these questions, ways to strengthen and improve your procedures will become apparent. You may want to build in safeguards that will take "ammunition" away from any potential critics or skeptics. And, as a result, you will have a stronger and more compelling evaluation.

Ultimately, the evaluation design you use will be based on several considerations: the amount of time you have in which to conduct the evaluation, the cost in materials and personnel, the administrative and political constraints, the purpose of the evaluation, and the concern that the results be reliable and valid. Muscatello (1988) identified these and several other factors in a discussion on choosing which program to evaluate and assessing the difficulty associated with evaluating any program.

Finally, Wholey (1987) identified four problems that prevent an evaluation from being used to improve program performance:

1. Lack of definition (of the problem to be addressed, the intervention, the expected outcomes or impact).
2. Lack of a clear logic of testable assumptions.
3. Lack of agreement on evaluation priorities and intended uses of the evaluation.
4. Inability or unwillingness to act on the basis of evaluative information.

Evaluators may not always be able to convince policymakers to act on the findings produced in their evaluation reports. However, by attending to the first three points made by Muscatello and trying to think like a "competent" evaluator, you will go a long way toward insuring that your evaluation product will make a useful contribution.

QUESTIONS FOR CLASS DISCUSSION

1. Identify local, state, or national programs for which you would like to conduct cost-effectiveness evaluations. Discuss the program outcomes for these. Is there a choice of more than one outcome indicator per program? List all of the relevant indicators.
2. Without referring back to the text, make a list of the various evaluation designs which have been presented in chapters 4 and 5, and then rank order these based on perceived credibility.
3. Using the same list of evaluation designs, decide which designs you think would be the easiest to use and the designs that you will most likely use sometime in the future.
4. Although it is known that client satisfaction studies typically are positively biased, discuss why this form of evaluation is used so often in evaluating university faculty.
5. Discuss the advantages and disadvantages of the Hammond and Judicial models in terms of their cost, feasibility, and potential information yield.

MINI-PROJECTS: EXPERIENCING
EVALUATION FIRSTHAND

1. You have been hired to conduct an evaluation of a hospice program. How will you determine if this is a "good" hospice program? Unlike most social and human service programs, it is unrealistic to expect that the clients of the hospice program will improve. Because they are terminally ill, most of them die within several months after becoming clients. Design an evaluation plan using a design discussed in this chapter. Discuss specifics such as: what information will be sought, how the sample will be obtained, and any instruments to be used.
2. A friend of yours has recently been put in charge of a school-based program which provides supportive services to teen parents. He asks for your advice. Although the school system wants these teen parents to graduate from high school, the system seems to have no other notion as to what the program should do. Help your friend out. Identify some program goals and objectives. Using an evaluation design discussed in this chapter, discuss what data would be needed to convince school board members that this is a "good" program.
3. Propose a cost-effectiveness program evaluation design for a pro-

gram of your choosing. Identify the program, its goals and objectives, outcome indicators, and data collection procedures.

REFERENCES AND RESOURCES

Armstrong, K.A. (1983). Economic analysis of a child abuse and neglect treatment program. *Child Welfare*, 62 (1), 3–13.

Brooks, C.H. (1989). Cost differences between hospice and nonhospice care. *Evaluation and the Health Professions*, 12 (2).

Buxbaum, C.B. (1981). Cost-benefit analysis: The mystique versus the reality. *Social Service Review*, 55 (3) 453–471.

Coulton, C.J. (1979). *Social work quality assurance programs*. Washington, DC: National Association of Social Workers.

Cronbach, L.J. (1982). *Designing evaluations of educational and social programs*. San Francisco, CA: Jossey-Bass.

Cronbach, L.J. & Associates. (1980). *Toward reform of program evaluation*. San Francisco, CA: Jossey-Bass.

Decker, J.T., Starrett, R., & Redhorse, J. (1986). Evaluating the cost-effectiveness of employee assistance programs. *Social Work*, 31 (5), 391–393.

Greenfield, T.K., & Attkisson, C.C. (1989). Steps toward a multifactorial satisfaction scale for primary care and mental health services. *Evaluation and Program Planning*, 12.

Hammond, R.L. (1975). Establishing priorities for information and design specifications for evaluating community education programs. *Community Education Journal*, March/April.

Heath, B.H., Hultberg, R.A., Ramey, J.M., & Ries, C.S. (1984). Consumer Satisfaction: Some new twists to a not so old evaluation. *Community Mental Health Journal*, 20 (2), 123–134.

Holosko, M.J., Feit, M.D. (eds.). (1988) *Evaluation of Employee Assistance Programs*. New York: Haworth Press.

Kalman, T. (1983). An overview of patient satisfaction with psychiatric treatment. *Hospital and Community Psychiatry*, 34 (1), 48–54.

Lebow, J.L. (1987). Acceptability as a simple measure in mental health program evaluation. *Evaluation and Program Planning*, 10, (3), 191–195.

Lebow, J.L. (1982). Consumer satisfaction with mental health treatment. *Psychological Bulletin*, 91 (2), 244–259.

Levin, H.M. (1987). Cost-benefit and cost-effectiveness analyses. *Evaluation Practice in Review*. New Directions for Program Evaluation, no. 34. San Francisco, CA: Jossey-Bass.

Levin, H.M. (1983). *Cost-Effectiveness: A Primer*. Beverly Hills, CA: Sage.

Levin, H.M., Glass, G.V., & Meister, G.R. (1987). Cost-effectiveness of computer-assisted instruction. *Evaluation Review*, 11 (1), 50–72.

Levine, M. Brown, E., Fitzgerald, C., Goplerud, E., Gordon, M.E., Jayne-Lazarus, C. Rosenberg, N., & Slater, J. (1978). Adapting the jury trial for program evaluation: A report of an experience. *Evaluation and Program Planning*, 1, 177–186.

Masters, S., Garfinkel, I., & Bishop, J. (1978). Benefit-cost analysis in program evaluation. *Journal of Social Service Research*, 2 (1), 70–93.

Mayer, R.R. (1985). *Policy and program planning; A developmental perspective.* Englewood Cliffs, NJ: Prentice–Hall.

McBride, M.E., Bertrand, J.T., Santiso, R., & Fernandez, V.H. (1987). Cost effectiveness of the APROFAM program for voluntary surgical contraception in Guatemala. *Evaluation Review*, 11 (3), 300–326.

McCrady, B., Longabaugh, R., Fink, E., Stout, R., Beattie, M., & Ruggieri-Authelet, A. (1986). Cost effectiveness of alcoholism treatment in partial hospital versus inpatient settings after brief inpatient treatment: 12-month outcomes. *Journal of Consulting and Clinical Psychology*, 54 (5), 708–713.

Mor, V., Greenr, D.S., & Kastenbaum, R. (1988). *The hospice experience.* Baltimore, MD: Johns Hopkins University Press.

Muscatello, D.B. (1988). Developing an agenda that works: The right choice at the right time. *Evaluation utilization.* New Directions for Program Evaluation, no. 39. San Francisco, CA: Jossey–Bass.

Nagel, S. (1983). Nonmonetary variables in benefit-cost evaluation. *Evaluation Review*, 7 (1), 37–64.

Newman, F.L., & Sorensen, J.E. (1985). *Integrated clinical and fiscal management in mental health; A guidebook.* Norwood, NJ: Ablex.

Roid, G.H. (1982). Cost-effectiveness analysis in mental health policy research. *American Psychologist*, 37 (1), 94–95.

Rocheleau, B., & Mackesey, T. (1980). What, consumer feedback surveys again? *Evaluation and the Health Professions*, 3 (4), 405–419.

Royse, D. (1985). Client satisfaction with the helping process: A review for the pastoral counselor. *Journal of Pastoral Care*, 39 (1), 3–11.

Russell, M. (1990). Consumer satisfaction: An investigation of contributing factors. *Journal of Social Service Research*, 13 (4), 43–56.

Seiner, K., & Lairson, D.R. (1985). A cost-effectiveness analysis of prenatal care delivery. *Evaluation and the Health Professions*, 8 (1), 93–108.

Shepard, D.S., & Thompson, M.S. (1979). First principles of cost-effectiveness analysis in health. *Public Health Reports*, 94, 535–543.

Simons-Morton, B.G., Brink, S., & Bates, D. (1987). Effectiveness and cost effectiveness of persuasive communications and incentives in increasing safety belt use. *Health Education Quarterly*, 14 (2), 167–179.

Skaburskis, A. (1987). Cost–benefit analysis: Ethics and problem boundaries. *Evaluation Review*, 11 (5), 591–611.

Smith, N.L. (1985). Adversary and committee hearings as evaluation methods. *Evaluation Review*, 9 (6), 735–750.

Sorensen, J.E. (1983). *Accounting and budgeting systems for mental health organizations.* Rockville, MD: U.S. Dept. of Health and Human Services, National Institute of Mental Health.

Spensley, J., Edwards, D., & White, E. (1980). Patient satisfaction and involuntary treatment. *American Journal of Orthopsychiatry*, 50 (4), 725–727.

Solberg, A. (1983). Community posthospital follow-up services. *Evaluation Review*, 7 (1), 96–109.

Sorensen, J.E., & Grove, H.D. (1978). Using cost-outcome and cost-effectiveness analyses for improved program management and accountability. In C.C. Attkisson, W.A. Hargreaves, M.J. Horowitz, and J.E. Sorensen (Eds.), *Evaluation of human service programs.* New York: Academic Press.

Thompson, M.F. (1980). *Benefit-cost analysis for program evaluation.* Beverly Hills, CA: Sage.

Vandivort, R., Kurren, G.M., & Braun, K. (1984). Foster family care for frail elderly: A cost-effective quality care alternative. *Journal of Gerontological Social Work,* 7 (4), 101–114.

Weinrott, M.R., Jones, R.R., & Howard, J.R. (1982). Cost-effectiveness of teaching family programs for delinquents: Results of a national evaluation. *Evaluation Review,* 6 (2), 173–201.

Wholey, J.S. (1987). *Using program theory in evaluation.* New Directions for Program Evaluation, no. 33. San Francisco, CA: Jossey-Bass.

Wolf, R.L. (1975). Trial by jury; A new evaluation method. *Phi Delta Kappan,* 57, 185–187.

Zelman, W.N. (1987). Cost per unit of service. *Evaluation and Program Planning,* 10 (3), 201–207.

CHAPTER 6

Instruments for Program Evaluation

The evaluation design provides an overall strategy or plan of procedures to be used in an evaluation effort. Once the evaluator has an approximate plan for how to conduct the evaluation, it is necessary to polish and refine the plan. This next step involves identifying, locating, or developing specific mechanisms for collecting the data needed for the evaluation. Researchers and evaluators operationally define and measure key variables with "paper-and-pencil" instruments. We tend to think of these instruments as questionnaires, although they may not always ask questions of respondents. Some instruments are composed of a number of statements (items) to which the respondent may indicate levels of agreement or disagreement. Other instruments may ask a respondent if certain statements are true or false. Regardless of their format, these instruments form the basis for our measurements—so that we can detect changes in our clients as a result of our interventions.

While measuring instruments are used to help us categorize clients in terms of those whom the program either did or did not help, the use of these instruments also gives us the capacity to go well beyond this basic classification. These psychometric instruments allow us to discriminate among the "successful" clients and to identify those whose progress could be described as slight, moderate, or major. Measuring instruments allow us to use quantification to move beyond subjective opinions ("I think these clients have improved") into a domain where we can discuss the amount of change or improvement. ("This group of clients is 37 percent more assertive than they were at the time of pretest." Or, "At the time of the posttest, 55 percent of the intervention group reported no clinically significant symptoms.")

Objective instruments provide evaluators with a certain amount of precision in arriving at the magnitude or intensity of clients' problems and in determining any consequent change in those problems. We are afforded this precision because instruments allow us to quantify abstract or intangible concepts such as self-esteem or assertiveness. These instruments allow us to translate subjective perceptions of problems and concepts into numeric values.

Evaluation instruments are not just plucked from thin air. They must be selected with care. A hastily chosen instrument could provide unreliable or worthless information. It is important to select instruments that not only are psychometrically strong, but also are good indicators of what the programs are attempting to accomplish. Consider the following scenario.

Jim Gradstudent was asked to evaluate a residential treatment center for youth who had experienced some trouble with the juvenile justice system. He had noticed that several of the most successful residents there seemed to have experienced an increase in self-esteem by the time they were released. One afternoon while in the university library he found a self-esteem instrument that looked as if it could be used for the program evaluation. After deciding upon a One Group Pre/Posttest Design, Jim made a number of photocopies of the self-esteem instrument and began administering it to new admissions. Eleven months later he had collected forty-two pre- and posttests from residents who had been discharged from the treatment center. He was surprised to learn that there was very little difference in the pre- and posttest self-esteem scores. Does this mean that the residential treatment program was unsuccessful?

As you think about this scenario, the lack of information in several areas should cause you to raise questions. First of all, is increasing the resident's self-esteem a clearly articulated goal of the residential treatment center? If it is not, would use of a self-esteem inventory to evaluate the whole program be a reasonable measure? Even if it is an important goal of the program, how likely is it that the youth in treatment will actually experience an increase in self-esteem? (Will this occur in a majority of the youth?) What other goals may lend themselves to measurement? (If the major goal of the program is to prevent these youth from becoming involved in the juvenile justice system again, could recidivism be used as an indicator of the program's success?) Additionally, in this particular scenario, we don't know anything about the instrument itself—how "good" is the instrument? Assuming that increasing self-esteem is a valid outcome for this residential program, it would be critically important that a "good"' instrument be used. In order to decide that an instrument is "good," we need to discuss some guidelines for the adoption and selection of evaluation instruments.

■ Selecting an Evaluation Instrument _____

The process of selecting a psychometrically strong evaluation instrument starts with operationally defining how "success" in a program is to be measured. What is a successful client or a successful program outcome? Of course, the successful client will be one who improves, but improves along what lines? As you can see below, in some programs the criteria of success are obvious:

Program	Major Goal
Alcohol and drug treatment programs	To help clients maintain sobriety
Day treatment for the severely mentally ill	To help clients live in the community
Juvenile and adult criminal justice diversion programs	To help clients avoid subsequent arrests
Employment and training programs	To help clients obtain competitive employment
Adoption programs	To obtain a permanent placement
Child protection programs	To protect and prevent future abuse or neglect

Such programs as these do not always require paper-and-pencil instruments to evaluate their outcomes. In some cases, no instrument is required; programs can be evaluated with the data already in their possession. It is very likely, for instance, that a mental health center will know how many or what percent of its clients in the day treatment program became hospitalized during the course of a year. It should not be difficult for adoption workers to determine the number of or percentage of children for whom a permanent placement was obtained. Forensic programs ought to be able to determine which of their clients are rearrested. Such programs as these can often be evaluated in terms of *behavioral outcomes.* If a drug treatment program requires its clients to periodically come in for urine analysis, the percentage of unsuccessful clients (those with "dirty" urine) can be calculated rather easily without the addition of any other tests or questionnaires. Success can be operationally defined as so many tests showing "clean" urine. The use of this kind of data to measure progress is nothing new. Florence Nightingale is said to have kept statistics on the mortality of British soldiers. She kept track of hospital deaths by diagnostic categories in order to show that improvements in sanitation reduced fatalities. Because of her efforts, the mortality rate dropped from 32 percent to 2 percent within six months (M.A. Nutting and L.L. Dock, 1907, cited in Meisenheimer, 1985).

Behavioral data can also be obtained through video or audiotaping of interactions. For instance, to determine if parents interact more appropriately with their young children after a nurturing program, videotaping sessions with parents and their children could be arranged. While there might be some concerns with "staged" behavior, a benefit of videotaping is that facial expressions and general demeanor can be observed. Rating scales can be developed so that there is a quantitative count or rating on the presence or absence of desired behaviors. The tapes can also be used by clients for learning from self-observation, as well as for demonstrating progress.

However, behavioral outcomes are not as easy to measure with every program. For instance, suppose you are the director of a program that provides drug prevention programming for elementary school children. The goal of your program is to prevent these children from becoming addicted as adolescents or adults. Most programs of this type will not have the ability to do any sort of follow-up study three, five, or ten years later to see if the prevention programming resulted in fewer persons with drug dependency problems than in the control group. As a consequence, these and other programs without an ability to measure behavioral outcomes must consider success in terms of clients increasing their *knowledge* about a given problem or in terms of changing clients' *attitudes.*

Sometimes prevention programs measure whether the program recipients have increased their knowledge about a given problem. In AIDS prevention programs, for instance, the goal could be to provide sufficient information about how AIDS is transmitted so that program participants have an increased knowledge about its transmission. One could envision a pretest of twenty items and the typical respondent (before the intervention) getting four or five items correct. After the intervention (assuming that the educational presentation is effective), the typical respondent might answer correctly eighteen or nineteen items on the posttest. This would indicate that respondents' knowledge about AIDS had been increased.

For other programs, the main goal may be to change the participants' attitudes about some behavior or practice. For instance, if you were administering an intervention program for men who batter—the evaluator might use a behavioral measure (arrests, incidents of battering) as an outcome measure, but it would also be possible to determine if program participants had a change in attitudes about battering. The goal of the program might be to help batters become more empathetic—to put themselves in the place of the victim—and to view battering as unacceptable behavior. In this instance, the evaluator may not want to measure batterers' knowledge about domestic violence but to change attitudes regarding its acceptability. The theory here would be that if attitudes change, so will behavior. Behavioral measures are not limited to just clinical settings. As an evaluator for a city's public services, you might monitor the number of citizen complaints in various divisions.

Often, it is much easier to measure attitudes and knowledge than behavior. It is relatively easy to determine if adolescents have become more knowledgeable about drugs or if they have developed attitudes favorable to the use of illicit drugs. It is much more difficult to determine if program recipients sell, buy, or use illegal drugs once they are away from school. Using the men-who-batter example, even after a treatment program has been completed, battering may still occur in the home but go unreported. An evaluator might be tempted to conclude that an intervention program was successful because there were no rearrests among the program participants, when in reality battering was still occurring but perhaps less often or in a somewhat less severe form. A major advantage of paper-and-pencil measures is that they can easily be administered in the classroom or office and for this reason outcome data can usually be obtained quicker than some behavioral measures (such as clients being rearrested or hospitalized).

A major disadvantage of focusing on knowledge and attitudes is that they may not be directly related to behavior. For example, clients may have knowledge that drug use is bad for them but continue with destructive drug use. (Think of how many persons smoke cigarettes even though the surgeon general's warning is printed on each pack.) Clients can increase their knowledge about alcoholism (or a number of other problems) and yet not change their behavior. We and our clients may have attitudes which are inconsistent with personal behavior. (Some very conservative legislators may favor legalization of illegal drugs not because they use illegal drugs themselves but simply as a way of trying to manage the national problem of drug abuse.) A woman might be in favor of women having a right to an abortion while not viewing that as an acceptable option for herself. The connection between attitudes, knowledge, and behavior is tenuous as best. Probably the "best" measure in any situation would be one closest to the intent of the program intervention. Because it is not always possible to observe behavioral changes or to get reliable measures of specific behaviors, evaluators use instruments to measure changes in attitudes or knowledge.

■ Reliability

An instrument or questionnaire is said to be **reliable** when it consistently and dependably measures some concept or phenomenon with accuracy. If an instrument is reliable, then administering it to similar groups yields similar results. A reliable instrument is like a reliable watch—it is not subject to extraneous factors such as temperature, humidity, physical appearance of the person using it, day of the week, cycle of the moon, and so forth.

The reliability of instruments is generally reported in a way that resembles a correlation coefficient—it will be a numerical value between 0 and 1. Nunnally (1978) says that in the early stages of research one can work with instruments having modest reliability (by which he means .70 or higher), that .80 can be used for basic research, and that a reliability of .90 is the minimum where important decisions are going to be made with respect to specific test scores.

Most professional journal articles carry information on the scales or instruments used in the study. (A scale is a cluster of items measuring a single concept. An instrument may contain one or more scales. For instance, in a study of attitudes about AIDS, an instrument might contain a knowledge of AIDS scale, a fear of AIDS scale, and an empathy towards persons with AIDS scale.) If no information is reported on the scale, instrument, or questionnaire, it cannot be assumed to have reliability.

What does it mean when an instrument does not have even modest reliability? It means that when the instrument is administered to a group of persons, not all of them will understand or interpret the items in the same way. For instance, suppose I am interested in measuring knowledge about AIDS and I develop the following item: "It is possible to get AIDS from gay employees in restaurants or bars." Six out of ten individuals may interpret this item as asking whether food-handlers can transmit AIDS by handling plates, silverware, or breathing on food. However, if four out of every ten individuals read into the item the question of whether AIDS is transmitted by having sex with the employees of gay restaurants and bars, then this item would detract from rather than contribute to the making of a reliable instrument. While one single item will seldom make a whole scale unreliable, several vague items that can be interpreted differently by various individuals will cause problems with reliability.

There are several ways to determine if an instrument has reliability.

Researchers sometimes administer the instrument to the same group on more than one occasion to see how closely the results correspond or correlate. (This is known as test-retest reliability.) A second approach is to devise parallel or alternate forms of the instrument and compare the results of both versions.

If you develop a scale to measure a single concept, it is possible to use computer programs such as the *Statistical Package for the Social Sciences* (SPSS-X) to determine the scale's reliability. The Reliability procedure provides an item analysis and computes coefficients of reliability. This procedure considers how well a group of items cluster together (the scale's internal consistency) and it indicates which items do not correlate well with the rest. If the items are dropped, the scale's reliability coefficient would improve. This is a simple procedure to do (especially if you already plan to use a computer to help you analyze your data) and ought to be done if you have developed your own scale for use in the evaluation. Knowing whether the instrument is reliable or not has important implications relative to the confidence you can place in your evaluation findings.

■ Validity

An instrument is said to be **valid** when it measures what it was designed to measure. Let's say that you are developing a self-esteem inventory and in a sudden flash of inspiration it occurs to you that a high level of self-esteem would be indicated if respondents could identify the twenty-seventh president of the United States. If you incorporate a number of similar items into your self-esteem inventory, you probably would not create a self-esteem scale but rather a scale that measures knowledge of American history. This scale would very likely not be valid for measuring self-esteem.

There are various ways to go about demonstrating that an instrument has validity. Sometimes experts are asked to review the scale to see if the entire range of the concept is represented. (This is known as **content validity**.) For instance, if you were developing a scale to measure progress in the treatment of bulimia and did not include the behaviors of eating uncontrollably, binge eating, or intentionally vomiting, then you would not have covered the entire range of behaviors that ought to go into a scale designed to measure progress in treating bulimia. Sometimes the term **face validity** is used when one's colleagues look over an instrument and agree that it appears to measure the concept. Neither content nor face validity is sufficient for establishing that the scale has "true" validity.

Concurrent validity is demonstrated by administering to the same subjects the new scale and another scale that has previously been determined (proven) to have validity. If the two scales correlate well, then the scale is said to have concurrent validity.

Predictive validity is demonstrated when scores on the new scale predict future behavior or attitudes. If you have developed an instrument to predict which parents are likely to abuse their children and three years later you find that a high percentage of these parents did abuse their children, then your instrument would have predictive validity.

Construct validity is an on-going, confirmatory process that builds upon other validity efforts. The evidence for construct validity comes from how well the scale differentiates along expected lines. For instance, suppose you develop an instrument to measure attitudes about drug usage. You would have evidence of construct validity if it showed that college students attending Baptist colleges held antidrug attitudes and that known drug abusers in a court-ordered treatment program had prodrug attitudes. Such findings would show that the instrument could discriminate between those who had positive and those who had negative attitudes about drugs. An instrument that cannot make these kinds of discriminations (e.g., between those who benefited and those who did not benefit from a program) would be of no use to program evaluators.

While reliability and validity have been presented as separate concepts, they are interrelated in a complex fashion. If an instrument can be empirically demonstrated to have validity (and we're not talking about just face or content validity), then it can generally be assumed to have adequate reliability. However, a reliable instrument may not be valid for the purpose we want to use it. That is, an instrument may provide dependable measurements, but of some concept unrelated to what we thought we were measuring. However, both reliability and validity ought to be demonstrated as evidence that an instrument is psychometrically strong. This is not an either/or choice. The evaluator should try to obtain information about the instrument's reliability and validity before adopting it. If you know nothing about the reliability and validity of an instrument, it is important to realize that the results obtained from its use will have very little meaning. One obvious way of avoiding having to establish that your new scale has reliability and validity is to use instruments that already have been demonstrated to have sufficient reliability and validity. For a good example of the ways authors go about establishing that their instruments have reliability and validity, refer to the description of work with the Addiction Severity Index contained in McLellan et al. (1985).

■ Locating Appropriate Instruments

Let's assume that the evaluator and/or the evaluation committee have decided to measure the program outcome with a self-esteem inventory. The next problem is to locate a self-esteem scale. This process starts with the literature review that was conducted to find how others had evaluated their programs and the evaluation designs they used. Evaluations of similar programs in journal articles will contain brief descriptions of instruments that were employed. Instruments can also be located by browsing through journal articles. When you locate a relevant one, turn to the references at the end of the article to find the citation for the author or the source referencing the instrument. Occasionally, a complete scale will be contained within a journal article. (See, for example, Doelling and Johnson, 1989, for the Foster Placement Evaluation Scale, contained within an article.)

Sometimes students say, "I want to start a new group in the nursing home, but I don't know which instrument to use." I respond with a series of questions about the goals of the group or program—what it was designed to accomplish. Then we usually discuss what data can readily be obtained and what is feasible to measure. On occasion, I instruct students to do some library research to learn more about a given problem. Suppose the new group in the nursing home is designed to help members adjust to being away from loved ones or their homes. The intent of the group is to help group members become less lonely. There should be some evaluation literature on similar group approaches from which the student can find descriptions of instruments and references for other studies that may have used different instruments or approaches.

Once in the library the student may consult a reference like *Psychological Abstracts, Social Work Research & Abstracts*, or *Index Medicus* (a comprehensive abstract service oriented to medical and mental health problems) and look under such headings as "loneliness," "depression," "nursing homes," "adjustment to nursing homes," "elderly," "aged," and "geriatric patients" until sufficient references are found. With a little searching, references directly relevant to the planned evaluative effort can be located. These articles may describe in detail the evaluation plan, the instrument that was used, the results of other evaluation efforts, and other useful information. Very rarely, however, will the journal articles reproduce the entire instrument used. Often more searching is required to locate the instrument. It may be necessary to contact the author to request a copy of the instrument used in his or her study.

An advantage of going through the abstracts to find relevant articles on a given problem or program is that reviewing these articles helps the evaluator to ground the evaluation effort in terms of theoretical models and explanations. However, if the evaluator (for pragmatic reasons, of course) is concerned with locating an instrument quickly, there are several collections of instruments worth examining.

The most recent collection of instruments is entitled *Measures for Clinical Practice: A Sourcebook* (1987) by Kevin Corcoran and Joel Fisher. The instruments in this volume are divided into those for children, for adults, and for couples and families. All have been empirically tested, are brief (under forty-five items each), and are easy to administer. These are sometimes called rapid assessment instruments (Levitt & Reid, 1981), and you need not be a psychologist to administer or interpret them. These instruments measure such concepts as anxiety, assertion, depression, self-concept, loneliness, guilt, satisfaction with life, social fear, stressful situations, and marital happiness.

Hudson (1982) has developed a number of instruments useful to social workers and other human service professionals, and these can be examined in a small volume entitled *The Clinical Measurement Package: A Field Manual*. While all of these scales have been copyrighted, they are available for purchase and cover such useful areas as contentment, self-esteem, marital satisfaction, sexual satisfaction, parental attitudes, a child's attitudes toward his or her mother and father, family relations, and peer relations. Hudson's instruments are each twenty-five items in length, and studies have shown that "enough data have been obtained to strongly support the validity and reliability of the entire package" (p. viii). Individuals with scores above thirty are usually found to have a "clinically significant problem."

The *Handbook of Scales for Research in Crime and Delinquency* (1983) contains a number of scales designed to measure attitudes toward the law, police, and law-abidingness; parolability; self-reported delinquency; delinquency potential; hostility; and aggression.

The advantage of browsing through these three publications is that they afford you an opportunity to visualize the scales. However, it is not always possible to see examples of instruments without purchasing them. Useful reference guides exist to help you locate instruments, but these generally do not contain test specimens. For instance, Conoley and Kramer, editors of the *Tenth Mental Measurements Yearbook* (1989), have assembled reviews of close to four hundred commercially available tests. The publication is organized like an encyclopedia—reviews of tests are found alphabetically by test title. The classified subject guide lists a number of tests under "personality" that may be of interest to social workers.

Other reference guides that describe and catalog tests include:

Educational Testing Service. (1988). *The ETS Test Collection Catalog. Volume 2: Vocational Tests and Measurement Devices.* New York: Oryx Press.

Educational Testing Service. (1989). *The ETS Test Collection Catalog. Vol. 3: Tests for Special Populations.* New York: Oryx Press.

Goldman, B.A. and Busch, J.C. (1982). *Directory of Unpublished Experimental Mental Measures.* New York: Human Sciences Press.

Hamill, D.D. (1989). *A Consumer's Guide to Tests in Print*. Austin, TX: Pro-ED.

Keyser, D.J. and Sweetland, R.C. (1984). *Test Critiques*. V1–7. Kansas City, MO: Test Corporation of America.

Keyser, D.J. and Sweetland, R.C. (1987). *Test Critques Compendium: Reviews of Major Tests from the Test Critiques Series*. Kansas City, MO: Test Corporation of America.

Sweetland, R.C. & Keyser, D.J. (1983). *Tests: A Comprehensive Reference*. Kansas City, MO: Test Corporation of America.

Sweetland, R.C. and Keyser, D.J. (1986). *Tests: A Comprehensive Reference for Assessments in Psychology, Education, and Business* Kansas City, MO: Test Corporation of America.

Still other volumes describing and containing instruments that may be useful to you are:

Chun, Ki-Taek, Cobb, S., & French, J.R., Jr. (1975). *Measures for Psychological Assessment: A Guide to 3000 Original Sources and Their Applications*. Ann Arbor, MI: Institute for Social Research.

Fredman, N., & Sherman, R. (1987). *Handbook of Measurements for Marriage and Family Therapy*. New York: Brunner/Mazel.

Lake, D.G., Miles, M.B., & Earle, R.B., Jr. (1973). *Measuring Human Behavior: Tools for the Assessment of Social Functioning*. New York: Teachers College Press.

McDowell, I. & Newell, C. (1987). *Measuring Health: A Guide to Rating Scales and Questionnaires*. New York: Oxford University Press.

Robinson, J.P., Athanasiou, R., & Head, K.B. (1969). *Measures of Occupational Attitudes and Occupational Characteristics*. Ann Arbor, MI: Institute for Social Research.

Another approach to locating instruments is to write to publishing companies that specialize in selling research instruments. Corcoran (1988) has listed over thirty such firms that could be contacted. Not to be overlooked are individual investigators who develop instruments and then form their own publishing companies to sell and market them. Examples of this are the Brief Symptom Inventory (BSI) and the Symptom Checklist 90-R (Derogatis, 1973, 1983) and the Child Abuse Potential Inventory (Milner, 1979). The evaluator finds references to these instruments in journal articles and then may purchase the authors' manuals that discuss reliability and validity, interpretation, characteristics of the normative samples, and other references on the instrument.

A final approach is to contact a faculty member at a university who is known to engage in research. These faculty members may have collections of useful instruments or be able to make recommendations of instruments. Even if they don't personally have the instrument you need, they may be able to refer you to other faculty who will have what you need.

It is not possible to list all of the instruments that are available for use in program evaluations. Several collections of instruments already exist and mention has been made of these. By no means, however, are all of the "good" instruments contained in these reference books. Often, instruments are developed for a specific purpose and the final report is not developed into a journal article. As a rule, journals do not have the space to reproduce instruments that were used in studies. When you find a potentially interesting instrument in a journal article you may have to write the author of the study to request a copy. This can be problematic when the article is not recent and the author has moved or died. (And sometimes university faculty just do not answer their mail or return phone calls very expeditiously.) When this obstacle is encountered, it may be possible to locate other (more accessible) authors who have used the same instrument by looking up the original author (and the corresponding journal reference) in the *Social Sciences Citation Index*. This index will list other authors who have cited the original author in their bibliographies. So, with a little library research, it may be possible to locate even an obscure instrument. When every effort has been made to locate appropriate instruments and none have been found, then it may be time to consider developing your own instrument.

■ Constructing "Good" Evaluation Instruments

A student recently asked me to assist her in getting some reliability data on an instrument she had developed. As a serious and conscientious student she had conducted a thorough literature search and could find no instrument to measure the concept in which she was interested. She talked with knowledgeable persons in the field, developed a list of questions, and reviewed and revised them. In short, she did about everything she could have been expected to do. When we computed the alpha coefficient (reliability) for her ten-item scale with some initial data, it turned out to be a puny .35—not good enough to use with her project. Consequently, the project soon stalled. This example is not intended to scare you or to convince you to avoid developing your own instruments—sometimes it is necessary to develop new instruments. However, if reliable and valid instruments are available for use, it makes little sense to create another instrument.

Developing good instruments requires much more explanation than an introductory evaluation text can provide. However, it is possible to point out some errors commonly made when constructing instruments or developing questionnaires.

Look at the examples of the questions in figure 6.1. Can you identify anything wrong with these questions?

In the first question, you should notice that there are two positive evaluation choices ("excellent" and "good"), but only one negative possibility. Respondents have two opportunities to say something good about the program but only one to indicate dissatisfaction. This response scale is biased towards (more likely to get) positive feedback about the program than negative feedback. It is not balanced. A better way to handle this would be to provide the response categories of "excellent," "good," "undecided," "fair," and "poor."

The problem with the second question is that "often" is not defined. What does often mean to you? Once a week? Once a month? Daily? The same difficulty would exist if the term "regular" were used (e.g., "Do you attend A.A. meetings regularly?).

The third question doesn't get specific responses. One could be sin-

Figure 6.1: Examples of Poorly Constructed Questions

1. Please rate the quality of our services:
   a. excellent   b. good   c. poor

2. Do you come here often for help?
   a. yes   b. no   c. don't know

3. What is your marital status?
   a. single   b. married   c. divorced

4. How long have you been a client with us?
   a. six months or less
   b. under a year
   c. one year or longer

5. What is your income?
   a. $10,000 to $20,000
   b. $20,000 to $30,000
   c. $30,000 or more

6. Do you not make a practice of shopping only on weekends?
   a. yes   b. no   c. undecided

7. Do you have a male relative and a female relative over fifty-five years of age living at home with you?
   a. yes   b. no   c. undecided

8. Approximately how many minutes do you dream each evening?
   a. under 15   b. 16 to 30   c. more than 31 minutes

9. Wouldn't you agree that clients should keep their accounts current with the agency?
   a. yes   b. no   c. undecided

gle because one had never married, because one was a widow or widower, or because one had been married and was in the process of legally dissolving it. On some occasions, it may be important to list as a separate response those who are "separated."

In the fourth question, there is a problem with the response set. Note that the response categories are not mutually exclusive. If one had been a client for exactly six months, both "a. six months or less" and "b. under a year" would be correct. There is also a problem with overlapping response categories in item five. A client with a $20,000 income might select a. because it was the first category he or she read, or b. because it suggests a desired income category. An additional problem with the income question is that "income" is a vague term. Is the intent of the question to identify the principal wage earner's annual salary? Or, does the question seek to know the total family income from all sources? Confusion about whether the question is asking for take-home (net) or gross pay is also likely.

Question six creates problems because the word "not" makes the question more complex than it needs to be. Many people will have to read the question a second time. Some individuals will inadvertently fail to see "not." Also, note that "shopping" is not defined. Does shopping refer to all shopping—shopping for essentials as well as nonessentials? What if one runs out of milk and stops to pick up a quart on the way home from work Thursday evening? Is stopping to buy a newspaper or a magazine considered to be shopping?

Item seven is called a "double-barreled" question. It asks two things in one sentence. It is entirely possible to have a male relative over the age of fifty-five living at home without having a female relative over fifty-five residing there—and vice versa. How would you respond to this question if you had only the male relative fifty-five or older but not the female living at home?

Item eight asks for information that the respondent cannot be reasonably expected to have. Most of us do not know how long we dream each evening. This question asks for information that can only be conjecture. Absurd questions and those which ask for information that respondents don't have not only may yield worthless data but on occasion may provoke an angry response resulting in respondents refusing to continue any further with the interview or the questionnaire.

When constructing questionnaires and developing items for instruments, one must be careful to use vocabulary that will be understood by the potential respondents. Avoid jargon and technical talk. Do not use street talk or terms that not everyone will understand. A student recently told me about an experience where a street person approached him and asked if he had a "pull." The student thought that street person meant "pool." After further discussion, the student realized that a cigarette was being requested.

Item nine is an example of a leading question. Few people tend to disagree with a question that suggests the answer. Further, there is an issue here of social desirability. Few people tend to disagree with normal social conventions (e.g., cleanliness, being sober on the job). We all want to be liked by other people, and there is a tendency to give responses that are "acceptable" even if that is not what we really believe or how we really act. It may not be easy for clients whose behavior is excessive or outside of "normal" social behavior to admit the true extent of their problem. For example, few active alcoholics will admit to being an alcoholic—yet they might admit to "occasionally drinking more than they should." Terms such as "alcoholic," "junkie," "addict," and "delinquent" are stigmatizing to respondents, and most individuals will not deliberately choose a response that characterizes them as being flawed, deviant, or markedly different from the rest of humanity.

Finally, there are important considerations in terms of what questions are asked first. As a general rule, it is better to ask sensitive questions (such as those about income, age, sexual practices) toward the end of the questionnaire. The theory is that individuals are more likely to respond to these items once they have become involved in the process of completing the questionnaire (or in the case of interviews, established rapport with the interviewer). For further assistance in the development of questionnaires, refer to Dillman (1978), Bradburn and Sudman (1979), Schuman and Presser (1981), Sudman and Bradburn (1982), and Alreck and Settle (1985).

■ Example 1: Constructing a Questionnaire

Susie Caseworker was employed as a hospital social worker in a rural community. She was one of two social workers responsible for patients in a rural hospital. While Susie liked her job, one annoying problem was that the Emergency Room staff could page her and she would have to drop what she was doing and race to the Emergency Room. She was constantly being interrupted and taken away from her patients in order to be of assistance in the Emergency Room. In her opinion, this happened with enough frequency to justify the hospital hiring another social worker solely for assignment in the Emergency Room. She discussed this with the hospital administrator, who said that he would make a decision once she had documented the need for an Emergency Room social worker. The five questions in figure 6.2 are those that Susie prepared as part of that effort. Her intention was to give the survey to each nurse and physician who worked in the Emergency Room. Let's evaluate the questions Susie was going to ask.

Figure 6.2 shows how difficult preparing an instrument can be. Consider the information which these five questions will produce. Will these

Figure 6.2: Emergency Room Survey

Place an "x" by the answer that best corresponds to your thinking.

1. There are times when a social worker could be utilized in the Emergency Room.
   ( ) never   ( ) seldom   ( ) occasionally   ( ) frequently   ( ) always

2. When I worked with a social worker, he/she acted in a professional manner.
   ( ) never   ( ) seldom   ( ) occasionally   ( ) frequently   ( ) always

3. When I needed a social worker, one was readily available.
   ( ) never   ( ) seldom   ( ) occasionally   ( ) frequently   ( ) always

4. I see cases where family members are not coping well with a relative's illness or injury.
   ( ) never   ( ) seldom   ( ) occasionally   ( ) frequently   ( ) always

5. I have seen situations in the Emergency Room where social workers could have done counseling.
   ( ) never   ( ) seldom   ( ) occasionally   ( ) frequently   ( ) always

questions provide the kind of evidence that will convince the hospital administrator of the need for an Emergency Room social worker? How can these questions be interpreted or misconstrued? What additional questions would you want to ask?

A potential problem with the first question is that it assumes that physicians and nurses know how and on which occasions a social worker could be utilized. If physicians and nurses don't know exactly what it is that a social worker does, then it is entirely possible that they would under- or overestimate the number of occasions when a social worker could be appropriately employed. These Emergency Room workers may not know when a social worker "ought" to be utilized. Do they think social workers are to be used to hold the hand of a person in pain? Or to provide grief counseling only when the chaplain isn't around? Are social workers to empty bedpans or watch small children when there is no one else to supervise them? Better information might be obtained if the Emergency Room staff were asked to identify the needed activities to be performed by social workers or the occasions when a social worker could be used.

A related but missing question could be developed to identify times that a social worker was most needed. There may be shifts (such as between 11 P.M. and 7 A.M. on weekends when there are more emergencies requiring assistance from a social worker. It may be that the existing hospital social workers can adequately cover the Emergency Room during weekdays, but that the greatest need for a social worker is on the weekends and evenings.

It might be helpful to ask the Emergency Room staff respondents to enumerate the number of times during an average day, weekend, and evening shift when the services of a social worker would be beneficial. Here, too, the response set is important. Knowing that respondents indicated that a social worker could have been used an average of twenty-five times per shift is a lot more powerful information than knowing the most frequent response was "occasionally" or "frequently."

The second question inappropriately attempts to assess the professionalism of the existing social work staff. Professionalism is not the issue at hand. The inclusion of this question does not help to assess the need for a social worker in the Emergency Room.

The problem with the third question is that there is no way to know how many occasions the respondent might have had a need for a social worker. The emphasis appears to be on availability. If a social worker was needed five times last week and was readily available all five times, would the respondent check "frequently" or "always"? Although it is not clear, perhaps the author of this question was trying to explore the time lag between the request for the social worker and the amount of time it took the social worker to disengage from other duties and to appear in the Emergency Room. If the social workers can always respond within a five or ten minute period, perhaps there is no need to add another social worker just for the Emergency Room. If this is the case, the evaluator might want to ask the question, "What is the longest you have had to wait for the social worker to disengage from other responsibilities and to travel to the Emergency Room?" This question could be followed by another: "About how often does this occur?"

Question four is vague and could be improved by asking how often (in terms of times per shift, week, or month) are cases observed where family members need brief counseling or referral from a social worker.

Question five seems to repeat the first question. It could be improved by listing a number of situations in which it is likely that Emergency Room staff would want to have a social worker available to assist. Once again, a frequency count of the times a social worker was needed (during a standard time period) would supply better information that the vague "occasionally" or "frequently."

■ Example 2: Evaluating Inservice Training _____

John Practitioner had responsibility for training social workers in a large state agency. John wanted to evaluate a major new training program for supervisors that he firmly believed would make them more effective managers. Knowing how participants at professional training sessions and workshops typically give positive feedback (remember our discussion about client satisfaction studies?), John was determined to go beyond asking "Did the presenter do a good job?" "Was the presentation clear and well organized?" or, "What is your overall rating of this workshop?" Instead, John wanted to know how the week-long workshop would impact trainees' as they performed their jobs. He developed the instrument in figure 6.3. Will this instrument help him to know the impact the workshop had on the trainees?

These questions, drawn from a longer instrument, are straightforward and easy to understand. They do not seem to be vague, double-barreled, stigmatizing, and so forth, problems we discussed earlier. There is only one major problem with this collection of items—they measure the respondents' *attitudes* about whether the training has assisted them. John Practitioner has missed the mark if he is truly interested in the "effect" of the intervention. Despite his best intentions, John has prepared a questionnaire that essentially is just another version of other consumer satisfaction efforts.

There is nothing wrong with this if that is what the evaluator wanted to accomplish. But in John's case, he wanted to measure the effect or outcomes of the workshop—the transferability to solving problems on the job. What John really wanted to measure are such things as:

1. absenteeism (is there less absenteeism after the workshop than before?)
2. operating costs (are costs lower?)
3. documentation of records (are a greater percentage of records in compliance with quality assurance standards?)
4. accident rates (are there fewer accidents?)
5. productivity (does productivity increase?)
6. performance ratings (do performance ratings of supervisors improve?)

Figure 6.3: Evaluation of the Supervision Workshop

1. Will this training help you reduce absenteeism among your staff?
   ( ) very little   ( ) moderately   ( ) very much

2. Will this training help you with the operating costs of your office?
   ( ) very little   ( ) moderately   ( ) very much

3. Will this training help you deal with staff's documentation of records?
   ( ) very little   ( ) moderately   ( ) very much

4. Will this training help you reduce accident rates among your staff?
   ( ) very little   ( ) moderately   ( ) very much

5. Will this training help you to increase the productivity of your employees?
   ( ) very little   ( ) moderately   ( ) very much

6. Will this training help you to get improved ratings from your district manager?
   ( ) very little   ( ) moderately   ( ) very much

In devising this instrument, John decided not to examine the increase in knowledge or applied skills that could be measured with a paper and pencil test. Without recognizing it, John had developed a consumer satisfaction instrument that examined participants' opinions or attitudes about the workshop. Given his concerns and interests, John would have been better advised to obtain behavioral data such as absenteeism, operating costs, and accident, performance, and productivity rates for the preceding quarter or year for the departmental supervisors' use and to compare those rates with the data after training. John need not worry about what the participants *thought* about the training as long as it produced demonstrable results.

■ A Sampling of Instruments

For those of you who are not familiar with testing and what paper-and-pencil instruments may actually look like, I have secured the permission of several authors to reproduce all or portions of their instruments. (You will be able to tell from the description whether the whole instrument is shown.) Though a small sample, these demonstrate the great variety of instruments available for program evaluation. Because some of these instruments are protected by copyright, you cannot reproduce them and use them for your own purposes. Read the section on "Availability" in order to know whether you must purchase the scale or request permission to use it.

As you review these instruments, ask yourself how they might be used in a program evaluation effort. What hypotheses or questions would they help you explore? What programs or special populations could they be used with?

Whenever you choose an instrument for evaluation purposes, it should be psychometrically strong (having good reliability and validity) and be sensitive to changes that could occur as a result of the intervention. Look at the instrument in terms of both pre- and posttest applications. Some good assessment instruments do not make good posttest measures because of their wording. Additionally, Corcoran and Fischer (1987) have noted that an instrument should have a practical value (if it does not reflect the clients' problems then there is no need to use the instrument); the instrument should also be acceptable in terms of length, sophistication, cost, and ease in scoring and interpretation. The instrument should not be offensive to the client, and ideally it should be relatively nonreactive. (That is, measuring the behavior should not bring about its change.) Finally, the instrument should have appropriateness—it should provide useful information about progress, while not being a burden upon clients or the staff. The ideal instrument will not have complex instructions (making it easy to administer and to take) and will not require much time to complete or to be scored.

■ CES-D Scale

Description
Developed by the staff at the Center for Epidemiologic Studies, National Institute of Mental Health, the CES-D is a brief self-report scale designed to measure depressive symptomatology in the general population (Radloff, 1977). It was developed from previously existing scales and was designed not to distinguish primary depressive disorders from secondary depression or subtypes of depression but to identify the presence and severity of depressive symptomatology for epidemiologic research, needs assessment, and screening (Radloff & Locke, 1986).

Psychometric Data
This depression scale has been found to have high internal consistency (.85 in the general population and .90 in the patient sample) and acceptable test-retest stability. The CES-D scores discriminate well between psychiatric inpatient and general population samples and moderately well among patient groups with varying levels of severity. The scale has excellent concurrent validity, and substantial evidence exists of its construct validity (Radloff, 1977).

Availability
The CES-D Scale is in the public domain and may be used without copyright permission. The Epidemiology and Psychopathology Research Branch is interested, however, in receiving copies of research reports that have utilized the instrument.

Scoring
Because the CES-D is a twenty-item scale, it is easily scored. Responses are weighted 0 for "Rarely or none of the time" to 3 for "Most of the time." Items 4, 8, 12, and 16 are reverse-scored (given a 3 for "Rarely" and 0 for "Most"). The range of possible scores is 0 to 60. High scores indicate the presence and persistence of depressive symptoms.

For further reference
Radloff, L.S. & Locke, B.Z. (1986). The Community Mental Heath Assessment Survey and the CES-D Scale. In Weissman, M.M., Myers, J.K., and Ross, C.E., (Eds.). *Community Surveys of Psychiatric Disorders*. New Brunswick, NJ: Rutgers.

Radloff, L.S. (1977). The CES-D Scale: A self-report depression scale for research in the general population. *Applied Psychological Measurement*, 3 (1), 385–401.

Weissman, M.M., Sholomskas, D., Pottenger, M., Prusoff, B.A., & Locke, B.Z. (1977). Assessing depressive symptoms in five psychiatric populations: A validation study. *American Journal of Epidemiology*, 6 (3), 203–214.
Comstock, G.W. & Helsing, K.J. (1976). Symptoms of depression in two communities. *Psychological Medicine*, 6, 551–563.

CES-D Scale

Circle the number for each statement which best describes how often you felt or behaved this way-during the past week

	Rarely or None of the Time	Some or a Little of the Time	Occasionally or a Moderate Amount of Time	Most or All of the Time
	(Less than 1 Day)	(1-2 Days)	(3-4 Days)	(5-7 Days)

DURING THE PAST WEEK:

1. I was bothered by things that usually don't bother me	___	___	___	___
2. I did not feel like eating; my appetite was poor	___	___	___	___
3. I felt that I could not shake off the blues even with help from my family or friends	___	___	___	___
4. I felt that I was just as good as other people	___	___	___	___
5. I had trouble keeping my mind on what I was doing	___	___	___	___
6. I felt depressed	___	___	___	___
7. I felt that everything I did was an effort	___	___	___	___
8. I felt hopeful about the future	___	___	___	___
9. I thought my life had been failure	___	___	___	___
10. I felt fearful	___	___	___	___
11. My sleep was restless	___	___	___	___
12. I was happy	___	___	___	___
13. I talked less than usually	___	___	___	___
14. I felt lonely	___	___	___	___
15. People were unfriendly	___	___	___	___
16. I enjoyed life	___	___	___	___
17. I had crying spells	___	___	___	___
18. I felt sad	___	___	___	___
19. I felt that people disliked me	___	___	___	___
20. I could not get "going"	___	___	___	___

Courtesy Department of Health & Human Services.

■ *Inpatient Consumer Satisfaction Scale (ICSS)*

Description

The ICSS was designed to measure consumer satisfaction among public psychiatric inpatient units. Three factors were identified using the ICSS. The first related to satisfaction with services, the second with respect and dignity shown to the patient, and the third with the treatment

---

PATIENT SATISFACTION SURVEY

WE ARE INTERESTED IN YOUR OPINIONS ABOUT YOUR STAY IN THE HOSPITAL.

DIRECTIONS: Please circle the answer that best represents your opinion
on each statement.

SD - Strongly Disagree   A - Agree
D - Disagree   SA - Strongly Agree
N - No Opinion

EXAMPLE:

SD (D) N A SA   The quality of service was good.

SD D N ·A SA	1. Sometimes I felt "put down" by the staff.
SD D N A SA	2. Counseling was helpful therapy for me.
SD D N A SA	3. I am satisfied with services I· received.
SD D N A SA	4. I feel better as a result of coming to the hospital.
SD D N A SA	5. The professional staff (doctors, nurses, psychologists and social workers) generally did not seem concerned about my improvement.
SD D N A SA	6. The nursing staff was willing to listen and talk to me in a helpful way.
SD D N A SA	7. This hospital stay helped me learn how to cope with my problems.
SD D N A SA	8. I am more hopeful about my future after my stay in the hospital.
SD D N A SA	9. It was clearly explained to me why I had to come to the hospital.
SD D N A SA	10. While in the hospital, I felt like I had no control over my life.
SD D N A SA	11. Activities (music, crafts, exercise) were a helpful part of my treatment.
SD D N A SA	12. I felt like I could be myself in the hospital.
SD D N A SA	13. Other patients staying on the ward frightened me.
SD D N A SA	14. The reasons for taking medications were explained to me.
SD D N A SA	15. Talking to my therapist was helpful to me.
SD D N A SA	16. There was not enough privacy on the ward.
SD D N A SA	17. Talking with my doctor was helpful to me.

---

environment. Item means, standard deviations, and percent satisfied/ dissatisfied are contained in the primary reference and can be used for comparison when the ICSS is used in different facilities.

Psychometric Data
Internal reliability of the three factors were an acceptable .92, .80, and .70. Because this is a relatively new instrument, there presently is no information on its concurrent validity. In terms of content validity, the instrument does seem to sample a wide range of topics that are likely to be associated with consumer satisfaction with inpatient services. (Contrast the thirty-three items in this scale with the eight items in the CSQ developed by Larsen, Attkisson, Hargreaves, and Nyguyen, 1979. Compare also with Greenfield and Attkisson, 1989, and Nyguyen, Attkisson, and Stegner, 1984). Construct validation was shown in that the three factors were replicated in a second sample of inpatients discharged from acute inpatient psychiatric units and in the patients' high level of satisfaction with services (as is typically found in similar studies using different instruments).

Availability
Persons interested in using this scale should contact William R. Holcomb, Ph.D., Superintendent, Fulton State Hospital, 600 East 5th, Fulton, Missouri, 65251-1798.

Scoring
All items were scored on a five-point Likert scale with 1 equaling "Disagree strongly" and 5 equaling "Agree strongly."

For further reference
Holcomb, W.R., Adams, N.A., Ponder, H.M., & Reitz, R. (1989). The development and construction validation of a consumer satisfaction questionnaire for psychiatric inpatients. *Evaluation and Program Planning*, 12, 189–194.

■ Child Abuse Potential Inventory

Description
The CAP Inventory is a 160-item questionnaire with a primary clinical scale, the physical child abuse scale, and six factor scales measuring distress, rigidity, unhappiness, problems with child and self, problems with family, and problems with others. Additionally, it contains three validity scales: the lie scale, the random response scale, and the inconsistency scale to check for "faking good," "faking bad," or randomly re-

sponding. An ego strength scale has recently been developed to measure emotional stability from items in the CAP Inventory. Milner (1988) noted that it is appropriate to use the CAP Inventory to measure program effectiveness and identified several studies showing decreases in abuse scores for abusive and neglectful parents as a result of intervention.

CAP INVENTORY FORM VI

Joel S. Milner, Ph D
Copyright. 1977, 1982, 1984. Revised Edition 1986
Printed in the United States of America

Name: _____   Date: _____ ID#: _____

Age: _____ Gender: Male _____ Female _____   Marital Status: Sin__ Mar__ Sep__ Div__ Wid__

Race: Black __ White __ Hispanic __ Am. Indian __   Number of children in home _____

Other (specify) _____   Highest grade completed _____

INSTRUCTIONS: The following questionnaire includes a series of statements which may be applied to yourself. Read each of the statements and determine if you **AGREE** or **DISAGREE** with the statement. If you agree with a statement, circle **A** for agree. If you disagree with a statement, circle **DA** for disagree. Be honest when giving your answers. Remember to read each statement; it is important not to skip any statement.

●○○○

1.	I never feel sorry for others	A	DA
2.	I enjoy having pets	A	DA
3.	I have always been strong and healthy	A	DA
4.	I like most people	A	DA
5.	I am a confused person	A	DA
6.	I do not trust most people	A	DA
7.	People expect too much from me	A	DA
8.	Children should never be bad	A	DA
9.	I am often mixed up	A	DA
10.	Spanking that only bruises a child is okay	A	DA
11.	I always try to check on my child when it's crying	A	DA
12.	I sometimes act without thinking	A	DA
13.	You cannot depend on others	A	DA
14.	I am a happy person	A	DA
15.	I like to do things with my family	A	DA
16.	Teenage girls need to be protected	A	DA
17.	I am often angry inside	A	DA
18.	Sometimes I feel all alone in the world	A	DA
19.	Everything in a home should always be in its place	A	DA
20.	I sometimes worry that I cannot meet the needs of a child	A	DA
21.	Knives are dangerous for children	A	DA
22.	I often feel rejected	A	DA
23.	I am often lonely inside	A	DA
24.	Little boys should never learn sissy games	A	DA
25.	I often feel very frustrated	A	DA

●○○○

Psychometric data

There is an extensive body of research on the CAP Inventory. (See, for instance, Milner & Wimberley, 1979, 1980; Milner, 1986, 1989; Milner, Charlesworth, Gold, Gold & Friesen, 1988.) Internal consistency estimates for the abuse scale range from .91 to .96. Test-retest reliabilities for the abuse scale are also strong. A number of cross-validation studies indicate the abuse scale has overall classification rates in the low 80 percent to low 90 percent range. Predictive validity has been demonstrated in a longitudinal study showing a significant relationship between elevated CAP abuse scores and subsequent confirmed physical child abuse. Construct validity has similarly been reported by a number of investigators. Recently, Wolfe et al. (1988) found significant decreases in abuse scores for a group of at-risk parents given a behavioral training program.

Availability

This instrument is copyrighted. You will need to purchase the manual and copies of the instrument from PSYTEC, Inc., P.O. Box 564, DeKalb, Illinois 60115.

Scoring

Scoring templates, scoring sheets, and computer scoring programs can be purchased along with the instrument from PSYTEC.

For further reference

Milner, J.S. (1989). Applications and limitations of the Child Abuse Potential Inventory. *Early Child Development and Care*, 42, 85–97.

Milner, J.S. (1986). *The Child Abuse Potential Inventory: Manual*, 2d ed. Webster, NC: Psytec Corp.

Milner, J.S., Charlesworth, J.R., Gold, R.G., Gold, S.R., & Friesen, M.R. (1988). Convergent validity of the Child Abuse Potential Inventory. *Journal of Clinical Psychology*, 44 (2), 281–285.

Milner, J.S., Gold, R.G., & Wimberley, R.C. (1986). Prediction and explanation of child abuse: Cross-validation of the Child Abuse Potential Inventory. *Journal of Consulting and Clinical Psychology*, 54 (6), 865–866.

Milner, J.S., & Robertson, K.R. (1989) Inconsistent response patterns and the prediction of child maltreatment. *Child Abuse & Neglect*, 13 (1), 59–64.

Milner, J.S., & Wimberley, R.C. (1979). An inventory for the identification of child abusers. *Journal of Clinical Psychology*, 35, 96–100.

Milner, J.S. & Wimberley, R.C. (1980). Prediction and explanation of child abuse. *Journal of Clinical Psychology*, 36, 875–884.

Thomasson, E., Berkovitz, T., Minor, S., Cassle, G., McCord, D., & Milner, J.S. (1981). Evaluation of a family life education program for rural "high risk" families. *Journal of Community Psychology, 9,* 246–249.

Wolfe, D.A., Edwards, B., Manion, I., & Koverola, C. (1988). Early intervention for parents at risk of child abuse and neglect: A preliminary investigation. *Journal of Consulting and Clinical Psychology, 56,* 40–47.

■ Brief Symptom Inventory

Description

The Brief Symptom Inventory (BSI) is a fifty-three item self-report inventory designed to identify psychological symptom patterns of psychiatric, medical, and normal populations in about ten minutes. A condensed version of the Symptom Checklist 90 (SCL-90), the BSI is scored in terms of nine primary symptom dimensions: somatization, obsessive-compulsive, interpersonal sensitivity, depression, anxiety, hostility, phobic anxiety, paranoid ideation, psychoticism, and three global indices. The General Severity Index is a summary measure of the general level of pathology and is the most important of these indices. The BSI has been widely used, and norms are available for adolescents, college students, the elderly, psychiatric outpatients, and psychiatric inpatients, as well as for nonpatients.

Psychometric Data

The BSI has very acceptable internal consistency reliabilities, ranging from .71 on the Psychoticism scale to .83 on Obsessive-Compulsive. Test-retest reliabilities are good, ranging from a low of .68 to a high of .91. The three global indices all have test-retest reliabilities above .80. Convergent validity has been demonstrated for the BSI with the MMPI. Construct validity has been shown when a factor analysis on a 1,000 psychiatric outpatient sample confirmed the construction of the symptom dimensions.

Availability

The BSI is protected by copyright and must be purchased from Clinical Psychometric Research, Inc., P.O. Box 619, Riderwood, MD 21139. The telephone number is 301-321-6165.

Scoring

Instructions for scoring the BSI are contained in the *BSI Manual.* BSI Profile Forms are available for nonpatient adults, adolescents, outpatient psychiatric adults, and inpatients. Microcomputer programs can also be purchased to score the BSI. Modules can be purchased for desktop scanning of BSIs.

For further reference
Cochran, C.D., & Hale, W.D. (1985). College students norms on the Brief
Symptom Inventory. *Journal of Clinical Psychology*, 41, (6),
777–789.

BSI

SIDE 1

INSTRUCTIONS:

Below is a list of problems people sometimes have. Please read each one carefully, and circle the number to the right that best describes HOW MUCH THAT PROBLEM HAS DISTRESSED OR BOTHERED YOU DURING THE PAST 7 DAYS INCLUDING TODAY. Circle only one number for each problem and do not skip any items. If you change your mind, erase your first mark carefully. Read the example below before beginning, and if you have any questions please ask about them.

SEX

MALE ○

FEMALE ○

NAME: _____

LOCATION: _____

EDUCATION: _____

MARITAL STATUS: MAR ___SEP ___DIV ___WID ___SING ___

DATE			ID. NUMBER	AGE
MO	DAY	YEAR		

EXAMPLE

HOW MUCH WERE YOU DISTRESSED BY:

VISIT NUMBER: _____

		NOT AT ALL	A LITTLE BIT	MODERATELY	QUITE A BIT	EXTREMELY
1.	Bodyaches	0	1	2	(3)	4

HOW MUCH WERE YOU DISTRESSED BY:

			NOT AT ALL	A LITTLE BIT	MODERATELY	QUITE A BIT	EXTREMELY
1.	Nervousness or shakiness inside	1	0	1	2	3	4
2.	Faintness or dizziness	2	0	1	2	3	4
3.	The idea that someone else can control your thoughts	3	0	1	2	3	4
4.	Feeling others are to blame for most of your troubles	4	0	1	2	3	4
5.	Trouble remembering things	5	0	1	2	3	4
6.	Feeling easily annoyed or irritated	6	0	1	2	3	4
7.	Pains in heart or chest	7	0	1	2	3	4
8.	Feeling afraid in open spaces	8	0	1	2	3	4
9.	Thoughts of ending your life	9	0	1	2	3	4
10.	Feeling that most people cannot be trusted	10	0	1	2	3	4
11.	Poor appetite	11	0	1	2	3	4
12.	Suddenly scared for no reason	12	0	1	2	3	4
13.	Temper outbursts that you could not control	13	0	1	2	3	4
14.	Feeling lonely even when you are with people	14	0	1	2	3	4
15.	Feeling blocked in getting things done	15	0	1	2	3	4
16.	Feeling lonely	16	0	1	2	3	4
17.	Feeling blue	17	0	1	2	3	4
18.	Feeling no interest in things	18	0	1	2	3	4
19.	Feeling fearful	19	0	1	2	3	4
20.	Your feelings being easily hurt	20	0	1	2	3	4
21.	Feeling that people are unfriendly or dislike you	21	0	1	2	3	4
22.	Feeling inferior to others	22	0	1	2	3	4
23.	Nausea or upset stomach	23	0	1	2	3	4
24.	Feeling that you are watched or talked about by others	24	0	1	2	3	4
25.	Trouble falling asleep	25	0	1	2	3	4
26.	Having to check and double check what you do	26	0	1	2	3	4
27.	Difficulty making decisions	27	0	1	2	3	4
28.	Feeling afraid to travel on buses, subways, or trains	28	0	1	2	3	4
29.	Trouble getting your breath	29	0	1	2	3	4
30.	Hot or cold spells	30	0	1	2	3	4
31.	Having to avoid certain things, places, or activities because they frighten you	31	0	1	2	3	4
32.	Your mind going blank	32	0	1	2	3	4
33.	Numbness or tingling in parts of your body	33	0	1	2	3	4
34.	The idea that you should be punished for your sins	34	0	1	2	3	4
35.	Feeling hopeless about the future	35	0	1	2	3	4

Copyright© 1975 by Leonard R. Derogatis, Ph. D.

Please continue on the following page ▶

Derogatis, L.R., & Melisaratos, N. (1983). The Brief Symptom Inventory: An introductory report. *Psychological Medicine*, 13, 595–605.

Glaser, R., & Kiecolt-Glaser, J.K. (1985). Stress-related impairments in cellular immunity. *Psychiatry Research*, 16 (3), 233–239.

Gould, M.S., Shaffer, D., & Kaplan, D. (1985). The characteristics of dropouts from a child psychiatry clinic. *Journal of the American Academy of Child Psychiatry*, 24, (3), 316–328.

Hale, W.D., Cochran, C.D., & Hedgepeth, B.E. (1984). Norms for the elderly on the Brief Symptom Inventory. *Journal of Consulting and Clinical Psychology*, 52, 321–322.

Nathan, R.G., Nixon, F.E., Robinson, L.A. Bairnsfather, L., Allen, J.H., & Hack, M. (1987). Effects of a stress management course on grades and health of first-year medical students. *Journal of Medical Education*, 62, 514.

Northouse, L.L. (1988). Social support in patients' and husbands' adjustment to breast cancer. *Nursing Research*, 37 (2), 91–95.

Pekarik, G. (1983). Improvement in clients who have given different reasons for dropping out of treatment. *Journal of Clinical Psychology*, 39, (6), 909–913.

Verinis, J.S., Wetzel, L., Vanderporten, A., & Lewis, D. (1986). Improvement in men inpatients in an alcoholism rehabilitation unit: A week-by-week comparison. *Journal of Studies on Alcohol*, 47, 85–88.

■ Rosenberg Self-Esteem Scale

Description

The Rosenberg Self-Esteem Scale was developed using over five thousand high school juniors and seniors from ten randomly selected schools in New York State. Since the instrument has been in existence almost thirty years, it has seen wide use. Crandall (1973), in a chapter discussing the measurement of self-esteem, ranked the scale fourth out of thirty-three measures in perceived overall quality. Norms are available for many different groups.

Psychometric data

Good internal consistency has been reported (Guttman scale reproducibility coefficient of .92, Cronback's alpha was .77). Test-retest reliability correlations of .85 and higher have been obtained. Rosenberg (1965) has presented a great deal of data on the construct validity of this measure. The Rosenberg Self-Esteem Inventory has been shown to correlate (.59) with the Coopersmith Self-Esteem Inventory.

Availability

This scale is in the public domain and may be used without securing permission. Should you wish to contact the author, his address is: Dr. Morris Rosenberg, Department of Sociology, University of Maryland, College Park, MD, 20742-1315.

```
                        Rosenburg Self-Esteem Scale


Instructions:


BELOW IS A LIST OF STATEMENTS DEALING WITH YOUR GENERAL FEELINGS ABOUT YOURSELF.
IF  YOU AGREE WITH THE STATEMENT, CIRCLE A.  IF YOU  STRONGLY AGREE, CIRCLE  SA.
IF YOU DISAGREE, CIRCLE D.  IF YOU STRONGLY DISAGREE, CIRCLE SD.


                                    Strongly              Dis-      Strongly
                                    Agree      Agree      agree     Disagree

     (1)  On the whole, I am satisfied with    SA         A         D         SD
          myself.

     (2)  At times I think I am no good at all. SA         A         D         SD

     (3)  I feel that I have a number of good   SA         A         D         SD
          qualities.

     (4)  I am able to do things as well as     SA         A         D         SD
          most other people.

     (5)  I feel I do not have much to be       SA         A         D         SD
          proud of.

     (6)  I certainly feel useless at times.    SA         A         D         SD

     (7)  I feel that I'm a person of worth,    SA         A         D         SD
          at least on an equal plane with
          others.

     (8)  I wish I could have more respect      SA         A         D         SD
          for myself.

     (9)  All in all, I am inclined to feel     SA         A         D         SD
          that I am a failure.

    (10)  I take a positive attitude toward     SA         A         D         SD
          myself.
```

Scoring
Using the Likert procedure, responses are assigned a score ranging from 1 to 4. Items 1, 3, 4, 7, and 10 are reverse scored. (For example, item 1, "On the whole I am satisfied with myself," the "strongly agree" response is assigned a score of 4 and "Strongly disagree" is assigned a score of 1.) This procedure yields possible total scores ranging from 10 to 40. The higher the score, the higher the self-esteem.

For further reference
Crandall, R. (1973). The measurement of self-esteem and related constructs. In J.P. Robinson and P.R. Shaver (Eds.), *Measures of Social Psychological Attitudes*, rev. ed. Ann Arbor, MI: Survey Research Center, Institute for Social Research.
Dobson, C., Goudy, W., Keith, P., & Powers, E. (1979). Further analysis of the Rosenberg Self-Esteem Scale. *Psychological Reports, 44,* 639–641.
Hensley, W.E., & Roberts, M.K. (1976). Dimensions of Rosenberg's Self-Esteem Scale. *Psychological Reports,* 38, 583–584.
Rosenberg, M. *Society and the Adolescent Self-Image.* Princeton, NJ: Princeton University Press, 1965.
Wylie, Ruth C. (1989). *Measures of Self-Concept.* Lincoln: University of Nebraska Press.

■ Adult-Adolescent Parenting Inventory

Description
The Adult-Adolescent Parenting Inventory (AAPI) is designed to provide an index of risk for abusive and neglecting parenting and child-rearing behaviors. Items were developed from four constructs about abusive and neglecting parenting: inappropriate parental expectations of the child, lack of empathy toward the child's needs, parental value of physical punishment, and parent-child role reversal. The AAPI consists of thirty-two items and takes about twenty minutes to complete. It is written at the fifth grade reading level and can be administered orally to nonreaders.

Psychometric data
Approximately three thousand adolescents have participated in the field testing of the inventory. Items in each of the four constructs produced an internal reliability equal to or greater than .70. The total test-retest reliability of all items was .76. In terms of diagnostic and discriminatory validity, research with the AAPI has shown that abused adolescents express significantly more abusive attitudes than their nonabused peers. Abusive adults express significantly more abusive attitudes than nonabu-

Adult-Adolescent Parenting Inventory
AAPI

	Strongly Agree	Agree	Uncertain	Disagree	Strongly Disagree
1. Young children should be expected to comfort their mother when she is feeling blue.	SA	A	U	D	SD
2. Parents should teach their children right from wrong by sometimes using physical punishment.	SA	A	U	D	SD
3. Children should be the main source of comfort and care for their parents.	SA	A	U	D	SD
4. Young children should be expected to hug their mother when she is sad.	SA	A	U	D	SD
5. Parents will spoil their children by picking them up and comforting them when they cry.	SA	A	U	D	SD
6. Children should be expected to verbally express themselves before the age of one year.	SA	A	U	D	SD
7. A good child will comfort both of his/her parents after the parents have argued.	SA	A	U	D	SD
8. Children learn good behavior through the use of physical punishment.	SA	A	U	D	SD
9. Children develop good, strong characters through very strict discipline.	SA	A	U	D	SD
10. Parents should expect their children who are under three years to begin taking care of themselves.	SA	A	U	D	SD
11. Young children should be aware of ways to comfort their parents after a hard day's work.	SA	A	U	D	SD
12. Parents should slap their child when s/he has done something wrong.	SA	A	U	D	SD
13. Children should always be spanked when they misbehave.	SA	A	U	D	SD
14. Young children should be responsible for much of the happiness of their parents.	SA	A	U	D	SD
15. Parents have a responsibility to spank their children when they misbehave.	SA	A	U	D	SD

Please go to next page.

sive adults. Standardized norms for the AAPI have been based on samples of over one thousand nonabusive adults, 780 abusive adults, 300 abused adolescents, and 6,480 nonabused adolescents. Bavolek (1984) has reported that parents completing a comprehensive parenting and nurturing program significantly increased their parenting attitudes upon completion of the program.

Scoring

The AAPI is available in two forms, A and B. Scoring stencils are used with AAPI profile worksheets in order to plot the standard scores. A computerized version of the AAPI is also available with reusable diskettes.

Availability

The AAPI is protected by copyright. You will need to purchase the manual, copies of the instrument, and other supplies from Family Development Resources, Inc., 219 East Madison Street, Eau Claire, Wisconsin, 54703. The telephone number is 715-833-0904.

For further reference

Bavolek, S.J. (1989). Assessing and teaching high-risk parenting attitudes. *Early Child Development and Care, 42,* 99–112.

Bavolek, S.J. (1984). An innovative program for reducing abusive parent-child interactions. *Child Resource World Review, 2,* 6–24.

Bavolek, S.J., Kline, D., & McLaughlin, J. (1979). Primary prevention of child abuse: Identification of high risk adolescents. *Child Abuse and Neglect: International Journal, 3,* 1071–1080.

Fox, R.A., Baisch, M.J., Goldberg, B.D., & Hochmuth, M.C. (1987). Parenting attitudes of pregnant adolescents. *Psychological Reports, 61,* 403–406.

■ Chapter Recap and Final Thoughts _____

This is an important chapter. In addition to containing samples of instruments, it provides information about where to locate instruments and how to identify "good" instruments, and makes some suggestions about writing or constructing one's own evaluation instrument. However, several other topics need to be mentioned. First, in deciding upon an instrument to use in a program evaluation effort, the evaluator should consider whether an instrument is likely to be sensitive to change as a result of the intervention or involvement in the program. Some traits (e.g., intelligence) are not thought to vary much over the course of several months (or even years). So, even if you locate a psychometrically sound intelligence test, you may not find much pretest/posttest difference with your clients because under normal circumstances, intelligence does not change. Similarly, questionnaire response choices where greater variation is allowed (e.g., 10 or 7 point response scales) allow for greater sensitivity to change than 3 point scales (e.g., "Good," "Fair," "Poor").

Second, when you design questionaires or evaluation instruments, be mindful of how the data will be analyzed. With open-ended questions ("What one thing would you change about this program if it were within your power to do so?"), the enormous range and variety of responses that are usually obtained are difficult to categorize. Limit yourself to a small number of open-ended questions.

From a data analytic standpoint, closed-ended questions (those where the response set is provided) are superior to open-ended questions. They are easier to code and put into the computer, they can be aggregated to make scales with numerical values, and they may require less of the client's time. On the other hand, closed-ended questions do not provide the rich detail that comes from open-ended questions. The choice between close-ended and open-ended questions should not be "either/or." Both types of questions can be used advantageously.

QUESTIONS FOR CLASS DISCUSSION

1. What is wrong with the following questionnaire items?
   a. True or False: Rape seldom takes place during daytime hours or in the victim's home.
   b. Describe your mother's condition during pregnancy.
   c. Yes or No: Have you ever been involved in any accidents?
2. Barbara Daydreamer designed a three item questionnaire to be used as a pre- and posttest instrument to measure adolescents' knowledge of alcoholism as a disease. Later she was surprised to find that there were no significant differences between pre- and posttest scores. How would you explain this?
3. Because her colleagues had so many problems with her previous questionnaires, Barbara designed a new one. This time she developed the following items as prototypes. What advice would you give to her?
   a. When you are an adult, what are the chances that you will be a drinker?
      _____ I am certain I will never drink
      _____ I don't think I will drink
      _____ I am not sure
      _____ I think I will drink
      _____ I am sure I will drink

   b. Have you ever had a drink of an alcoholic beverage?

     ____ No

     ____ Yes

     If yes, how many last week? _____

4. Discuss the relative merits of the instruments displayed in this chapter. What practical applications are there? In what ways are the instruments limited?

MINI-PROJECTS: EXPERIENCING EVALUATION FIRSTHAND

1. Find and read "Reliability and Validity of the MAST, Mortimer-Filkins Questionnaire, and CAGE in DUI Assessments" by H. D. Mischke and R. L. Venneri, in *Journal of Studies in Alcohol* (1987) 48 (5), 492–501, or "Rating Scales for Marital Adjustment," by D. F. Harrison and D. J. Westhuis, in *Journal of Social Service Research* (1989) 13 (1), 87–105. Summarize what one of the articles reported and then write a brief (three-page) paper on what you learned about evaluating the psychometric properties of instruments.

2. In one paragraph or more, outline a social service program with which you are familiar. Then, locate a paper-and-pencil instrument which will enable you to successfully operationally define your key outcome variable(s) for a program evaluation. If possible, obtain a copy of the instrument you found and bring it to class to share. Be prepared to discuss the strengths and weaknesses of the instrument.

3. For a problem often seen in clients of social service programs (e.g., fear of failure, dependency, lack of assertiveness), devise a ten item scale that could be used to quantitatively show improvement as a result of intervention.

REFERENCES AND RESOURCES

Aday, L.A. (1989). *Designing and conducting health surveys: A comprehensive guide*. San Francisco, CA: Jossey-Bass.

Alreck, P.L., & Settle, R.B. (1985). *The survey research handbook*. Homewood, IL: Irwin.

Bradburn, N., & Sudman, S. (1979) *Improving interview method and questionnaire design*. San Francisco, CA: Jossey-Bass.

Brodsky, S.L., & Smitherman, H.O. (1983). *Handbook of scales for research in crime and delinquency*. New York: Plenum Press.

Conoley, J.C., & Kramer, J.J. (Eds.). (1989). *The tenth mental measurements yearbook*. Lincoln: University of Nebraska Press.

Corcoran, K.J. (1988). Selecting a measuring instrument. In R.M. Grinnell, Jr., *Social work research and evaluation*. Itasca, IL: Peacock.

Corcoran, K., & Fischer, J. (1987). *Measures for clinical practice: A sourcebook.* New York: Free Press.

Curtis, P.A., Rosman, M.D., & Pappenfort, D.M. (1984). Developing an instrument for measuring psychosocial assessment in clinical child welfare. *Child Welfare,* 63 (4), 309–318.

Derogatis, L.R., Lipman, R.S., & Covi. L. (1973). The SCL-90: An outpatient psychiatric rating scale—Preliminary report. *Psychopharmacology Bulletin,* 9 (1), 13–27.

Derogatis, L.R., & Melisaratos, N. (1983). The Brief Symptom Inventory: An introductory report. *Psychological Medicine,* 13, 595–605.

Dillman, D.A. (1978). *Mail and telephone surveys: The total design method.* New York: Wiley.

Doelling, J.L., & Johnson, J.H. (1989). Foster placement evaluation scale: Preliminary findings. *Social Casework,* 70 (2), 96–100.

Edleson, J.L. (1985). Rapid-assessment instruments for evaluating practice. *Journal of Social Service Research,* 8 (3), 17–31.

Greenfield, T.K., & Attkisson, C.C. (1989). Steps toward a multifactorial satisfaction scale for primary care and mental health services. *Evaluation and Program Planning,* 12 (3), 271–278.

Hudson, W.W. (1982). *The clinical measurement package: A field manual.* Homewood, IL: Dorsey Press.

Larsen, D., Attkisson, C.C., Hargreaves, W., & Nguyen, T. (1979). Assessment of client/patient satisfaction: Development of a general scale. *Evaluation and Program Planning,* 2, 197–207.

Levitt, J.L. & Reid, W.J. (1981). Rapid-assessment instruments for practice. *Social Work Research and Abstracts,* 17 (1), 13–19.

McDowell, I., & Newell, C. (1987). *Measuring health: A guide to rating scales and questionnaires.* London: Oxford University Press.

McLellan, A.T., Luborsky, L., Cacciola, J., Griffith, J., Evans, F., Barr, H.L., & O'Brien, C.P. (1985). New data from the Addiction Severity Index: Reliability and validity in three centers. *Journal of Nervous and Mental Disease,* 173, (7), 412–423.

Meisenheimer, C.G. (1985). *Quality assurance: A Complete guide to effective programs.* Rockville, MD: Aspen Systems Corp.

Nguyen, T.D., Attkisson, C.C., & Stegner, B.L. (1984). Assessment of patient satisfaction: Development and refinement of a service evaluation questionnaire. *Evaluation and Program Planning,* 6, 299–314.

Nunnaly, J.C. (1978). *Psychometric theory.* New York: McGraw-Hill.

Radloff, L.S. (1979). The CES-D Scale: A self-report depression scale for research in the general population. *Applied Psychological Measurement,* 3, 385–401.

Robinson, J.P., & Shaver, P.R. (1980). *Measures of social psychological attitudes.* Ann Arbor: Institute for Social Research, University of Michigan.

Schuman, H., & Presser, S. (1981). *Questions and answers in attitude surveys.* New York: Academic Press.

Sudman, S., & Bradburn, N.M. (1982). *Asking questions: A practical guide to questionnaire design.* San Francisco, CA: Jossey-Bass.

CHAPTER 7

Pragmatic and Political Considerations

While program evaluations are conducted because of a commitment to providing the best possible services or because of a need to know if one program is better than another, other catalysts for evaluation are personality clashes and power struggles within an organization. The novice evaluator would be well advised to remember that often evaluation is perceived or experienced as a political activity. Sonnichsen (1989) has noted that evaluation is often viewed metaphorically as a sporting event where there are "victims and victors" (p. 15). Program evaluations may be sponsored with the "hidden agenda" of showing that a certain program manager is inept and incompetent so that a more favored employee can be promoted to that position.

The decision to conduct a program evaluation may also stem from a vague perception that the program is not working quite the way it should. A troubled agency may hire an evaluator to document suspected problems such as inadequate supervision and incompetent or abrasive leadership. Sometimes there are visible symptoms of organizational dysfunctioning—staff morale may have deteriorated or staff turn-over may have become problematic.

An administrator may also employ a program evaluator to show that the criticism that he or she has been receiving is unwarranted. Decision makers who desire to reduce or eliminate popular programs in the community may need "evidence" from a program evaluation to convince others that the program is not as effective or cost-efficient as other approaches.

Within any organization, there are likely to be as many opinions as to the "real" purpose and value of an evaluation as there are reasons for conducting the evaluation. As a result, some staff will be supportive and helpful, others will be threatened because the evaluation was "imposed." Staff who feel this way may attempt to undermine the evaluation effort. The evaluator may be seen as an investigative reporter, a critic, a "spy," a benevolent consultant, or some combination of these. Kennedy (1983) noted that:

> Evaluation is an inherently contradictory activity. . . . Evaluators are expected to help organizations achieve their goals, yet because organizations may consist of parts whose goals are incompatible, helping one group may entail hindering another. . . . Evaluators are often expected to observe organizational activities from an objective position, yet their credibility may depend on being perceived as sympathetic friends. Most of these tensions are inherent in the task of evaluation. (P. 519)

The program evaluation literature contains many references to the political nature of program evaluation. Coffee (1989), in discussing opinions toward evaluators, noted that some individuals view evaluators as "mean-spirited, politically motivated, rewarded only for finding out what is wrong. . ." (p. 59). Chelimsky (1987) in an article entitled "What Have We Learned about the Politics of Program Evaluation?" noted that "the choice of the program to evaluate emerges in *real terms* from the political process, with the determination of the types of policy questions to be asked being a function of the decision makers" (p. 10). Cronbach (1980) in his book *Toward Reform of Program Evaluation* summarized his major points in a number of theses. Several of these speak to the political arena in which evaluators must operate. For instance, "the evaluator has political influence even when he does not aspire to it"; "evaluators' professional conclusions cannot substitute for the political process"; and, "a theory of evaluation must be as much a theory of political interaction as it is a theory of how to determine facts" (p. 3).

Muscatello (1989), in writing about his experience as manager of an evaluation team within a large public organization, observed that evaluators are sometimes asked by decision makers to develop data to verify or legitimize decisions that have already been made—an activity, he said, to which purists in the evaluation field may take exception. Other political implications for the evaluator are also apparent in that the "good evaluator" will work with the "good manager" to "ensure that the conclusions and recommendations reached during the study are overlaid first with relevant policy considerations, and then with the realities of organizational politics, organizational environment, and future business strategies" (p. 17). Muscaletto further cautions:

> If this overlay process does not take place, implementation becomes far less practical and the effectiveness of the evaluation function is diminished, along with its value to the organization. For any segment of his or her business, the chief executive officer has the right to ask, "Why do I need this function and/or these people?" Certainly it is a healthy company whose officers ask each segment of the business, "What have you done for me lately?" If the manager of a program evaluation unit cannot demonstrate impact for the evaluation function, then the logical business decision is to eliminate the unit itself. (P. 17)

This theme has also been discussed by Chelimsky (1987) who has written, "We must be useful to others if we are to be successful. That means understanding the political system in which evaluation operates, and understanding the information needs of those policy actors who use evaluation" (p. 17).

Regardless of the motivation for conducting a program evaluation, it will threaten some portion of the agency's staff. If the staff feel that they are being scrutinized in a situation where there is no examination of the administrative hierarchy, they will feel threatened. On the other hand, if the staff feel that the problems lie not with their functioning but at the administrative level and the evaluation will detect this, they will be less threatened. Evaluators must be mindful that anyone fearing loss of job or other negative repercussions from an evaluation will feel threatened. Even if staff do not fear loss of job but feel that the program has been unjustly singled out, they will feel threatened.

If staff feel threatened, they are likely to be less cooperative than the evaluator would desire. While they may not be as vicious as to slash the tires on the evaluator's car, they may quite pleasantly refuse to complete questionnaires or forms that are needed by the evaluator. They may be "too busy" to review their closed client records or to contact active clients for evaluation purposes. They may "forget" to return questionnaires on the date requested, or they may have "lost" the evaluator's instructions. If the evaluation requires ongoing data collection and the evaluator is not in the agency on a regular basis and has not designed adequate data collection mechanisms, the resulting data may be collected sporadically, only when it was convenient, or perhaps not at all. Passive-aggressive staff may argue, "We are here to help clients . . . not to use them as guinea pigs. We are too busy helping—we don't have the luxury of time to conduct research!"

Evaluators should not underestimate the amount of power that they are perceived to have by persons within the organization being evaluated. Thompson (1989) has described the evaluator as a "power broker." Part of the reasoning for this is that the evaluator can speak and act for others in positions of authority. Evaluators can stimulate action and change by speaking for and acting as agents for those who are reluctant to do so on their own. By gathering information and focusing on the important issues, the evaluator assists the decision makers in becoming more knowledgeable (and therefore more powerful).

Perhaps the evaluator will be viewed by some agency staff as a "hired gun" who has come into the agency to do away with certain staff by documenting their inefficiency or ineffectiveness. According to this line of thinking, the hired gun takes orders from those who did the hiring. The evaluator will not be seen as objective or even as interested in hearing the "truth" because of ties to those who are paying the consulting fees.

The evaluator may be pressured by the administrator or administration to show that a program is successful—whether it is or not. Because of the potential for losing funds, administrators may be anxious that even negative findings be worded in such a way as to present the program in the best possible light. They may ask the evaluator to emphasize the positive points (see Kytle & Millman, 1986, for instance), to include anecdotal accounts from satisfied clients or favorable remarks of influential persons in the community (even though these individuals may know little about the program). Similarly, administrators may be concerned with the order in which the findings are presented. They may want the favorable points made early in the evaluation report and the negative points buried deep in the report. House (1986) has cautioned **internal evaluators** (staff evaluators employed full-time by an organization) against confusing the interests of the organizations with those of individual administrators with whom they identify personally.

Regardless of whether you are an internal evaluator or an **external** (contract) **evaluator**, you will find that program evaluation is almost always conducted in a political arena. A finding that pleases one group may make another group unhappy. It can be expected that political pressures will vary in strength depending on what is at stake. The wise evaluator will be sensitive to any factors (political or otherwise) that can have a biasing effect. Accordingly, several guidelines have been drafted to assist you in managing political pressures that may attempt to influence the outcome of your program evaluation.

■ Guidelines for Evaluation in Politically Charged Arenas

1. **Maintain your independence.** There may be some pressure from within the organization to present the results in a favorable light. This problem is reported quite often in evaluation literature (see Worthen & White, 1987, and Kytle & Millman, 1986, for example). Prepare for such pressures. Suggest ahead of time that some of the findings may be positive and some may be negative. Let it be known that information from a variety of perspectives will be gathered and examined.

   The evaluator's autonomy is less likely to be compromised when there is a clear notion of the purpose of the evaluation and what the evaluator's role will be. As an evaluator, will you be a consultant making suggestions to help a program grow and improve? Or will you be a "fact finder" who uncovers and diagnoses unhealthy programs so that the administration can perform "surgery"? Insist upon a contract that states explicitly the evaluation sponsors' expectations of you and the evaluation product.

   Your independence is safeguarded when, in the process of negotiating a contract, you insist upon editorial authority in writing the evaluation report. Do not allow the evaluation sponsor to have final authority for writing or revising your evaluation report. (However, it is often a good idea to brief key personnel once you have a draft copy of the report ready. Sometimes such briefings can provide the evaluator with a different perspective or new way of interpreting the data. Briefings may also serve the useful purpose of keeping the administration from being totally surprised by negative findings. The little bit of additional time this may require is well worth its expenditure in a politically charged arena—a director will have time to prepare a response or implement corrective actions even before the report becomes "official.")

2. **Negotiate a contract.** One way to reduce confusion about the evaluator's role and the purpose of the evaluation is to draft an agreement or contract. These contracts can be complex or simple and will vary widely depending upon the amount of time and remuneration involved, the intricacy of the evaluation, and the amount of trust between the evaluation sponsor and the evaluator. (Worthen and White [1987] and Herman, Morris, and Fitz-Gibbon [1987] can be consulted for additional information on negotiating a contract). Essentially, these agreements should cover:

   a. The purpose or focus of the evaluation. (Incorporate a list of the questions that the evaluation sponsor wants answered or hypotheses that will be investigated.)

b. The beginning and ending dates of the evaluation. (At a minimum, it is important to specify deadlines when the evaluation products must be finished.) On some occasions, it may also be advisable to describe the sponsor's expectations of a final product—in terms of appearance, the amount of detail it will contain, and so forth.

c. The evaluation methodology; data, staff, and facilities needed. (Will the evaluation design necessitate the use of control groups? Will random assignment of clients be necessary? Will it be necessary to obtain sensitive information from clients? What other data will be necessary to access? How many and what employees will need to assist?)

d. The budget needed. (Not only is agreement important on the consultant's fee, but also there should be a definite budget for such items as travel, supplies, printing, secretarial services, and so on. It is also important to specify the payment schedule—when the evaluator can be expected to be paid.)

e. Ownership of the data and editorial authority. (At the end of the evaluation, who keeps the computer printouts, completed questionnaires, and other data? You may need the data, or at least access to it, should you decide to write an article for a professional journal. Further, it should be clear who will write and have editorial authority over the final evaluation report, and to whom it will and can be disseminated.)

In some instances, it is necessary for the evaluator to gather some information about the program or agency before an evaluation design and data collection procedures can be recommended. This design phase (sometimes called a feasibility study) may be negotiated separately so that the evaluator can later submit a realistic estimate for conducting the actual evaluation.

3. **Attempt to obtain evaluative information from as many sources as is feasible.** Be inclusive rather than exclusive. Talk to clients, staff, board members, citizens in the community—in short, talk to anyone who may have an opinion about the program. Use more than one evaluation design if time and resources allow. Consider the worst case scenario—what would you be able to conclude if the evaluation model you have planned does not work as it was intended? What other sources of data would be available for evaluation? Along this line Michael Quinn Patton (1982) has written, "In my judgment it is not practical to base one's entire practice on a single model in the hope (or expectation) that said model will always work" (p. 43).

4. **Explain and communicate the purpose of the evaluation and its methodology to staff and other interested parties.** Schedule a staff meeting and allow the staff to raise questions and interact with you. You may even want to use a committee of practitioners for advisory purposes. They can provide you with feedback with regard to the evaluation procedures. They will know the educational level and abilities of the clients and, if they want to help you, may be able to point out ways to get around certain organizational obstacles or barriers. At a minimum, allowing staff to raise questions will help reduce the level of anxiety they have about the evaluation. Providing staff with information will help suppress some of the rumors that may surface about the "real" purpose of the evaluation. I find that the involvement of staff provides a richer and more comprehensive evaluation than can be obtained when they are not involved. Since they are likely to know the serious problems with the program, it is good evaluation practice to keep staff both informed and involved. Staff and administrators are also more likely to use the results of the evaluation if they participated in the process and their interest was kept at a high level.

While it may seem like just common sense, it is vitally important that any instructions or directions be communicated clearly. Staff and clients will not be as familiar with the evaluation methodology or the instruments as the evaluator. They may require detailed instructions, special training, or additional preparation. (I once heard of an evaluation where the staff were given a rather lengthy questionnaire with practically no instructions at all. In the absence of guidelines, the staff improvised. Some requested additional instructions, others "guessed" at what the evaluator wanted.) On the other hand, we can also overdo the instructions. They can be too complex for busy people to quickly comprehend. If instructions are not readily understood, they are not likely to be followed. There should be virtually no confusion due to the complexity of evaluation procedures or feelings of frustration as a result of the "burden" that is imposed upon clients, staff, or members of boards of directors.

■ Other Pragmatic Problems

While navigating the shoals of agency politics, the evaluator must be alert to day-to-day problems that arise when he or she is not able to personally supervise the evaluation. An evaluator once told me of her frustration when staff affiliated with a special project kept broadening the eligibility criteria in order to provide services to a greater number of needy persons. The evaluator discovered this much later when she followed-up on service recipients and found out that they did not meet the criteria of persons for whom the project had been designed to help. Many of the service recipients could not be included in the evaluation. Much too late to do anything about it, the evaluator had a much smaller group of service recipients to evaluate than had been planned. To make matters worse, somewhere along the line the staff had quit trying to randomly assign clients to the "regular" or the "intensive" intervention programs. They had begun using their own criteria to decide who could best benefit from the programs.

"War stories" of this type abound. Most evaluators have vivid memories of evaluations gone awry. While it would be rare for an evaluation to experience no problems at all, the experienced evaluator learns to anticipate problems before they occur and plan for them. For instance, in planning for a large scale survey to be mailed, the evaluator needs not only to calculate the amount of time required to type the questionnaires, stuff and address the envelopes, and sort the mail by zip codes in time for the post office to deliver them but also to allow for an extra day or two for secretaries to get sick, computers to break down, and holidays and vacation days. Things that may have never happened before may occur at a critical time. For this reason, many evaluators estimate the amount of time taken for certain tasks beyond their control (e.g., the delivery of the mail) and then double their estimates to give a comfortable "cushion" in case unanticipated problems arise. Even for those activities that are within your control, the unexpected can happen and can result in missing a deadline if the planning does not allow for some "slippage."

■ Determining Sample Size

Another pragmatic concern is, "How many clients do I sample?" or, "Have I interviewed enough?" The problem is in knowing how large the sample should be. A common assumption is that 10 percent of the population makes an adequate sample. Yet, this rule of thumb could provide too small a sample (in the case of small populations) or too large a sample (when there is a large population). To understand what size sample is appropriate, we need to consider margin of error and confidence intervals. **Margin of error** refers to the precision of our findings. A margin of error of 5 percent means that the actual findings could vary by as much as 5 points either positively or negatively. A consumer satisfaction survey, for instance, with a 5 percent margin of error associated with a finding of 65 percent of clients "highly satisfied" with services would mean that the true value in the population could be as low as 60 percent (65 − 5 = 60) or as high as 70 percent (65 + 5 = 70). This 5 percent margin of error is pretty standard. If, however, you require greater precision, (e.g., plus or minus 2 points), then you will need to increase your sample size.

The other term that is important to understand is confidence interval. The **confidence interval** is a statement of how often you could expect to find similar results if the survey were to be repeated. Since every survey varies slightly (depending upon who is selected to be in the sample), the confidence interval informs about how often the findings will fall outside the margin of error. For instance, in a sample developed to have a 95 percent confidence interval with a 5 percent margin of error, the results would miss the actual values in the population by more than 5 percent only one time in 20 samples. In 95 out of 100 samples, the results would fall within the 5 percent margin of error.

There are two ways to determine the appropriate sample size for your evaluation effort. One approach is to find reference books or text books that contain tables to aid in determining necessary sample sizes. An example is Chester McCall's (1980) *Sampling and Statistics Handbook for Research in Education: A Technical Reference for Members of the Research Staff of the National Education Association and Its State and Local Affiliated Association.* McCall has prepared tables that allow you to determine sample size based on levels of confidence (99 to 90 percent), and margins of error (1 to 5 percent) when the absolute proportion of the trait, characteristics, or attitude in the population is not known. (When the level of the expected attitude, trait, or characteristic is unknown, a conservative estimate of 50 percent is used. Somewhat smaller samples can be developed when the known proportion in the population is less than 50 percent.)

A second approach is to actually calculate the sample size and adjust for the desired margin of error, confidence interval, and population proportion. The following formula (found in Krejcie and Morgan, 1970) can be used:

Sample Size $= X^2 NP(1-P) \div d^2(N-1) + X^2 P(1-P)$.

Where: X^2 = 3.841 (the table value of chi-square for 1 degree of freedom at the 95% confidence level)

N = the population size

P = the population proportion (without other evidence, this is assumed to be .50)

d = the margin of error or degree of accuracy needed (e.g., .05)

From this formula, I have calculated sample sizes for the populations in table 7.1.

Note that when the population is small, sample sizes constitute a larger proportion than when the population is very large. For example, 24 would be needed to make the necessary sample when the client population is 25 (a proportion of 96 percent) where only 357 would be needed when the population was 5,000 (a proportion of 7 percent). As the population size increases, the sample size increases at a slower or diminishing rate. Sample size remains relatively constant as it approaches 380, so that a sample of 384 is needed whether the population is 50,000 or 1,000,000 (given a 5 percent margin of error and 95 percent confidence).

The 5 percent margin of error and 95 percent confidence are regarded as providing all the precision needed for most research and evaluation purposes in the social sciences. However, there may be occasions when greater or less precision is required. If, for instance, you would be comfortable with a 90 percent confidence level and a 5 percent margin of error, smaller samples could be used. By substituting 2.71 for the chi-square value of 3.841, you can determine that for a population of 500, the

Table 7.1 Appropriate Sizes of Simple Random Samples with a 5% Margin of Error and 95% Confidence Level Assuming a Population Proportion of 50%

Population Size	Sample Size
25	24
50	44
75	63
100	80
150	108
200	132
250	152
300	169
400	196
500	217
750	254
1,000	278
2,000	322
4,000	351
5,000	357
10,000	370
15,000	375
20,000	377
25,000	378
50,000	381
100,000	384
1,000,000	384

90 percent confidence level requires a sample size of 176, and with a population of 1,000 a sample of 213 is needed. Compare these with the sample sizes in table 7.1.

Although it is seldom necessary to have more confidence than 95 percent or to decrease the margin of error below 5 percent, when greater precision and confidence is necessary, the formula can similarly be adjusted. To compute a sample size that would provide a 99 percent level of confidence and a margin of error of 3 percent, you would substitute 6.64 for the chi-square value of 3.841 in the above formula and .03 for d (the margin of error). For populations of 500 and 1,000, this would result in samples of 394 and 649, respectively.

Either table 7.1 or the formula provides the evaluator with a means for determining the necessary sample size to obtain accurate estimates. In both instances, it is understood that a random selection process will be used to select the sample. (Consult a text on basic research methodologies if you don't know how to draw a random sample.)

There are occasions when it is not necessary to use a random selection process. For instance, you may want to talk to all six administrators in an agency. Or, there may be only twenty-five clients enrolled in a program. It would make more sense to interview all of the clients than it would to go through a random selection process and to choose twenty-four. There are times when evaluators use **nonprobability samples** (sometimes called samples of convenience, or accidental, purposive, or availability samples). An example of a sample of convenience would be interviewing the first fifteen clients who walked past your office in the afternoon. Such a procedure might on the surface appear to generate a random sample, but it is possible that all fifteen walking past your door were returning from a special program or a field trip; they might all have been new clients and gotten lost while looking for the exit. The problem with using nonprobability samples is in not knowing how representative or how closely the sample resembles the "true" population. The nonprobability sample could be very biased, yet it would be difficult for the evaluator to always know this. Nonprobability samples do not provide you with a means for determining margin of errors or confidence level.

Also, keep in mind that 20 to 30 percent response rates are not uncommon with mail surveys. If you had a thousand clients in your program and if you randomly selected 278 to receive a questionnaire, you might plan on getting back fifty to eighty. It is also possible that you might receive as few as twenty-five. What problems would there be if you evaluated a program using a small minority of clients? You cannot assume that a minority of responders have the same experiences, opinions, or behaviors as those who did not respond. Because you have less than a majority of the sample responding, you have a self-selected group that is very likely biased. You would have lost the advantage of drawing the initial sample randomly. To give your evaluation credibility, one of the most important things you can do, besides drawing an adequately sized random sample, is to get a response rate greater than 50 percent. There are several ways to go about this—sending postcard reminders, mailing a second questionnaire, and so forth. For additional information on how to improve your response rates, refer to Dillman (1978), Alreck and Settle (1985), or Fink and Kosecoff (1985).

There are times when some policymakers tend to put more emphasis on the number of responders than on the response rate. A conservative U.S. Congressman changed his stance on legislation to ban the manufacture of semiautomatic weapons based on the number of responses received from a congressional mailing. Representative Hubbard noted that he mails out 230,000 newsletters and gets back responses from 37,000 (a 16 percent response rate). When asked if he was concerned about relying on unscientific results, Hubbard said, "Unscientific? It's convincing at times. It tells me the same things I'm hearing in town meetings . . . in my district" (*Lexington Herald-Leader*, October 13, 1989).

■ Ethical Considerations _____

Due to past abuses of human subjects by researchers (see for instance, Jones, 1981; Conot, 1983; Faden & Beauchamp, 1986; Grundner, 1986), federal legislation now exists that protects American citizens from harmful research. Investigators affiliated with organizations that receive federal funds for conducting research (typically colleges, universities, hospitals, and other large public service organizations) must have their proposals reviewed by an Institutional Review Board (IRB). Review boards have been established in these research-conducting institutions and have the authority to approve, disapprove, or modify proposed research activities. Further, they periodically review ongoing research and may suspend or terminate any research previously approved that deviates from the original prospectus. Don't think because you are conducting an evaluation and not "pure" research that the review boards would not be interested in your activities. Evaluation is applied research and does come under authority of IRB review.

Evaluators who must directly contact clients or have access to identifying information about clients for their evaluations may need to have their proposals reviewed by an IRB. However, if you were planning to examine the effectiveness of a program using existing data already available to the public (e.g., school dropouts, arrests, or state hospital admissions), you may not need IRB review. On the other hand, if you are a graduate student and anticipate interviewing clients for a program evaluation and part of this data may become your dissertation, then you are likely to need IRB review. Should you be an employee of a small social service agency that receives no direct federal funding, your agency probably would not have an IRB review your evaluation proposal.

IRBs perform several levels of review. The most cursory of these (when the investigator asks for an exemption) requires only that a small summary of the proposed research or evaluation be written specifying the objectives, the subject population, how the subjects will be recruited, the research procedures, and any potential physical, psychological, social, or legal risks to subjects. A full review requires a lengthier application and sometimes a personal appearance before the IRB to explain or defend the proposal.

Exemptions are usually routine when such activities as those listed below are planned:

1. Research conducted in established or commonly accepted educational settings, involving normal educational practices such as instructional strategies or the effectiveness of instructional techniques, curricula, or classroom management methods.
2. Research involving the use of educational tests (e.g., aptitude, achievement, or diagnostic) if information taken from these sources is recorded in such a manner that subjects cannot be identified directly or through identifiers linked to the subjects and if any disclosure of the subjects' responses outside the research would not place the subjects at risk of criminal or civil liability or be damaging to the subjects' financial standing, employability, or reputation.
3. Research involving survey or interview procedures and observation of public behavior when it meets the conditions specified in (b) above.
4. Research involving the collection or study of existing data, documents, or records if these sources are publicly available or if the information is recorded by the investigator in such a manner that subjects cannot be identified directly or through identifiers linked to the subjects.
5. Research and demonstration projects conducted by or subject to the approval of federal department or agency heads which examine or evaluate public benefit or service programs or procedures for obtaining benefits or services under those programs, including possible changes to programs or procedures.
6. Research involving survey or interview procedures and educational tests when the respondents are elected or appointed public officials or candidates for public office or where federal statutes require the confidentiality of the personally identifiable information will be maintained through the research and thereafter.

However, exemptions generally are *not* available when certain vulnerable populations are to be used in the study (e.g., children, prisoners, and the mentally disabled), or when there is deception of subjects, or techniques that expose the subject to discomfort or harassment beyond levels normally encountered in daily life. Further, exemption is not available when the information obtained from medical or agency records is recorded in such a way that subjects can be identified directly or through identifiers linked to the subjects.

■ Ethical Guidelines

Several guidelines have been proposed (Royse, 1991) to assist researchers and evaluators in conducting ethical research.

Guideline 1: Research subjects must be volunteers

All of those participating in a research or evaluation effort should freely decide to participate. No coercion of any kind can be used to secure participants for a study. Subjects must also be competent to understand their choices. If they are not able to fully comprehend (e.g., individuals under the age of majority), then their legal caretakers must give permission, and the subjects still must assent. This means that even if parents have given permission for their children to participate in a research project, these children may still refuse to participate. The subject's right to self-determination must be respected, and the research participant is free to withdraw from the study at any time. In many instances, IRBs *require* that written permission be obtained from subjects of the research. Consent forms usually provide general but brief information on the nature of the project and indicate that the subject is free to withdraw consent and to discontinue participation in the project at any time without any penalty or loss of benefits. When evaluating a social service program, it is vitally important that recipients of services fully understand their right to refuse participation in a study and that this will in no way affect delivery of services to them in the present or any future time.

Guideline 2: Potential subjects should be given sufficient information about the study to determine any possible risks or discomforts as well as benefits.

Sufficient information includes an explanation of the purpose of the research, the expected duration of the subject's participation, the procedures to be followed, and the identification of any of those that might be experimental. The evaluator must be specific about any procedures that will involve the research subjects. If there are potential risks, these must be identified. Subjects should be given the opportunity to raise and have answered any questions about the study or any procedures that will be used. Subjects must also be allowed to inquire at any time (and have their questions answered) about procedures that are used. Consent forms should be written at a level of readability that the program participants can understand.

Guideline 3: No harm shall result as a consequence of participation in the evaluation.

While there is much less possibility of harm resulting from an intervention in the social or human services than from biomedical research, this guideline suggests that *no* harm should result. This guideline would be violated, for instance, if an evaluator contacted battered women some months after they had returned to an abusive situation and if there was a risk that talking to the evaluators might trigger another episode of violent assault.

More intangible although, no less important, clients can suffer emotional or psychological harm—as when their reputations are injured. For example, suppose a questionnaire is mailed to clients of a drug treatment or sexual offenders' program and one is accidentally sent to a client's work address and inadvertently opened by a secretary or is delivered to a neighbor and opened by mistake. This could result in the loss of a job or in the client's reputation being irreparably damaged. The potential for inadvertent harm of this type should concern every evaluator.

Guideline 4: Protection of sensitive information.

The privacy of human subjects is protected by:
a. allowing subjects to respond anonymously, if at all possible. If the research design cannot accommodate anonymity, protection is provided by:
b. separating any personally identifying information from the research data through the use of numeric or other special codes. Where complete anonymity is not possible (e.g., because pretests and posttest scores have to be matched for each subject), it may be possible to use Social Security numbers or specially created codes (such as the first four letters of a client's mother's maiden name and the last four digits of the client's own Social Security number) to help guard against unauthorized persons accidently recognizing or identifying program participants.

The privacy of human subjects is further protected by not capturing or reporting any personal information (names, addresses, phone numbers, or personal descriptors such as Mayor, Eminence,

Kentucky) that would result in research subjects being identified by persons other than the project's evaluators. When sensitive data must be obtained, it should be kept in locked cabinets or files until no longer needed and then destroyed (material to be protected includes master lists of codes, lists of respondents, mailing lists, completed questionnaires, and transcripts of interviews).

■ Ethical Dilemmas

Students and practitioners often have negative opinions about evaluation because they assume that the use of evaluation designs and randomization necessitates that some clients will be denied services. However, denying services to a group of clients solely for the purpose of creating a control group would not be approved by many institutional review boards. Fortunately, seldom would such a situation be required for an evaluation. There are less problematic ways to obtain control groups without running the risk of litigation or possible violation of professional ethics by denying services.

For instance, instead of an experiment, the evaluator may want to conduct a comparative study. With a quasi-experimental nonequivalent control group design, the evaluator does not deny the control subjects the intervention received by the experimental subjects but finds a control group in a different geographical area where the intervention may not be available. Or, the evaluator may decide to compare the experimental subjects with the service recipients of another, similar agency. In this scenario, the evaluator could compare clients receiving an intervention from Agency A with clients receiving the same intervention, but from Agency B. While not a strong design, there is a control group (and since they receive an intervention, there is no conflict of ethics).

In a slightly different scenario, some potential clients of a new intervention (e.g., a program designed to provide counseling to first-time shoplifters) may decide to pay a fine or even spend time in jail rather than to participate in a structured counseling program. This group of persons who choose not to participate makes a natural comparison group in terms of judging the effectiveness of the intervention received by others. At the end of two years, you might expect the intervention group to have fewer rearrests than the control (no intervention) group.

Long waiting lists are another source of control subjects. If there is a lengthy list of clients waiting for services, it might be possible to consider these as a control group (providing, of course, that the intervention is short enough that it would be concluded before those on the waiting list began receiving services). Clients on a waiting list might appreciate a periodic contact with an agency representative (even if it is limited to the administration of a pretest and posttest) because it would constitute evidence that they had not been forgotten by the agency and that they are still queued for services.

A fourth possibility is to continue the usual or regular services with some clients (this would be the control group) and provide another group with new and more intensive (experimental) intervention. For example, in an agency providing therapy to families in conflict, the control group would be assigned a social worker as usual. The intervention group might participate in a home-based therapy program of twelve to twenty hours each week during a six or eight week period of time. At the end of the study period, the evaluator would determine which group of families showed the most progress.

In programs for clients that have very similar problems, it may be possible to evaluate different modalities or ways of delivering the intervention without denying services. One group of clients might receive individual counseling, another could receive group counseling, and a third group might receive educational information through seminar type lectures with audiovisual aids. Of course, such decisions depend greatly on the type of problem, its severity, the population being served, as well as the agency itself. Many alternatives are available, and evaluators merely need to keep in mind that denial or withholding of treatment is seldom needed in order to obtain control groups.

Most evaluators of social service programs are not involved in any research where physical harm is likely to occur to the subjects in the study. Often, program evaluations rely upon data already available in the public or agency records. On other occasions, evaluations include surveys or interviews—which require a fair amount of cooperation from the participant. Harm to the subjects is much more likely to derive not from an intervention but from a third party's use of information gathered as part of the evaluation effort (especially when items pertain to admissions of illegal behaviors or acts.

If you perceive an ethical problem or need advice about how to avoid such a problem, and there is no institutional review board within your agency, the IRB at the university nearest to you may be able to provide some assistance. Additionally, many organizations have developed codes of ethics or have professional standards that address professional behavior. While these tend to be fairly general, in some instances they may help an evaluator decide the right course of action. Some are rather specific in addressing the holding of confidential information, protecting anonymity, lying, obtaining consent, and so forth. Others contain less specificity. Organizations with codes of ethics include:

American Association for Public Opinion Research
American Educational Research Association
American Evaluation Association
American Psychological Association
American Political Science Association
American Sociological Association
National Association of Social Workers

■ Chapter Recap

This chapter described some of the ways evaluation may be viewed. The evaluator needs to be sensitive to "hidden agendas" and perceptions about his or her role that may indicate a misunderstanding of actual purpose. It is important to discuss with all involved parties the planned evaluation and to address fears, concerns, and questions. One way to make the evaluation somewhat less burdensome on clients is to make use of scientifically selected random samples of clients. Procedures for determining appropriate sample sizes were explained. Finally, Institutional Review Boards were discussed as well as the evaluator's responsibility for insuring that any evaluation meets ethical guidelines.

While we are aware that information gleaned from clients benefits the evaluator and agency, it also benefits clients. Clients may directly benefit from improvements made to a program as a result of an evaluation. Positive arguments can be made for clients' participation in evaluation and research projects. Korchin and Cowan (1982) have noted that subjects may gain from some new therapeutic procedure. Even if that doesn't occur, participants may feel that the study was important and that they have made a contribution that will be of help to others. Participants may also feel honored to have been selected, or may have experienced an increase in self-worth as a result of receiving attention associated with being a participant in an evaluation. People are often flattered when asked to share their opinions or insights. Finally, research and evaluation projects can be interesting and may challenge the participant to think or grow in new or different ways.

Even when a new or experimental program is being compared with the regular or standard treatment, it would be hard to make the case that it is unethical to expose participants to the new program (where the traditional program was thought to be superior) or to argue that all the clients should receive the experimental intervention because it is not known which of the treatments is superior. As Moore (1985) notes, "No one is deliberately deprived of the best therapy, even though because of our ignorance one group will receive an inferior treatment. . . . Controlled and randomized experiments are the only method for discovering which therapy is superior" (p. 93). Our practice knowledge increases with each solid evaluation effort. Evaluation allows us to continually improve the services provided to our clients and, as a consequence, to improve the quality of their lives.

QUESTIONS FOR CLASS DISCUSSION

1. From students' knowledge of local agencies (but without disclosing the names of these agencies), discuss political pressures or agendas which might influence (either positively or negatively) any evaluation efforts.
2. Discuss ways in which the political pressures identified in answers to question 1 might be neutralized or negated.
3. Discuss the external evaluator's responsibility upon concluding that objectivity had been lost or that a program evaluation cannot be done well. Discuss whether the responsibilities would be any different if an internal evaluator were involved.
4. Suppose that a thorough evaluation concludes that a program in an agency is not effective or is not cost-effective. Discuss how the results might be alternatively used or misused by persons with different political aspirations.
5. Have students give estimates of the number of service recipients in programs with which they are familiar. Then, assume a survey must be made of this population. Using the table provided in this book, determine the sample sizes needed for a confidence interval of 95 percent with a 5 percent margin of error.
6. With the same client population groups in mind, discuss the advantages and disadvantages associated with using nonprobability samples of fifteen, fifty, and seventy-five clients.
7. What are the various ways people react when they learn there is going to be an evaluation of their program or agency? What is the most common response?

MINI-PROJECTS: EXPERIENCING
EVALUATION FIRSTHAND

1. Envision a scenario where an agency asks you to conduct a program evaluation. Prepare a contract that could result from the negotiations. Provide as many details as possible.
2. Obtain a copy of the exemption certification form used by an institutional review board at a nearby university. Complete the form as if you were proposing a program evaluation at a local social service agency.

3. Draft a consent form to be signed by clients who need to release personal information for a planned program evaluation. Briefly explain the nature of the project and what the clients are expected to provide, and include a statement informing clients that they have the right to refuse to participate without any penalty or loss of benefits. Compare your product with a model or copy obtained from the institutional review board at a nearby university.

4. How have human subjects been abused in the name of research? Using the resources of your library, write a small paper which highlights unethical or inhumane research projects from prior years. You might want to start by looking at some of the experimentation conducted by Nazi doctors on human subjects. Relative to the United States, see Jones (1981) or learn more about the controversy that has swirled around Laud Humphreys or Stanley Milgram.

REFERENCES AND RESOURCES

Alreck, P.L., & Settle, R.B. (1985). *The survey research handbook*. Homewood, IL: Richard D. Irwin.

American Psychological Association. (1985). *Standards for educational and psychological testing*. Washington, DC.

Baumrind, D. (1985). Research using intentional deception: Ethical issues revisited. *American Psychologist*, 40 (2), 165–174.

Boruch, R.F. (1987). Conducting social experiments. *Evaluation practice in review*. New Directions for Program Evaluation, no. 34. San Francisco, CA: Jossey–Bass.

Chelimsky, E. (1987). What have we learned about the politics of program evaluation? *Evaluation Practice*, 8 (1), 5–21.

Coffee, J.N. (1989). Advice for the evaluated. *Evaluation and the federal decision maker*. New Directions for Program Evaluation, no. 41. San Francisco, CA: Jossey–Bass.

Conot, R.E. (1983) *Justice at Nuremberg*. New York: Harper & Row.

Cronbach, L.J., Ambron, S.R., Dornbusch, S.M., Hess, R.D., Hornik, R.C., Phillips, D.C., Walker, D.F., & Weiner, S.S. (1980) *Toward reform of program evaluation*. San Francisco, CA: Jossey–Bass.

Dillman, D.A. (1978). *Mail and telephone surveys: The total design method*. New York: Wiley.

Faden, R.R., & Beauchamp, T.L. (1986). *A history and theory of informed consent*. New York: Oxford University Press.

Fink, A., & Kosecoff, J. (1985). *How to conduct surveys: A step-by-step guide*. Beverly Hills, CA: Sage.

Grundner, T.M. (1986). *Informed consent: A tutorial*. Owings Mill, MD: Rynd Communications.

Herman, J.L., Morris, L.L., & Fitz–Gibbon, C.T. (1987). *Evaluator's handbook*. Newbury Park, CA: Sage.

House, E.R. (1986). Internal evaluation. *Evaluation Practice*, 7, (1), 63–64.

Jones, J.H. (1981). *Bad blood: The Tuskegee syphilis experiment.* New York: Free Press.

Kennedy, M.M. (1983). The role of the in-house evaluator. *Evaluation Review*, 7 (4), 519–541.

Kimmel, A.J. (1988) *Ethics and values in applied social research.* Beverly Hills, CA: Sage.

Korchin, S.J. & Cowan, P.A. (1982). Ethical perspectives in clinical research. In P.C. Kendall and J.N. Butcher (Eds.), *Handbook of research methods in clinical psychology.* New York: Wiley.

Krejcie, R.V., & Morgan, D.W. (1970). Determining sample size for research activities. *Educational and Psychological Measurement*, 30, 607–610.

Kytle, J., & Millman, E.J. (1986). Confessions of two applied researchers in search of principles. *Evaluation and Program Planning*, 9, 167–177.

McCall, C. (1980). *Sampling and statistics handbook for research in education: A technical reference for members of the research staff of the National Education Association and its state and local Affiliated Association.* Washington, DC: National Educational Association.

McLemore, J.R., & Neumann, J.E. (1987). The inherently political nature of program evaluators and evaluation research. *Evaluation and Program Planning*, 10 (1), 83–94.

Moore, D. (1985). *Statistics: concepts and controversies.* New York: Freeman.

Monahan, J. (1980). *Who is the client? The ethics of psychological intervention in the criminal justice system.* Washington, DC: American Psychological Association.

Muscatello, D.B. (1989). Evaluation and the management process. *Evaluation Practice*, 10 (3), 12–17.

Patton, M.Q. (1982). *Practical evaluation.* Beverly Hills, CA: Sage.

Royse, D. (1991). *Research methods for social workers.* Chicago, IL: Nelson–Hall.

Siebert, J.E., & Stanley, B. (1988). Ethical and professional dimensions of socially sensitive research. *American Psychologist*, 43 (1), 49–55.

Sonnichsen, R.C. (1989). Program managers: Victims or victors in the evaluation process. *Evaluation and the federal decision maker.* New Directions for Program Evaluation, no. 41, San Francisco, CA: Jossey–Bass.

Thompson, R.J. (1989). Evaluator as power broker: Issues in the Maghreb. *International innovations in evaluation methodology.* New Directions for Program Evaluation. San Francisco, CA: Jossey–Bass.

Wise, R.I. (1980). The evaluator as educator. New Directions for Program Evaluation, no. 5. San Francisco, CA: Jossey–Bass.

Worthen, B., & White, K. (1987). *Evaluating educational and social programs: Guidelines for proposal review, onsite evaluation, evaluation contracts, and technical assistance.* Boston, MA: Kluwer–Nijhoff.

CHAPTER 8

Making Sense of Evaluation Data

Once you have gathered all the data that you intend to collect, the next step is to analyze the data. The purpose of analysis is to provide answers to questions that were previously raised. If hypotheses were stated, analysis of the data informs as to whether the hypotheses are supported by data. Condense the data (sometimes massive amounts of data) until some meaningful patterns, trends, or relationships emerge.

Periodically, I find it necessary to scribble a note as I am walking to or from class to remind me of meetings or special things I am supposed to do. Once, I found a scrap of paper in my pocket on which was written:

SEA

TING

The note made no sense whatsoever. Since my family and I occasionally take a summer vacation beside the ocean, I began considering whether there was something about the sea I was supposed to remember. After I had exhausted all possible associations

173

between the sea and things I was supposed to so, I moved to the next word. Again, I could not decipher "TING." Sometime later, when I was standing before a class of about fifty students, it dawned on me that I had wanted to make a seating chart. In much the same way, analysis involves examining data until something intelligible emerges.

Regardless of the program you are evaluating, it is very likely that at some point you will need to use one or more statistical procedures. There will be times when you will want to conclude there were statistically significant differences between pre- and posttests or between the control and intervention groups. If the differences between groups are markedly different (say 45 percent of those in the control group are successful compared to 83 percent of those in the intervention group), it may be possible to conclude that the intervention was an unqualified success, and perhaps no one will challenge it. However, what if the intervention group had only five participants and the control group was based on scores from two hundred different individuals? Would you still feel secure about concluding that the intervention was an unqualified success? In computing a probability level, statistical procedures take into account the number of individuals and the variation in their scores. Most evaluators cannot determine if observed differences between groups are statistically significant by visual observation alone.

The argument for using statistical procedures in analyzing evaluation data is that they provide objective evidence that the program was or wasn't successful—information not dependent upon the evaluator's whims or judgment. Avoiding the use of statistical procedures when they are needed not only is amateurish but also suggests incompetence. Statistical procedures lend credibility and professionalism to your final report. Even though your audience may not understand what a t-test is or how to compute a chi square, your usage of these statistical procedures helps you to determine if differences are "real" and helps your audience to have faith in your ability and expertise. In some instances, the use of statistical procedures may help defuse hostility by removing an element of subjectivity.

If large amounts of data are collected and need to be analyzed, you may want to use a computer to help with management and analysis of the data. Preparing data to be entered into the computer is not difficult and can be easily learned. Descriptive terms (like *male* or *female*) are converted to numerical values (0, 1) for computer processing. (For a lengthier explanation of how to code data for machine processing, refer to chapter 9 in Royse (1991).

While there are many statistical software programs to choose from, the *Statistical Package for the Social Sciences* (SPSS-x) is one found on most large computers used by universities. (It can also be purchased for personal computers.) To help you understand the ease with which computers can be used to analyze data, this chapter has examples of commands in SPSS-x that produce useful computer products. But before you can begin discussing how to analyze data on the computer, you need to know how to make sense of data. This is explained in the following sections.

■ Univariate Analysis

Univariate analysis looks at one variable at a time. There are several reasons for doing this. First, you might want to know how many respondents with a certain characteristic have been obtained. (If you were concerned with the variable of marital status, you may want to know how many questionnaires have been completed by divorced respondents. If the sample is too small, the evaluator may decide to increase it.) The examination of the variables one at a time can sometimes indicate that a certain group of individuals was inadvertently missed or that the range of responses was compressed (all of the possible responses were not represented). Univariate analysis helps the evaluator develop a "feel" for the data. Typically, the data are arranged in either ascending or descending order to facilitate finding "gaps" or missing values. Univariate analysis begins the process of making sense of data collected for a program evaluation.

All too frequently, evaluators who have only a cursory knowledge of analysis think they have analyzed the data when all they have done is to report what data were obtained. I once came across an "evaluation" of a program that consisted of more than thirty pages of data that looked something like that in table 8.1.

The pretest and posttest values were average scores on a five point

Table 8.1   Evaluation Summary

	Parents		Professional Staff	
	Pretest n = 62	Posttest n = 47	Pretest n = 32	Posttest n = 24
Q1	3.24	4.54	3.50	4.30
Q2	3.20	3.60	3.80	4.50
Q3	3.70	3.90	3.50	4.20
Q4	2.80	3.10	2.00	2.30
Q5	2.50	2.22	2.00	3.30
Q6	2.30	2.80	2.22	2.45
Q7	2.60	4.70	3.40	4.00
Q8	3.40	4.00	4.40	5.00
Q9	2.10	1.75	4.50	2.60

Figure 8.1

88	94	66	73	81
77	78	65	97	69
73	90	90	94	82
75	87	79	99	74
86	91	75	85	91

scale where 1 = poor, 3 = fair, and 5 = great. Respondents had been asked to evaluate training that they had received at a series of workshops held around the state. The data were arranged by date and locality in which the training was provided. While the "evaluator" had listed the questions used in the final evaluation report, there was no information on the reliability or validity of any scale(s) contained on the instrument.

Not only is thirty pages of such data tedious to wade through, it is also difficult to know what to conclude. For instance, are the increases shown above (e.g., Q2 increases from 3.20 to 3.60 under the column headed Parents) statistically significant? If they are not statistically significant, then they are not really increases at all but represent scores that are essentially equivalent. What the "evaluator" did not realize is that it is the *overall* scores and not the item-by-item scores on an instrument that should be used for analysis. It is the *collection of items* which makes an instrument reliable. Any one item may or may not be useful for detecting significant change or improvement. In this instance, the evaluators concluded (I suppose by visual inspection) that the training increased participants' knowledge "in all areas—indicating that the training sessions were effective." This conclusion could very well be unwarranted. The evaluator does not know (nor does the reader of the evaluation report know) if participants' scores were significantly improved. This can only be learned when a statistical test is employed. Further, unless we know more about the instrument, it is entirely possible that it was unreliable. Perhaps it would show improvement even when another more reliable instrument would not. In this instance, how important would the evaluators' findings be? What effect do you think the loss of subjects between the pretest and posttest would have?

Analysis is more than displaying the responses or data that were obtained. Look, for instance, at the example of data display in figure 8.1.

These data look as if they could be test results of some kind. However, until we know more about the data it is extremely difficult to interpret what these numbers may indicate. Could these be the ages of persons in a nursing home? The weights of students enrolled in a class of fifth graders? The I.Q. scores of children enrolled in a remedial math class? Let's assume that they are the results of a final examination in an undergraduate research class. Knowing this much, we now may develop a strategy for trying to understand the data. We might, for instance, array the data in terms of the highest and lowest scores (figure 8.2).

By simply arraying the data, we can easily identify that the highest score was 99 and that the lowest was 65. Further, if we knew that grades ·were awarded according to the following scheme, then we would also know that there are six A's, eight B's, eight C's, and three D's on this particular test.

$$
\begin{aligned}
A &= 100 - 91 \\
B &= 90 - 81 \\
C &= 80 - 71 \\
D &= 70 - 61
\end{aligned}
$$

Now we understand a little more what the data may mean (figure 8.3).

Generally, we start analysis by looking at the data one variable at a time (univariate analysis) to see what we have. Often, evaluators use computers to array their data. An ordered array of data showing the number of in-

Figure 8.2: An Array of Sources

99
97
94
94
91
91
90
90
88
87
86
85
82
81
79
78
77
75
75
74
73
73
69
66
65

Figure 8.3

	99
"A" Range	97
	94
	94
	91
	91
	90
	90
"B" Range	88
	87
	86
	85
	82
	81
	79
	78
	77
"C" Range	75
	75
	74
	73
	73
	69
"D" Range	66
	65

stances each value occurs is called a **frequency distribution.** Note in the example in table 8.2 that the data have been grouped by response category.

From even a cursory glance, we can determine that very few respondents (about 3 percent) gave the program a poor rating. In fact, almost half of the respondents gave the program a good rating. By combining those who rated the program either "Good" or Excellent," we could determine that 81 percent of respondents were pleased with the program.

In the next example, table 8.3, you can see how a frequency distribution (univariate analysis) can help you to understand who has been included and who may be missing from your sample. We can see that there are many more older than younger respondents. Note that there are no respondents between the ages of twenty-two and thirty. In fact, the median age for this sample is sixty-one years. If the clients in your program are known to be much younger, a distribution like this may suggest that the sample is biased—that the younger clients' opinions are not reflected to the degree one might expect.

Besides wanting to understand who responded and who didn't (the make-up of your sample), another reason for looking at each variable individually is to determine if any errors were made in preparing or recording the data. This would be immediately obvious, in table 8.3, for instance, if you knew that there were no fifteen-year-olds in the outpatient program.

Table 8.2   Client Ratings of Quality of Program

("How would you rate the quality of our outpatient program?")

Rating	Frequency	Percent	Cumulative Percent
Excellent	173	33.0	33.0
Good	254	48.4	81.4
Fair	80	15.2	96.6
Poor	18	3.4	100.0
Total	525	100.0	

Table 8.3   Respondents' Ages

Age	Frequency	Percent	Cumulative Percent
15	1	1.8	1.8
22	2	3.6	5.5
30	1	1.8	7.3
32	1	1.8	9.1
34	2	3.6	12.7
38	1	1.8	14.5
39	1	1.8	16.4
42	1	5.5	18.2
43	1	1.8	20.0
44	3	5.5	25.5
48	2	3.6	29.1
52	3	5.5	34.5
57	2	3.6	38.2
58	4	7.3	45.5
61	3	5.5	50.9
64	2	3.6	54.5
65	5	5.5	63.6
66	2	3.6	67.3
67	2	3.6	70.9
68	2	3.6	74.5
70	5	9.0	83.6
71	2	3.6	87.3
72	3	5.5	92.7
75	3	5.5	98.2
81	1	1.8	100.0

The fifteen-year-old listed there may have been a fifty-one-year-old for whom the digits were transposed. Before further analysis is done with this variable, the correct age should be checked on the original questionnaire.

There are times when an evaluator is limited to univariate analysis. On these occasions, frequency distributions provide arrays for understanding the range of scores and the number of cases or respondents associated with each value. Another advantage of having a computer produce frequency distributions is that the evaluator can request measures of central tendency such as the mean, median, or mode. The **mean** is the arithmetic average of scores. This is useful for understanding the "typical" case or client. However, the mean can easily be distorted when there are a few extreme scores (e.g., a seventy-three-year-old taking classes with nineteen-year-olds pulls the average away from nineteen and toward the other end of the spectrum). The **median** is another measure of central tendency, but one that is less influenced by extreme scores. The median is the middle category or value in an array of scores. The **mode** is the most common category or value.

In addition to these measures of central tendency, other statistics (the standard deviation, the range) are often available from the computer printout produced by the SPSS-x command "Frequencies." A basic primer, such as those by Pilcher (1990), DiLeonardi and Curtis (1988), Weinback and Grinnell (1987), or Craft (1985), will help make these and other statistical concepts more understandable.

■ Bivariate Analysis

Once you have edited the data and corrected any mistakes and learned what you can from the univariate analysis, you are ready to begin looking at variables two at a time. This is called **bivariate analysis** of data. Evaluators look at variables two at a time to test hypotheses or to examine the strength of associations.

Consider, for example, a specially funded program designed to provide information about the transmission of AIDS to a population considered to be at "high risk" for contracting AIDS. The evaluator conducts pretests and posttests using a reliable instrument that measures knowledge about AIDS transmission. The evaluator has a series of pretest and posttest scores that look very much like the data in figure 8.1. Looking at these scores as they would be arrayed in a single frequency distribution would not help the evaluator to know if the program participants were actually more knowledgeable after receiving the educational presentation. To test the hypothesis that there was an improvement in knowledge after the presentation, the scores need to be separated into two groups:

Table 8.4   Summary Scores from an AIDS Education Presentation

	Pretest Score	Posttest Score
Intervention Group (n = 46)	65	85
Control Group (n = 115)	64	70

pretest and posttest. Then the evaluator can attempt to determine if any observed differences in the average scores are statistically significant.

You can tell by looking at table 8.4 that the intervention group improved its average score by 20 points from the time of the pretest to the posttest. However, the control group (who got no intervention) also showed some improvement. As an evaluator, you want to know whether the intervention group made significantly more improvement than the control group. In order to determine if there are important differences between the groups at posttest, the evaluator will need to conduct a **t-test**, a statistical procedure for comparing differences between two groups. The t-test can be computed manually or on a mainframe or a personal computer using statistical software. For instance, the procedure "t-test" in SPSS-x produces a summary report with a probability statement regarding the likelihood that the scores obtained from the two groups could have occurred by chance.

Usually, social scientists are interested in finding probabilities of .05 or less. Conducting a t-test and discovering a probability level of less than .05 would indicate that the average posttest scores for the control and intervention groups were not similar—that the intervention group's scores had improved quite a bit more than the control group's scores. In other words, there were real differences between the control and intervention groups at the time of the posttest. Further, it would be unlikely that the differences between the scores would have happened by chance alone. A probability of .04 would mean that differences in the two groups' average scores would have occurred by chance only 4 times out of 100.

Had the evaluator been able to randomly assign subjects to the experimental and control groups, it would not be necessary to conduct a t-test to determine if the two groups were equivalent at the time of the pretest. However, when random assignment is not possible and the evaluator is using a nonequivalent control group design, then a t-test could be used to establish that the groups were similar or equivalent at the beginning of the study.

Note that the t-test can be applied only on quantitative data measured at the **interval level** of measurement. These variables are some-times described as being continuous—variables such as weight, age, and scores from tests and scales. Intervals of equal length are required (the difference between 173 pounds and 172 pounds is the same as the difference between 101 and 100 pounds).

Different t-tests are available. If you were comparing pretest scores from a compulsive eating inventory administered to patients in one program with the pretest scores obtained from patients in a different hospital, you would use an independent samples version of the t-test. The independent samples version would also be used with the example in table 8.4, when the posttests of the control group were being compared to the posttests of the intervention group (two different groups are being compared). However, if you want to see if the 64 pretest average and the 70 posttest average for the control group is a statistically significant improvement, you need to use the paired samples version of the t-test (because the t-test is being conducted on only one sample where pre- and posttest scores are matched).

Sometimes evaluation designs require more than two groups. For instance, you might have a control group (no intervention), a group receiving intensive intervention, and another group receiving a less intense intervention. (Or, you might compare a control group with groups receiving inpatient and outpatient treatment.) When there are more than two groups, the t-test cannot be used. Instead, a statistical procedure known as **one-way analysis of variance** is used. (The SPSS-x command is "oneway".) This procedure is similar to the t-test, and the computer printout will provide mean scores for each group and a probability statement like the one produced with a t-test.

While the t-test and one-way analysis of variance are versatile tools for the evaluator to use, mention must also be made of **chi-square.** Chi square is another useful statistical procedure to use when doing bivariate analysis and the procedure of choice when the data are not interval but nominal. **Nominal data** are measured by categories—as when we classify people based on descriptive categorization (e.g., Democrat or Republican, Vietnam veteran, American Indian).

Let's assume that you are evaluating a program where numerical scores are not available. However, the staff have a well-established procedure for determining, at the point of closing a case, those clients for whom the intervention was successful and those for whom it was not successful. The new director asks you to draw a random sample of clients in the outpatient program and to determine the proportion who have successful outcomes.

Examining a sample of two hundred cases closed in the last six months, you find the following pattern:

Client Outcome	Cases	Percent
Successful	126	63%
Unsuccessful	74	37%
Total	200	100%

In this example, we are looking at only one variable, client outcome, that is measured by the categories of success or lack of success. This dependent variable is measured at the nominal level. As you share this data with the new executive director, she asks if you can determine if the program is more successful with female than with male clients. If we were to test the hypothesis that the staff were more successful with females than with males, chi square would be the appropriate statistic to use. The easiest way to compute this is to enter the data into a computer and use the computer to make statistical computations. In the SPSS-x program, a simple command like "crosstabs tables = success by sex" will produce a table like 8.5 and the corresponding chi square statistics.

It is difficult to tell by looking at table 8.5 whether there may be a statistically significant difference in the male and female success rates. We cannot conclude that there is a statistical difference in success rates without computing the chi square. In this example, the chi square is very low (less than 1), and the associated probability level is .54, which indicates that there is no statistically significant difference between the success (or failure) rates in this sample of male and female clients ($p < .05$ would mean there was statistical significance).

Table 8.5 Crosstabulation of Program Outcomes by Gender

Client Outcome	Female		Male
		I	
		+	
		I	
Successful	75	I	51
	(65%)	I	(60%)
		+	
		I	
Unsuccessful	40	I	34
		I	
	(35%)	I	(40%)
		+	
Total	115	I	85

	Chi-square	D.F.	Significance Level
	.37	1	.54

Now let's suppose that as you share this information with the executive director she tells you her hypothesis that clients with successful outcomes received more treatment than those who were not judged to be successful. To test this hypothesis you would use a t-test, because the dependent variable of interest is the number of treatment episodes (a variable measured at the interval level).

Table 8.6 shows that, on the average, clients with successful outcomes received 12.4 episodes of treatment, while unsuccessful clients received 4 episodes. We can understand whether the differences between these two groups are statistically significant by looking at the entry under "2-Tail Probability." Since the probability of obtaining the F value that was actually produced is less than .05, we can assume that the variances within each of the groups are not similar. Therefore, we should go to the t-value under the heading of "Separate Variance Estimate." Looking under that column, we find that the probability associated with that t-value would have occurred by chance less than 1 time in 1,000. In other words, the average number of treatment episodes received by the successful clients and the unsuccessful clients is statistically significant (p < .001). (Had the 2-tail probability been larger than .05, we would have used the t-value associated with the "Pooled Variance Estimate".)

If we were interested in going a step farther, we could test the hypothesis that successful women clients received more intervention than successful men. Once again, we would use a "t-test" command that would produce a printout like that in table 8.7.

We can see in table 8.7 that the successful female clients did in fact receive more intervention than the male clients. Successful female clients averaged thirteen treatment episodes compared to slightly over eleven for successful male clients. These differences are only marginally significant, because a probability level of .07 exceeds the standard criterion of .05.

Table 8.6   T-test for Examining Success by Number of Treatment Episodes

Variable	Number	Mean	F Value	2-Tail Probability	Pooled Variance Estimate t-value	Probability	Separate Variance Estimate t-value	Probability
Group 1 (Failure)	74	4.08	7.01	.000	12.0	.000	14.65	.000
Group 2 (Success)	126	12.44						

Table 8.7   T-test for Examining Successful Outcomes by Sex

Variable	Number	Mean	F Value	2-Tail Proba-bility	Pooled Variance Estimate		Separate Variance Estimate	
					t-value	Probability	t-value	Probability
Group 1 (Female)	75	13.2						
			1.37	.24	1.83	.07	1.88	.06
Group 2 (Male)	51	11.3						

■ Multivariate Analysis of Data

Multivariate analysis of data usually refers to the use of such procedures as multivariate analysis of variance, multiple regression, and discriminant analysis—subjects taught in intermediate level statistics courses. However, we can begin to understand the usefulness of a multivariate perspective by constructing a table that will allow us to examine three variables at once.

Let's assume that you have conducted an evaluation and presented the findings to your executive director. At this point, another question is raised, perhaps because a client complained about services in one of the agency's three satellite offices. The executive director suspects problems with one of the offices, because complaints tend to come primarily from that geographical area and only rarely from the other two sites. She asks you to look at the success rate for men and women clients for each of the agency's three locations. Table 8.8 provides an illustration of a table that presents three variables at one time.

As can be seen in table 8.8, 87 percent of the males receiving an intervention in Area 1 had a successful outcome—the best rate for either sex in any of the three areas. Males fared the poorest in Area 3, where only 41 percent had successful outcomes. Females did almost equally well in areas 1 and 2, and like males, did the poorest in Area 3. Overall, 40 percent of the male clients experienced a successful outcome compared to 60 percent of the females. Not only did the evaluator find that some locations seemed to be more successful with males than with females, it is also apparent that there are fewer successful clients produced at the Area 3 office than in the other two locations. Areas 1 and 2 were successful with a majority of their clients, but Area 3 was not.

Evaluators and researchers must be vigilant in their search for **extraneous variables** (variables which may be overlooked and not included in a study or evaluation but which influence the findings). Table 8.8 demonstrates how an evaluator concerned only with the dependent variable of a

Table 8.8   Successful Outcomes by Gender and Location

	Area 1	Area 2	Area 3	Row Total
Male Clients	23	25	37	136
Successes—Male	20	16	15	51
Percent of Male Clients	(87%)	(64%)	(41%)	(40%)
Female Clients	39	45	31	115
Successes—Female	26	31	18	75
Percent of Female Clients	(67%)	(69%)	(58%)	(60%)
Total Clients	62	70	68	200
Successes—Total	46	47	33	126
Overall Success Rate	(74%)	(67%)	(49%)	(63%)

program's overall success rate could be missing an opportunity to provide additional and valuable information to the program director. By controlling for the extraneous variables of location and gender, the evaluator provides the program director with a better understanding of how and where the program succeeds. In order to further improve the agency's success rate, the director will need to focus on increasing the number of successes in Area C. By anticipating that success may differ by location and client gender, the evaluator has improved the usefulness of the evaluation report. Armed with this information, the program director may want to test hypotheses or notions about why males have fewer successes than females or why the success rate is so low in Area C (e.g., poor morale, inadequate supervision, staff in need of training).

The evaluator can anticipate extraneous variables by keeping in mind that success with clients is seldom uniformly distributed across all clients. Evaluators need to speculate about the characteristics of clients who would be likely to show the least and the most progress. Programs may be differentially effective depending upon clients' education, financial and social resources, and so on. Besides the clients' characteristics, the evaluator ought to consider any relevant factor which could interact with the intervention or have an influence upon it. By identifying these variables and collecting information on them, the evaluator is able to comprehend the extent of their influence and produce an evaluation report containing real analysis.

■ Understanding Trends

Assume that you are evaluating a community's intervention program for persons who have been arrested the first time for driving while under the influence (DUI). After some deliberation, you decide that the best measure of the effectiveness of the intervention is the number of persons who are rearrested for DUI. Accordingly, you begin to gather your data. A pattern is revealed as you examine the data over a five-year period.

In table 8.9, we observe that while the number of DUIs remains about the same over the five-year period, it appears that the intervention is less effective over time. However, a number of alternative explanations are possible. First, the police may have added staff or are making a greater effort to arrest drunken drivers. Second, since there are more cars on the road with mobile phones, it is possible that more citizens are calling the police when they spot an inebriated driver—resulting in more drinking drivers being arrested. Third, judges and magistrates may be less inclined to dismiss charges of DUI. Without a control group, it is difficult to understand the increasing number of those who are rearrested each year for DUI.

Let's add a control group to the example. By examining DUIs and rearrests in another similar sized community, we might be able to better comprehend the trends in our own community (table 8.10).

While it is entirely possible that a greater proportion of DUIs in Community A are being rearrested than when the program first began, data

Table 8.9   DUIs And Rearrests, 1987–1991

	Number of DUIs	Program Recipients Rearrested
1987	385	31 (8%)
1988	380	38 (10%)
1989	377	38 (12%)
1990	390	55 (14%)
1991	372	60 (16%)

Table 8.10   DUI Rearrests during the Years 1987–1991

| | Community A (Intervention Mandated) | | Community B (No DUI Intervention | |
	Number of DUIs	Rearrested	Number of DUIs	Rearrested
1987	385	31 (8%)	340	48 (14%)
1988	380	38 (10%)	336	47 (14%)
1989	377	45 (12%)	351	53 (15%)
1990	390	55 (14%)	344	59 (17%)
1991	372	60 (16%)	360	70 (19%)

from Community B reflects a similar pattern of more rearrests. The conclusion that the program is becoming less effective over time does not seem to be warranted. In the preceding three years, Community A averaged 3 percent fewer rearrests than Community B. To understand why rearrests are increasing, the evaluator could look at whether the number of police or car phones have increased over the five-year period or determine if there had been changes in legislation (such as lowering illegal blood alcohol levels from .10 to .08) which would affect the total number of DUI arrests. Because of these and other possibilities, it would be wrong to compare the 1991 rearrest rates in Community A with the rates in 1987 and conclude that overall the intervention program was losing effectiveness.

In trying to make sense of trends, you must also be alert to seasonal trends or variations. I once examined the productivity of professional staff in a community mental health center after the installation of a new reporting system. I found that while the amount of client counseling showed dramatic improvement almost immediately after the new system began in August, productivity fell during a two-week period at Christmas. (This is understandable because fewer clients had problems during that period and a large percentage of therapists took vacation time and were not available.) After Christmas, productivity climbed some, then fell considerably during a period of extremely bad winter weather. But once again, productivity increased steadily reaching a high for the year during the second week of May.

At that point, some staff were ready to give credit for the increased level of productivity to the new reporting system. However, if you look closely at figure 8.4, you may see another explanation. Productivity may tend to be higher in the warm months of spring (March, April, May) than in the middle of summer or winter. What figure 8.4 may represent is a seasonal variation in productivity which may have been present under the old reporting system as well. There is not enough data provided to conclude that productivity is higher in May than it was in May of the prior year, for example. Even though there are twenty different measurements of productivity (corresponding to bi-monthly pay periods), the period of time covered is less than a year. We would be in a better position to conclude that productivity had significantly increased if we were able to compare 1991 with 1990 and 1989 productivity records. If we think about the period of time necessary to observe an intervention or program change as a "window," the larger the window the better chance we have of accurately comprehending the effects of that intervention or program change. It is almost always better to look through a larger window (look at more data) than to assess a potential trend by looking through too small a window (not enough data).

Figure 8.4: Individual Counseling Productivity: Advent of Management Information System

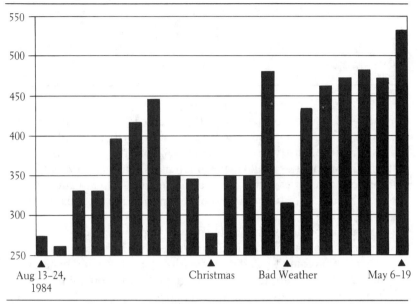

■ Using Statistics in Reports

Just as it is possible to fail to use statistics when they are needed, it is also possible to inundate the readers of your evaluation report with too much data—too many tables—and to cite the results of too many statistical tests. It is vitally important that you consider the audience who will be reading your evaluation report. You should not write over their heads and present statistical information that they are not likely to understand. With some audiences, you may want to note that statistically significant differences were found and not report the actual t or X^2 values. Usually it is not necessary to show any formulae used in the calculation of statistics (unless you are writing for a group of university professors). Present information that is important for understanding the major findings—not everything that is available from the computer printout. Keep tables as simple as possible.

Evaluators can get carried away with all of the information available to them. I saw a good example of this when a student was preparing a table of respondents' characteristics for a study she had completed. She could have simply reported the information on marital status as it is reflected in figure 8.5. Instead, she unnecessarily complicated things by adding all the rest of the information obtained from the computer printout. She included such information as the standard deviation (.911), the

Figure 8.5: Marital Status of Respondents

	Number	Percent
Single	8	14.5
Married	28	50.9
Separated/Divorced	10	18.3
Widowed	9	16.3
Total	55	100.0

kurtosis (− .439), the skewness (.518), the variance (.830), the median (2.0), the mean (2.33), the standard error (.124), and so forth. Such information makes very little sense when we are talking about the variable of marital status. (These statistics would make much more sense when variables are not discrete categories but instead are interval level data such as test scores.) Actually, the student could have reported the information without using a table.

There may be times when you will want to provide such information as standard deviations or skewness to your readers, but such technical information is not going to be digested easily by most lay audiences. One way to judge how much statistical detail to provide to your audience is to ask friends or colleagues to read your rough draft and give their opinion. Another way is to look at what information tends to be presented in research reports carried in the journal you read most.

It is not necessary to reproduce for your reader every table or statistically significant finding generated by the computer. Sometimes statistically significant findings can be trivial. For instance, a correlation of .15 is unsubstantial (about 2 percent of the variance in the dependent variable would be explained by the independent variable), yet it is statistically significant at p <.05. Even a strong statistical relationship might not have practical or substantive significance. Weinrott, Jones, and Howard (1982), for instance, found that youths in one type of group home had a mean GPA of 1.7 on a 4.0 scale. Comparison youths had a mean GPA of 1.4. While the difference in their GPAs were statistically significant, they were educationally negligible.

Remembering that evaluation is applied research, evaluators must keep in mind the pragmatic aspects of the findings. Even some findings that are not statistically significant may be important to report—especially those that result in recommendations or suggestions to the management. One way to display data so that it can be easily digested by audiences is with graphics like bar charts and pie charts.

A wide range of charts and graphs can be produced by statistical software programs. The charts shown in figure 8.6 were generated by my twelve-year-old son on his computer at home. Note that some are easier

Figure 8.6: Sample Charts Generated by a Computer

a. Failure and Success Rates by Program

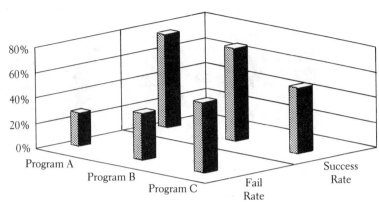

b. Success Rates by Program

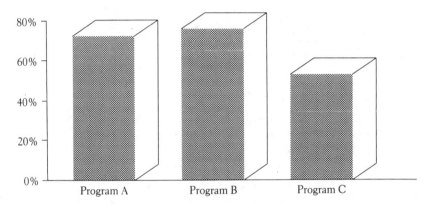

c. Clientele by Age Category

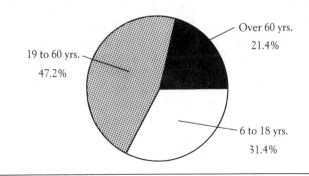

(*Continued next page*)

Figure 8.6: (*Continued*)

d. Success Rates by Program

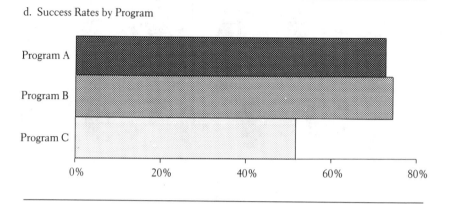

to grasp than others. This should also be a consideration when planning for presentation to a group. Even without a computer, you can design striking charts manually that will help you to clarify numerical data. (See the references at the end of this chapter for suggestions of useful books.)

■ Final Thoughts

In this chapter, I have provided an overview of how to start analyzing data. Obviously, there are many more sophisticated statistical procedures than could be presented here. Even if you don't have a computer at your disposal, some statistical procedures are relatively easy to compute manually. And, publications exist to assist you with this. (See, for example, Pilcher, 1990; DiLeonardi & Curtis, 1988; Fitz–Gibbon and Morris, 1987; Weinback and Grinnell, 1987; or Craft, 1990.)

Often, students are convinced that all they want to know about a program is whether the intervention correlated with successful outcomes. They anticipate that a correlation of .50 or so will convince the readers of their evaluation reports that the intervention was worthwhile. In fact, a **correlation** expresses only the amount or degree of relationship between two variables. For instance, we conducted a study and found a correlation of .51 between students' ages and the number of years of experience they had volunteering in social service agencies. Although .51 is a moderately strong correlation, only 26 percent of the variance in the dependent variable is explained by the independent variable. (The percentage of the variance explained is found by multiplying the correlation by itself.) Seventy-four percent of the interaction between the two variables was not explained.

What level of correlation can you expect in your studies? Nunnally (1978) noted that "correlations as high as .70 are rare, and the average of all correlations reported in the literature probably is less than .40" (P. 143). More recently, Rubin and Conway (1985) surveyed social work research literature and found that on the average 13 percent of dependent variable variance was explained; for evaluations of the effectiveness of clinical interventions it was approximately 10 percent.

There will be times when correlations are needed for program evaluations, but not often. Correlations indicate whether two variables are moving in the same direction—if the variables tend to increase or decrease together. They do not establish "proof" that one variable caused another. In the previous example, older students tended to have more years of experience in social service agencies, but their age did not "cause" them to volunteer. Similarly, volunteer experience did not "cause" the respondents to grow older.

Although I did not want to overlook mentioning correlations (they are useful for helping to gauge the influence of an extraneous variable and for identifying hypotheses to be tested in-depth in subsequent studies), they are not particularly helpful in establishing that one program is better than another. Correlations are easy to generate on the computer and relatively easy to understand, but they are not a powerful enough tool for program evaluation purposes.

While it is more common for students of evaluation to fail to use statistical procedures when they are needed than to overuse them, readers are cautioned against computing a large number of correlations or other statistical tests just to hunt for "statistically significant" findings. If enough statistical tests are computed, some statistically significant differences will be produced.

Suppose you had one dependent variable (e.g., recidivism) and you indiscriminately correlate forty separate socio-demograhic variables with this dependent variable. You could expect this "shotgun" approach would yield two statistically significant findings when significance is determined at the .05 level (i.e., .05 multiplied times 40 = 2). Even though these "significant" findings may not have been connected with the initial hypotheses or research questions, it sometimes is difficult to keep this in perspective when a bivariate test turns up something statistically significant. In your excitement over finding something statistically significant, you may forget that its occurrence was a fluke. The problem with conducting numerous bivariate tests is that a few significant results will occur if you conduct enough statistical tests, but such findings are likely to be related more to chance than to anything else. Avoid this problem by not computing correlations on all possible combinations of variables just to find something statistically significant. If you have many socio-demographic variables and you have no idea which of these will make the best predictors, use a more powerful statistical procedure (e.g., multiple regression analysis) to incorporate all of the variables simultaneously. However, even this method is no guarantee that all chance findings will be eliminated.

Finding significant differences just by chance is a **Type I error**. Type I errors lead you to conclude that a relationship exists between two variables (e.g., rejecting a null hypothesis) when there is no real relationship—merely a statistical fluke. Typically, we reduce the probability of making a Type I error by lowering the significance level. When it is terribly important to avoid making a Type I error, the traditional significance level of .05 can be lowered to .01 or less. However, by lowering the risk of a Type I error, the odds of making a Type II error are increased. In **Type II** errors, the null hypothesis is accepted when, in fact, there is a relationship between two variables.

Although social scientists seem to be more concerned with the risk of making Type I errors than Type II errors, it is possible to estimate the risk of committing a Type II error by using statistical power analysis. Tables have been prepared (Cohen, 1987) to enable evaluators to estimate the probability of committing a Type II error when using different statistical tests. While this is a relatively complex topic, Rubin and Babbie (1989) provide a simple explanation using one of Cohen's tables to show the relationship between sample size and the probability of rejecting the null hypothesis with correlation coefficients.

Statistical procedures are routinely used and, indeed, are essential for most evaluations based upon quantifiable data. However, the use of statistical procedures does not guarantee that the resulting information will be meaningful. It is quite possible that, because of the laws of probability, a few occurrences of statistical significance will be found when these findings have little value or meaning. Knowing that this is expected to happen when a large number of statistical tests have been produced will make it easier for the evaluator to discard them and to focus on the salient relationships. Don't be afraid to ask for statistical consultation when it is important to know such things as the probability of making a Type II error.

QUESTIONS FOR CLASS DISCUSSION

1. Ask students how much change they have in their pockets or purses. List all these amounts on the board. Manually prepare a frequency distribution. What is the mean? Would it make more sense to use a median to get a "truer" notion of the average amount of change held by students? Is this nominal or interval data?

2. Using the data obtained in question 1 as the dependent variable, ask the class to think of independent variables that could be used for bivariate analysis of the data. How might the data be grouped in several of these bivariate analyses? Would a t-test, oneway analysis of variance, or chi square be the appropriate statistical test?

3. Consider the data in figure 8.2 to represent the outcome data for a study the class is conducting. What is the outcome variable? What variables would be important to include in a bivariate analysis? What statistical procedures would be used?

4. A student once conducted an evaluation and in a report began analyzing the data along this line:

> Client A showed the most improvement. This is understandable in that he and his spouse seem to have ironed out the domestic difficulties which have plagued them for the past four years. Client B progressed less than other clients. Whether a coincidence or not, this client has not had an intimate relationship in the last five years. Client C made minimal progress, possibly because her boyfriend violated his parole and was returned to prison. Client D made great strides after acknowledging her earlier sexual trauma. Client E made minimal progress, possibly because her marriage of seventeen years broke up during this period. . . .

What is wrong with analyzing data in this manner? If the report consisted of only this type of information, would you conclude that there had been an analysis of the data?

5. Ask the class members to identify seasonal trends in the agencies in which they have worked, interned, or volunteered. Are these trends subtle or dramatic? When are the peak periods and times when fewer clients seek services?

6. Select a program outcome variable that would be a good gauge for the success of some social service program and make a list of extraneous variables. Then, create a table (like the one in table 8.8) that would control for the influence of extraneous variables.

7. Have the class look through journals, magazines, and newspapers in order to bring in examples of ways that data are summarized and reported in tables, charts, and graphs. Which examples are most easy to read, and which are the most difficult?

MINI-PROJECTS: EXPERIENCING EVALUATION FIRSTHAND

1. Visit the university computer center to learn what statistical software is available for their mainframe and personal computers. Are manuals for these programs in the library? Are consultants available to

assist you in working with these programs? Summarize what you learned from this visit in a brief report.

2. Using either real or fictitious data, test a hypothesis using statistical software on a computer. Be sure to state your hypothesis, how your data were obtained (or if they were manufactured), and the statistical procedure used. Submit the corresponding printout, circling the most important items.

3. Obtain an evaluation report and read it for the statistical procedures used. Write a brief paper summarizing: the hypothese tested, the procedures used, and your reaction to the evaluation report's use of statistical procedures. Were the appropriate procedures used? Were too few or too many used? Did the report clearly benefit from the use of statistics? What could have been concluded if no statistics were used?

REFERENCES AND RESOURCES

Cleveland, W.S. (1985). *The elements of graphing data.* Monterey, CA: Wadsworth.

Cohen, J. (1987). *Statistical power analysis for the behavioral sciences.* New York: Academic Press.

Craft, J.L. (1990). *Statistics and data analysis for social workers.* Itasca, IL: Peacock.

DiLeonardi, J.W., and Curtis, P.A. (1988). *What to do when the numbers are in: A user's guide to statistical data analysis in the human services.* Chicago, IL: Nelson–Hall.

Fitz–Gibbon, C.T., & Morris, L.L. (1987). *How to analyze data.* Program evaluation kit, 8. Newbury Park, CA: Sage.

Freiman, J.A., Chalmers, T.C., Smith, H., & Kuebler, R.R. (1978). The importance of Beta, the Type II Error, and sample size in the design and interpretation of the randomized control trial. *New England Journal of Medicine,* 299, 690–694.

Kraemer, H.C., & Thiemann, S. (1987). *How many subjects? Statistical power analysis.* Beverly Hills, CA: Sage.

Nunnally, J.C. (1978). *Psychometric theory.* New York: McGraw–Hill.

Patton, M.Q. (1982). *Practical evaluation.* Beverly Hills, CA: Sage.

Pilcher, D.M. (1990). *Data analysis for the helping professions.* Beverly Hills, CA: Sage.

Royse, D. (1990). *Research methods for social workers.* Chicago, IL: Nelson–Hall.

Rubin, A., & Conway, P.G. (1985). Standards for determining the magnitude of relationships in social work research. *Social Work Research and Abstracts,* 21 (1), 34–39.

Rubin, A., & Babbie, E. (1989). *Research methods for social work.* Belmont, CA: Wadsworth.

Schmid, C.F. (1983). *Statistical graphics.* New York: Wiley Interscience.

Tufte, E.R. (1983). *The visual display of quantitative information.* Chesire, CT: Graphics Press.

Vito, G.F., & Latessa, E.J. (1989). *Statistical applications in criminal justice.* Beverly Hills, CA: Sage.

Weinback, R.W., & Grinnell, R.M., Jr. (1987). *Statistics for social workers.* New York: Longman.

Weinrott, M.R., Jones, R.R., & Howard, J.R. (1982). Cost-effectiveness of teaching family programs for delinquents: Results of a national evaluation. *Evaluation Review,* 6 (2), 173–201.

CHAPTER 9

Writing the Evaluation Report

Many evaluators dread writing the report summarizing their evaluation efforts. This may stem from not knowing what to report, where to begin, how much detail to give, or which style to use. However, if the outline in this chapter is followed, the final report should be complete and cover all major bases. The outline is one that professionals in the field can use when writing reports for their peers or such groups as boards of directors as well as one that graduate and undergraduate students can use when preparing evaluation reports. While some minor modification may be needed, the same basic structure is used whether one is writing a thesis, an evaluation report, or an article for a professional journal, or applying to a funding source for a grant.

■ Major Content Areas for Evaluation Reports _____

1. Introduction
   a. Description of the problem
   b. Statement of the problem or questions to be explored

      c. Significance of the problem and rationale for studying it
2. Literature Review
      a. Theoretical and historical perspectives
      b. Identified gaps in the literature
      c. Reiteration of purpose of the evaluation
3. Methodology
      a. Evaluation design and data collection procedures
      b. Sampling design
      c. Description of subjects
      d. Description of instrumentation
      e. Procedures for analyzing the data
4. Findings (Results)
      a. Factual information presented (including tables, charts)
      b. Statistical and practical significance
5. Discussion
      a. Brief summary of the findings
      b. Explanation of any unexpected findings
      c. Application to practice
      d. Weaknesses or limitations of the evaluation
6. References
7. Appendices

While there is some merit in trying to find an evaluation report to use as a guide for writing your report, you could spend a considerable amount of time searching for a "good" evaluation report to use for a model. Even if you locate a report that you think might serve as a model, there is always the possibility that the report could be of questionable value. A "defective" model might be mistaken for an exemplary one if you are uncertain about the essential elements to be contained in an evaluation report.

An enormous diversity exists in the ways that evaluation reports are written. Some reports are so lengthy, that their bulk is intimidating. Others are too short—they may fail to include what you feel is important information. Sometimes authors will emphasize one question or concern at the expense of other issues. For these and other reasons, your time would be more profitably spent going to the library and locating several journal articles reporting evaluations in a relevant area. But even these can serve only as rough guides. Journals differ. Some journals require hefty bibliographies and a great amount of statistical or technical detail, and others that don't. Journals vary a great deal by the audience for whom they are written (e.g., scholars or practitioners). For those who are bewildered by the proper components to include in an evaluation report, the outline presented earlier is explained in greater detail.

■ Introduction

The purpose of the introduction is to describe why an evaluation was conducted. This is done by placing the program within some context or frame of reference. For instance, Stout and Rivara (1989) reviewed the evidence supporting sex education in the schools and start off with the following:

> The United States has the highest teen-age fertility rate of any developed nation, with more than 1 million teen-age pregnancies occurring in the United States each year, or about 3,000 per day.[1] ... In a 1982 national survey of urban areas, it was revealed that 75 percent of school districts offer sex education, although it was reported elsewhere that less than 10 percent of students are exposed to comprehensive, quality programs. Most of these programs are short, with 75 percent lasting for less than 20 hours.[3,4] (P. 375)

A similar article by different authors demonstrates again how a program designed to address a social problem is placed in a perspective in the introduction:

> Annually, in the United States, approximately 700,000 unmarried females aged nineteen years or younger become pregnant. Of these pregnancies, 85 percent are unintended.[1] The negative health and social outcomes of unintended, premarital, adolescent pregnancy and subsequent premarital childbirth and child-rearing present to the medical and public health communities a challenge of the greatest magnitude.[2] Over the past decade, numerous federal, state, and local efforts have been implemented to reduce the occurrence of unintended adolescent pregnancy. To date, however, there have been few reports of success in obtaining the outcome objective—significant reduction in unintended pregnancy among unmarried adolescents.[3,5] (Vincent, Clearie, & Schluchter, 1987, p. 3382)

From these brief excerpts the reader becomes aware of the extent of teen-age pregnancies as a social problem and begins to see the need for programs designed to reduce teen pregnancies.

The introduction ought to state the questions that were the catalyst for the evaluation. If the questions cannot be clearly stated, then it follows that the evaluation not only will be confusing to read, but may also not provide the type or kind of information needed by the decision makers.

In the fourth paragraph of the Stout and Rivara (1989) article, the reader learns what questions particularly concern the authors:

> The effort to implement these programs in communities raises several questions: Specifically, what evidence exists that sex education has any effect on

gain in knowledge and change in attitudes with regard to the material it presents? What effect do these programs have on sexual activity and contraceptive behavior? How are the ultimate target areas of adolescent pregnancy, abortion, and birth rates affected by these interventions? (P. 375)

While Stout and Rivara sought the answers to specific questions, some authors prefer to describe the purpose of the evaluation in a less direct manner. Sometimes the hypotheses or questions that directed the study are a little more veiled, but nonetheless serve to guide the evaluator's efforts. This can be seen in the following example:

> The current study was designed to rate the satisfaction of patients, their relatives, and clinicians with psychiatric evaluations and treatment plans, and to assess the degree to which initial satisfaction correlated with patient treatment compliance and clinical improvement. (Bulow, Sweeney, Shear, Friedman & Plowe, 1987, p. 290)

An example of stated hypotheses developed for an evaluation of a prepaid mental health plan for business can be found in Carpenter, Boyenga, and Schaible (1985):

1. The enrollee population under the prepaid plan will show a greater awareness of the community mental health center and its services than will persons in the service area not under the prepaid plan.
2. The enrolled population will express a more positive attitude toward the mental health center and the possibility of using its services than will persons in the community who are not covered by the prepaid plan. (P. 96)

Although examples of both specific and general questions to be explored can be easily found in the literature, I strongly believe beginning evaluators are better off investigating a small list of specific questions. Generally, the evaluation comes about because the people who fund or sponsor it have specific questions or hypotheses that they want answered or investigated. As a rule, it is easier to find the answers to specific questions than it is to more general questions (such as "What is the patient's quality of life after treatment?"). An evaluation is kept focused by the questions that are asked. If the questions are too general, it is easy for the evaluator to lose sight of the purpose of a program evaluation and to become concerned with trivial matters. Unless the study or research is exploratory, there ought to be specific questions or hypotheses that need to be examined. Constantly keep in mind that the purpose of the program evaluation is to provide useful information to program managers about how to improve their programs.

After the evaluator has: (1) described the problem or program being studied and (2) listed the specific questions to be explored, it is time to: (3) discuss the rationale for the study. In developing a rationale, sometimes it is necessary to inform the reader how the present evaluation is different from previous evaluations. In the next example ("A Preventive Intervention Program for the Newly Separated: Final Evaluations"), the authors establish that marital disruption is a stressful life event that has led agencies to develop preventive programs for persons experiencing marital disruption. The authors go on to state why they used thirty-month and four-year interviews in their evaluation of the program:

> The purpose of this report is to present the results of two final evaluations of such a preventive intervention program. Prior evaluations have examined the program six months after its inauguration and again eighteen months after its inauguration. (Bloom, Hodges, Kern, & McFaddin, 1985, p. 10)

It is always a good practice to state the rationale for the evaluation. Note how Velasquez and Lyle (1985) handle this in comparing the results of day treatment versus residential treatment for juvenile offenders:

> This article presents a case study of one public social service department's attempt to obtain and present program evaluation findings that would assist a county board of commissioners to determine whether day treatment provides a means for treating adjudicated juvenile delinquents and status offenders who might otherwise be placed in residential treatment settings. . . .
> A primary reason for the interest taken in this project by the county board was the method of funding. Unlike residential treatment, for which federal fiscal participation is available, the costs of the day treatment approach would be borne entirely by the county. Thus it was important that the study address the cost differences between the two service approaches. At the same time, it was necessary to avoid encouraging decision makers to fund such an approach solely on the basis of expected or actual cost savings. The therapeutic merit of both methods of treatment could not be ignored. (P. 146)

■ Review of the Literature

Once the parameters of the social problem or concern have been described and the purpose and rationale of the evaluation stated, the evaluator is ready to begin reviewing the pertinent literature. The purpose of the literature review is to summarize for the reader the major findings of other researchers and evaluators that are relevant to the evaluated program. It is necessary to identify major theoretical explanations of the social problem or phenomenon that prompted a human service program. Human service programs are always based upon readily identifiable assumptions that often can be easily traced to theoretical explanations of the phenomenon. For example, Majchrzak (1986), in reporting the results of a program designed to lower rates of unauthorized absenteeism (UA) among the Marines, has identified three models of absenteeism behavior:

> One type follows a "decision model" whereby UA is the result of a deliberate economic analysis with personal preferences weighed against sanctions, a second type follows a "pain avoidance model" in which UA is an impulsive act by those unable to cope with the military, and a third type follows an "adjustment model" in which UA is used as a means of resolving a problem not handled appropriately by the situation. (P. 254)

In order to further understand how these theoretical models may provide insight into the Marines' actual absenteeism behavior, interviews were conducted with a small group of Marines, and, later, a survey was conducted of all field battalion and company commanders stationed in the United States. These data were examined with battalion-level UA rates. Majchrzak (1986) then found that UA was strongly related to leaders' actions in the unit, although the data were not causal or specific enough to provide useful guidance to field commanders. However, from these efforts, "a program of effective leader actions was developed from previous literature and the tentative conclusions drawn to date in the research. This program was then experimentally implemented to determine its causal impact on UA" (p. 255).

The theoretical models upon which an intervention is based are important. Drug prevention programs might be based on a temperance model, a disease model, or developmental, sociocultural, or lifestyle risk-reduction models. We know that there are a lot of reasons why youth experiment with drugs. Some of these reasons have to do with self-definition, autonomy, social modeling, risk taking, peer pressure, and value formation (Braverman & Campbell, 1989). If the intervention is based upon a model or theoretical approach that has been discredited or for which there is little empirical support, this information needs to be communicated to the reader. Knowing that an intervention being evaluated is based upon an approach that is outdated or has weak grounding in research may give rise to questions about the program that might not have arisen otherwise.

The following demonstrates the necessity for doing a thorough review of the literature. Suppose you are asked to evaluate a program that provides intervention for persons arrested for Driving Under the Influence (DUI). You and the program sponsor agree that subsequent DUI arrests will be the dependent variable. How long a period of time after the intervention has ceased should be allowed to elapse before you can conclude that the program was successful? Six months after the first arrest? Twelve or eighteen months after the first arrest? By reviewing the literature, you would find an article in which Maisto, Sobell, Zelhart, Connors, and Cooper (1979) reported that the average period of time between first and second arrests for driving under the influence of alcohol, based on state driver's license records, was 23.5 months. Without reviewing the literature, overly optimistic results of the program's effectiveness would be obtained if too short a follow-up interval was designed.

Gaps in the literature

It is not uncommon for new or innovative programs to be launched that do not build upon prior evaluative or research studies. Evaluators of trailblazing programs will not have an abundance of literature to draw upon to help with understanding the significance of the impact made by the new intervention. For example, assume that virtually no evaluative studies have been conducted on programs designed to teach safety in a sheltered workshop to persons with mental retardation. You came to this conclusion after spending several weekends in the library. You read every listing under the broad topic of mental retardation and still come up empty-handed. What do you do?

In a situation like this, the evaluator tries to conceptualize an analogous problem for which there may be literature. For example, one of my graduate students was unable to find literature on the teaching of safe work practices in a sheltered workshop. However, she was able to find literature on a comparable problem—getting young children to use their safety belts. Research on efforts to promote the use of safety belts is an area where there is considerably more literature (see, for example, Sowers-Hoag, Thyer & Bailey, 1987) and though not directly relevant, it approximates the kind of problems one might experience in teaching safety issues to persons with mental retardation. One could also look at the research on safety belt promotion with adults (see, for example, Cope, Moy & Grossnickle, 1988).

Another way of providing a context for understanding the teaching of safe work habits would be to look at efforts to reduce hazards within a specific industry. Fox, Hopkins, and Anger (1987), for instance, conducted research on the use of a token economy to help reduce lost-time injuries in two dangerous open-pit mines. Employees earned stamps for being in work groups that experienced no lost-time injuries, for not causing injuries, and for making safety suggestions.

Each of these examples (the child and adult seat belt studies and the open-pit mining one) could have been found by searching abstracts under the descriptor "safety." However, relevant literature may also have been found by searching under different topics. Perhaps the teaching of job initiative to severely mentally retarded sheltered workers (McCuller, Salzberg & Lingnugaris/Kraft, 1987) would be seen as a problem similar to teaching this group about safety procedures. Sometimes it is possible to find other relevant articles serendipitously. I believe in helping serendipity (accidental discoveries) happen by browsing through journals likely to carry research related to the problem of interest, and by telling my friends about projects I am working on and asking them for any leads they may have on relevant literature.

A question that students sometimes ask is "How much literature should be reviewed?" Or "How do I know when I have reviewed enough literature?" These are difficult questions to answer because the amount of literature on one topic may be quite voluminous and on another rather scanty. The guidelines I suggest are these:

1. Make sure that the major (sometimes the first or classical) studies in the field are included in the literature review. You'll tend to see these studies cited time and time again. They establish the first efforts to explore or evaluate the problem. Subsequent studies have built upon what was learned in those early studies. Sometimes our perspectives aren't nearly broad enough. We may think that our new program is the first of its kind when actually there have been many prior and similar programs. Did you know, for instance, that sex education programs in public schools date back to the beginning of the century?

2. Include current studies of the problem in the literature review. (Besides searching *Psychological Abstracts* and *Social Work Research and Abstracts* for recent studies, the *Social Sciences Citation Index* can help you locate other journal articles on the same topic. Once you have found one or more major studies, use them as referents in the *Social Sciences Citation Index*. Articles that have cited the major study (referent) in their bibliographies are listed each year. Articles that list the referent study in their bibliographies are highly likely to be on the same topic and, therefore, to be of interest to you.

3. Assume that there is some relevant literature to be found. Often, students assure me that they cannot find any literature on their topic— having spent a total of three hours in the library. Depending upon the importance of the evaluation you are doing, you may have to spend twelve, sixteen, or thirty-six hours in the library to find useful literature. Like most other things, the more hours you spend searching, the more likely you are to find what you are seeking. But it is

more important to "work smart" than to merely put in hours. One student bitterly complained to me that she spent over eight hours reading through the *New York Times* on microfilm to find an exact reference she needed. It did not occur to her to ask the reference librarian for assistance. Had she done so, she would have discovered that a *New York Times Index* is produced each year. Using this reference, she could have found her citation in five minutes or less.

If you search all the right places for literature and still come up empty handed, spend a few dollars for a computer search. Brainstorm other topical or subject headings that may provide productive material. Discuss with friends or colleagues what kinds of problems or programs would be analogous and then look for examples of these in the literature. Double your efforts.

As a rough guide, if you have followed all of these suggestions and still have found only three or four relevant studies, then you know that there isn't a wealth of literature to draw upon. This is confirmed when, after much searching, you locate one more piece of relevant literature and on examining its bibliography, discover that it does not introduce you to any new studies. When do you have "enough" literature? Whenever you believe that you have a good understanding of the literature on the program or problem—from the earliest study to those appearing in the current year.

After you have reviewed the literature in your evaluation report (and there is no reason to go into great detail about all the findings in each and every study), restate for the reader the purpose of your evaluation. Depending upon the amount of the literature reviewed, it may be necessary to again indicate its uniqueness or similarity to prior efforts.

■ Methodology

The purpose of the methodology section of your report is to explain how you conducted your evaluation. You should give sufficient details to allow another investigator or evaluator to replicate the study. Commonly, subsections and subheadings are used to differentiate the various components of the methodology.

The first information often presented under the Methodology usually pertains to the subjects. Your readers will want to know how many there were, how they were selected, and something about their characteristics—such as the male/female composition, average age, and other demographic information. Here is a brief example from a study of families coping with heart disease (Dhooper, 1983):

The study sample consisted of forty families of hospitalized patients meeting the following criteria: (1) Age—60 years or less; (2) Diagnosis—First myocardial infarction; (3) Health status prior to illness—Absence of major illness; and (4) Marital status—Married and living with spouse. These families were selected because our purpose was to focus on a crisis rather than difficulties of a chronic problem. Five hospitals in the Metropolitan Cleveland area participated in the study. The ages of the sick members ranged from 32 to 60, and fifteen percent were female. (P. 23)

Although in explaining the purpose of your evaluation you may have already mentioned the evaluation design used, it is appropriate to go into a little more depth in the procedure subsection of the methodology. You may want to discuss how the random assignment and selection process was conducted. See, for example, how this was treated in a cost-effectiveness evaluation of alcoholism treatment (McCrady et al., 1986):

Informed consent was obtained and baseline data collected during the initial hospitalization. Subjects were randomly assigned on a 2:1 basis to either Partial Hospital Treatment (PHT; n = 114) or Extended Inpatient Treatment (EIP; n = 60). The number of subjects assigned to the two conditions was unequal because the hospital needed to have inpatient beds available; the 2:1 ratio did not jeopardize the power to detect significant results in the study. Patients assigned to the PHT were detoxified on an inpatient basis and then commuted from home, attending treatment 6½ hours per day, Monday through Friday. (P. 709)

The reader of the evaluation report not only needs to understand what evaluation design was used and how the data were collected, but also needs to be informed of the instruments employed in the evaluation. Roberts and Schervish (1988), in evaluating alternative juvenile offender treatment programs, described their method as follows:

In mid-July, 1985, the senior author developed and mailed a two-page questionnaire to juvenile correctional departments and state juvenile institutions in all 50 states and the District of Columbia. This constituted a sample of 151 agencies. A follow-up letter, with another copy of the questionnaire, was sent to the non-respondents in mid-September, 1985. By December 1985, responses had been received from 66 programs.

Program administrators were asked to provide the following information: their rationale for selecting the program; program objectives; [and] the number of juveniles completing the program each year. (P. 116)

It is not unreasonable to assume that readers will be interested in the reliability and validity of any instruments used. See how we (Royse & Toler, 1988) handled this in the next example:

> Beginning in June, 1986, both new and long-term patients at the outpatient dialysis center were asked to complete the Symptom Checklist 90-Revised. . . . The Symptom Checklist 90-Revised (Derogatis, 1983) is a 90-item self-report instrument measuring psychological stress with nine symptom scales and three global indices. The SCL-90-R uses a 5-point response scale ranging from "not at all" (0) to "extremely" (4). The reliability and validity of the SCL-90-R have been well documented. Test-restest and internal consistency coefficients have been reported to range from .77 to .90 on the nine dimensions (Derogratis, 1983). The SCL-90-R has been used in a broad variety of clinical and medical contexts and received positive independent evaluations. (P. 828)

One topic to be covered in the methodology section is how the data are to be analyzed. Data analysis should be planned at the time that the evaluation design is being considered. This is done so that evaluation does not produce data which cannot be analyzed as desired. (More rigorous analyses usually need interval level data.) This is the way Saunders and Parker (1989) discussed how their data were analyzed in an article on examining treatment follow-through of men who batter:

> Multiple regression analyses predicting dropout during assessment, during treatment, or at any point were conducted. Referral source was added hierarchically to the equation after all the other independent variables to determine its additive effect and to uncover possible suppression in its relationship with attrition. Finally, interaction terms that combined referral source and each independent variable (each standardized before multiplying) were constructed and tested for their unique contributions to attrition. (P. 23)

When you believe that you have provided enough information for the reader of your evaluation report to replicate your study (assuming that someone would desire to do so), then you are finished with this section and ready to move on to the next.

■ Findings

The Findings or Results section of your evaluation report contains what you have learned from collecting and analyzing your data. You provide the answers to the questions that were previously asked or information about the hypotheses that were tested. Just the facts are presented in this section—statistically significant differences, results of pre- and posttesting, and so on. The implications of the findings (what the findings may mean practically and pragmatically) are dealt with in the Discussion section of your report.

When evaluators have access to a computer and can easily prepare many crosstabulations and statistical tests, it is possible to produce (and perhaps tempting to force into the Results section) much more of this information than most readers would care to consume. The mass of data accumulated over a year or eighteen months or so of evaluating a program presents something of a problem to those writing evaluation reports, because they can be struck by a compulsion to "tell all." Wanting the sponsor to feel that the contract amount was truly earned, evaluators may compile such an awesome assemblage of tables, charts, and dry, boring paragraphs that only the boldest of academics would attempt to wade through that portion of the report.

Chelimsky (1987) acknowledged this problem: "To its author all of the evaluation's findings seem important. It is painfully difficult to trim surgically what is not relevant, to condense, to rank, to decide not only which finding is most important, but which is most important that is also manipulable by policy" (p. 15). Cronbach et al. (1980) referred to the problem of evaluators wanting to document everything as "self-defeating thoroughness."

It is unrealistic to expect that busy people will take the time to read tens of page of detailed tables or reproductions of computer printouts. It is the evaluator's responsibility to write for the audience who will be reading the evaluation report and to select the most important findings to highlight for that audience. Most evaluation reports are too technical if they contain more than six to eight tables. If the program being evaluated was complex and there are numerous important findings, the evaluator may want to prepare a technical report to accompany a smaller evaluation summary designed to be given to the group of decision makers and other interested members of the public.

Keep in mind that the most helpful of evaluation findings will (as advocated by Mowbray, 1988) contain standards for comparison. Evaluators should provide more than descriptive detail (e.g., 50 percent of the clients were male, 49 percent were over the age of thirty-five, all but one were right-handed). She illustrates the value of "anchors" for comparison with the statement "Fifty percent of geriatric hospital patients have physical health problems of a chronic nature." The reader is left uninformed as to whether 50 percent represents an improvement over what was expected or whether the situation was much worse than expected. Mowbray argues that "some standard must be included as part of the evaluation design and used in the analyses for comparison purposes. . . . Decision makers will expect the evaluator to interpret the results in prescriptive terms" (p. 52).

To help you decide what information needs to be reported and what is trivial, take a blank sheet of paper and make two columns; label one

"Insignificant" and the other "Significant." The results of statistical tests of hypotheses and information directly answering questions serving as catalysts for the evaluation should be placed in the "Significant" column. A finding can be significant even if not statistically significant. For example, suppose you find that there was no statistically significant difference in a social experiment using a control group and an intervention group. Since the reason for the evaluation is to see whether the intervention group performs better than the control group, the finding of no difference between the two groups is very important information.

Findings that are tangential or only superficially relevant are placed in the "Insignificant" column. For example, when evaluating the success of a program designed to teach public speaking skills to adults, you find that the ages of the participants' children correlates with the number of books read by the adults last year. This has no direct bearing on public speaking ability. Your task of deciding what to place in the evaluation report should be a great deal simpler once you have finished placing each of your findings in one of the two columns.

■ Discussion

The Discussion section is where the evaluator begins to interpret and explain the findings. In this section, the evaluator reveals why the results came out the way they did. Perhaps there was some source of bias that was not immediately obvious at the time the study was planned. Or, maybe the study was not implemented exactly as it had been proposed. The main purpose of the Discussion section is to help the reader make sense of the data reported in the previous section. For example, in an article entitled, "How Helpful Are Helplines? A Survey of Callers," Gingerich, Gurney, and Wirtz (1988) report in the Results section that more than half of the callers contacted one to two weeks after their initial call to a helpline rated their problems less severe at the time of the follow-up phone call. After the findings have been presented, the authors begin the Discussion section by writing:

> The findings of the present study must be interpreted with considerable caution, because the sample of respondents was not taken randomly. Clearly, selection factors may have influenced the counselors' decision to participate in the study, whom they chose to ask to participate, the callers who consented, and the callers who actually completed the follow-up interview. . . . The callers who were asked to participate in the study were probably considered by their counselors to be under less emotional stress . . . and possibly more positive toward the helpline than were other callers. (Pp. 638-639)

The authors go on to say that it would be tempting to conclude that the helpline produced the change in the clients' problems but that the study could not rule out several competing explanations. Explanations such as sampling biases are limitations. Every study or evaluation has some limitations, and it is the evaluator's responsibility to point out the major ones. McCrady et al. (1986) reported the following limitations:

> One limitation of the study is that 32 percent of the initial subjects did not participate in the extended follow-ups. Because there was no differential dropout rate from the two experimental groups, comparisons between the groups are appropriate, but the dropouts might affect the overall levels of treatment outcome across groups. (P. 712)

Also, quite appropriate in the Discussion section is a comparison to any similar (or dissimilar) findings contained in studies mentioned in the literature review section. A certain tidiness ensues when your findings are contrasted with those identified earlier in the paper as being the salient works in the field. The reader is then able to place your findings within the context of those that already have a place in the literature. Again, borrowing from McCrady et al., we can see how this might appear in brief form:

> Our findings, as well as two recent studies (LaPorte, McLellan, Erdlen, & Parente, 1981; Sobell, Sobell, & Maisto, 1984), have found no differences in outcomes between subjects who were easily followed and those who were not, and few differences between subjects who continued or discontinued in research follow-ups. (P. 712)

Some professional journals may require a separate section they call "Conclusion." Whether you use a separate Conclusion section or place your concluding thoughts in the Discussion section is a matter of individual taste or a journal's style. It is important, however, that you have conclusions. Did the program perform as it was designed? Should the program be continued? Are clients being helped? The answers to such questions as these make the evaluation relevant and interesting to those who will be reading your evaluation report.

■ References

If you cite studies in your evaluation report (and you probably should if you have done even a cursory review of the literature), then you owe it to your readers to provide a bibliography or a listing of these references. I find the APA style (the one used in this book) to be convenient. You insert the last names of the author and the year of the publication in the correct place in your report and then list the full citation at the end of the document. The APA stye does not use footnotes at the bottom of the page, and there is no danger of getting your notes in the wrong sequence or out of order, since the references are arranged alphabetically at the end.

■ *Appendices*

Appendices are usually found in long evaluation reports and typically include such items as a copy of instruments that were employed during the course of the evaluation, a sample copy of the instructions that were read or given to the subjects, cover letters that went out to participants, and perhaps bulky tables that you feel are important to include but too lengthy to place in the Results section. It is not always necessary to have an Appendix. For instance, if the data from your evaluation came from the health department, no mailings were done, and no questionnaires were given to respondents, then you may have no need for an Appendix at the end of your report. If you are writing a report of your evaluation for a journal article, it is usually necessary to limit the manuscript to sixteen to twenty pages, and an Appendix is not wanted. Anyone wanting additional technical information or copies of instruments is expected to contact the author.

■ Mistakes to Avoid

Over the years I have read a number of papers written by students in which they have reported an evaluation, or proposed an evaluation design for a specific program, supplied "dummy" data, and then discussed the findings. It is always interesting to see the diversity of the products created by students having access to the same lectures and texts. Occasionally, a student will make a major mistake for which I have no explanations. (A student once wrote an evaluation report where pre- and posttest scores were averaged together.) More often, students' mistakes come from going beyond their limited data (ignoring the fact that their samples were not random or representative), from not sufficiently defining their concepts, from using inadequate instruments, from not recognizing major sources of bias or limitations, or from failing to conduct any analysis except the univariate. These are all problems that you should recognize by now. However, just to make sure that your evaluation report doesn't contain any "fatal flaws," I have assembled several examples of problems that I tend to find from time to time. As you come across evaluation reports in your practice or in the literature and begin to read them more critically, keep your eyes open for these mistakes.

■ Misunderstanding the Purpose of the Literature Review

One student who was assigned to critique an evaluation report wrote, "Although I did not verify the articles reported in the literature review section, I assume that they, as conscientious authors, left no stone unturned." The purpose of the literature review is to familiarize the reader with what is known about the problem under investigation and the intervention that has been applied. The reader should have an intuitive feeling that the author of the evaluation report has provided enough information to understand the intervention, the theoretical model on which it was based, the ways these interventions have been evaluated in the past, and with what results. Your reaction may be that the literature review is too skimpy (important literature may have been missed) or that it seems appropriate. Normally, it is not your job to verify the existence of articles cited in the literature. (Unless, of course, you suspect that someone is making them up.)

■ Too Small a Sample

An example of a program that is likely to impact only a small number of clients is an intensive in-home family intervention program. Such programs are designed so that each caseworker has responsibility for two to four families at a time. If only one or two caseworkers are employed in a program like this and if the evaluation period runs for one year, the population of clients served by this program might range from twelve to about fifty.

Even if there were no attrition, twelve cases is too small a sample for a program evaluation, and twenty-four or even thirty-six cases is also pretty darn small. Inevitably, there is a loss of information when evaluative studies are conducted on programs like these. Some families move out of the area, families break up, children run away from home, and family members may be arrested or sent to prison, may become hospitalized, or may even die. Instead of having twelve or even fifty families at the end of the year, it would not be unrealistic for the evaluator to plan on being able to locate fifty percent or sixty percent of the families who were served earlier in the year for an evaluation follow-up. Even when families are located, they may not always agree to participate in the evaluation. The loss of data is a serious threat to the internal validity of a study and particularly so when the number of clients served was small in the beginning. When attrition is a serious problem, it may be difficult to convince others that the program is more successful than less expensive-programs. In such a program as this, it may be unrealistic to expect to conduct a rigorous evaluation at the end of the first year. Perhaps a formative evaluation is called for at that time and a more thorough one at the end of year two or at a time when a larger number of families have been served.

In an intensive program like this, another threat to the internal validity of the study would be the likelihood that these families were specially selected and not randomly assigned. Because only a small number of families can be served by this program, there is a greater probability that families who are believed to have the best chance of succeeding would be hand-picked.

A small sample may also create problems when the evaluator assumes that clients entering a program at one time of the year (e.g., during the summer months) are representative of clients entering the program at other times during the year. If you think that the clientele varies by season or other predictable cycle (for example, requests for services at the end of the month might be different from those at the beginning of the month), your sample should not be restricted to clients entering or served during part of that cycle or season. This would result in an unrepresentative cross-section of the total clients served by the program. (A student once informed me about a study she conducted of the active clients in her agency during the month of January. Since this agency was in a northern state, I asked if the January clients resembled the clients who requested service in July or April. She couldn't tell me because she did not draw a client sample from all twelve months of the year. Would there be a potential for drawing some erroneous conclusions using a sample of only January clients?)

■ Insufficient Information about Instruments

Students often think that a "good" evaluation is guaranteed if they are able to locate an already prepared instrument in the literature. The fact that an instrument has been photocopied or appears in print does not necessarily make it one that ought to be used in your evaluative study.

Occasionally, a student makes a statement in a paper to the effect that "two instruments were used to assess learning outcomes" but does not discuss who developed the instruments or for what purpose, whether the instruments are reliable, or if any studies have been done to show that they have validity. Neither is it sufficient to write, "This instrument has been researched for validity and reliability and proven to have both." The evaluator should provide sufficient information to enable the reader to determine for him- or herself that the instrument is sound. An informed reader of an evaluation report will want to know about the instruments used. How many items did the instrument contain? How was it administered? How has the instrument been used in other studies?

Another mistake to avoid is taking selected items from an already prepared scale or instrument and combining these with several new items. The resulting scale or questionnaire may not have as much reliability and/or validity as the old scale or instrument. Any adjustment, revision, or substitution made to an already prepared scale has the potential for affecting its psychometric properties. The more extensive these changes, the greater the likelihood that the instrument's reliability and validity have been changed in some way. You will not know whether the change is for better or worse unless additional psychometric studies are conducted with the revised instrument. So, if you find a good instrument that you want to use, try not to modify it unless it is absolutely necessary to make changes to fit a different population or age group.

■ Failure to Use a Control Group

Social work students seem to particularly dislike the concept of control groups. I suspect this is because they feel that there is something unethical about their use. What they often do not realize is that control groups can be constructed without denying clients services (this was covered in chapter 7). In many instances, it is impossible to make sense of evaluative data without a control group. Two brief examples will demonstrate this.

A former student asked me to help interpret some data he had prepared in conjunction with evaluating an inpatient mental health facility for emotionally disturbed adolescents. He was able to show that 75 percent did not return to the facility. I asked him if he knew what recidivism rates were reported in similar facilities in the area or in the literature, but he knew of none. While I could see that his evaluation was not one that I would be quick to label "superlative," I continued to try to help him interpret the data. I asked if there could be legitimate reasons why some of the adolescents might not return to the facility. In fact, there were some very good reasons why adolescents might not return to the same facility. They were not eligible to return if they had committed a felony, been arrested and sent to a detention facility, or moved out of state, or if their eighteenth birthday was within three months. These and other reasons could easily explain why a large proportion of the adolescents did not turn to the facility—and none of the reasons had anything to do with the effectiveness of the treatment they received.

Another student was doing a survey of social workers' attitudes about panhandlers. He spent quite a bit of time writing and refining a questionnaire. He collected his data, wrote his report, and just before the semester was over, came to talk to me about his project. He realized, too late to do anything about it, that while he knew what social workers' attitudes were, he couldn't conclude anything because he had no control group. He didn't know whether social workers were more empathic than other professionals or lay citizens toward panhandlers. If he had used a control group of non-social workers, the data from the social workers would have been more meaningful.

■ Presenting Individual Scores

It is the evaluator's job to condense, summarize, and otherwise make sense of all the data that has been collected. It is *not* necessary to inform the reader of an evaluation report of the pretest and posttest scores of every participant in the study. Instead, show the average pretest score for the control and intervention groups and the average posttest score. You may want to talk about the highest and lowest scores, or standard deviations, but very seldom would it ever be necessary to document each and every score. Generally, when this occurs in an evaluation report, I presume the author did not know how to go about analyzing the data and is trying to make up for this by presenting the reader with bulk rather than a perceptive grasp of the data.

■ Lack of Specificity

It seems that some writers of evaluation reports believe that others have the ability to read their minds. I make this assumption when I read a statement like the following: "Due to the controversial nature of the topic, every precaution was taken to ensure the anonymity of the persons taking part in the study." A reader with some understanding of these processes would want to know exactly what precautions were taken. Perhaps the writer meant that no names, addresses, or phone numbers were gathered. However, if Social Security numbers were used in order to match subjects at pretest and posttest, does this protect anonymity? Did the evaluator create a coding system to protect anonymity? Does protection of anonymity mean that the names were cut off or marked out by a student assistant before the questionnaires were given to the researcher? These questions would not have been raised if the author had been more specific.

■ Overgeneralizing

To understand this mistake, imagine an evaluation of an AIDS educational program for elementary school students. A study was completed of 250 fifth and sixth graders in one rural school district. Assume that the students are more knowledgeable about AIDS after the educational intervention than they were at the beginning. The evaluator concludes that the program is a success, and "the findings indicate that social workers across the United States should encourage school administrators to adopt comparable AIDS educational programs and expand these programs to all grades in their elementary schools."

The problem with this statement is, first of all, that since the population of students involved in this study came from only one rural school district, the author is overgeneralizing. There is no way of knowing, for instance, if the results would have been the same if students came from urban or suburban areas or even from different rural areas. Are students living in rural Montana different from those living in rural Mississippi or rural Vermont? Since the evaluation was limited to students in only one small school district, that is the only geographical area for which the intervention is known to have worked. It may be that the unique blend of socio-demographic characteristics found in the population receiving the intervention makes it quite unlike other populations of "typical" fifth and sixth graders.

Since no statement was made about there being a control group, there is always the possibility that the increase in knowledge about AIDS came from greater coverage of this topic on television or other media. Perhaps it came about because a respected person in the community died of AIDS and this became a popular topic of conversation—with a result that parents and other adults requested and distributed, on their own, informational brochures about AIDS to the fifth and sixth graders. Maturation is another threat to the internal validity to this study. As they grow older, fifth and sixth graders may become more interested in sex and related matters and begin a process of self-education about AIDS. This becomes more of a problem the longer the time interval between pretest and posttest.

Even if the program were a success with fifth and sixth graders, there is no evidence that the same program would work with younger children (second, third, or fourth graders). So, a statement that the program ought to be expanded to all grades is unfounded. It is a belief or value statement, not a finding of the evaluation. The statement that social workers should encourage school administrators across the country to implement such a program is based on the assumption that other school districts are doing nothing and that their children are ignorant of AIDS. Even without this intervention, children in other school districts may be more informed than the children in the rural school district receiving the intervention. Unless there is data for support, it is presumptuous to assume that all children across the United States need such an intervention. A sampling of students from around the state or from other school districts would help to establish that other fifth and sixth graders also need the intervention. This sample could also serve as a comparison or control group against which the "success" of the students receiving the educational intervention could be gauged.

■ *Lack of Consistency*

Periodically, I come across a report or a manuscript in which the following mistake has been made: analysis is conducted with variables without *a priori* foundation in the literature review. This problem seems to occur most often when evaluators or investigators try to find something statistically significant to report. Evaluators may be tempted to test for differences by gender, race, income, educational level, and so on until they find what is regarded as something of importance. However, if differences by sex, race, and so forth were not important enough to be included in the literature review or in the hypotheses, then the examination of these differences in the Results section is not logical. The converse is also true— the evaluation would be incomplete if the literature review and hypotheses were concerned with differences by sex, race, and so on, but the analysis failed to report these comparisons.

■ Checklist for Writing and Assessing Evaluation Reports

Using the topics that have been covered in this chapter, we can construct a simplified checklist for insuring that all the essential elements are contained within an evaluation report. (This checklist can also be used to help you evaluate reports you may be reading.)

Introduction
Does the Introduction provide a clear notion of:
a. the problem?
b. the program?
c. the purpose of the evaluation?
d. the rationale for the evaluation?

Literature Review
Does the Literature Review provide:
a. a relevant context for understanding prior programs and evaluation efforts of these programs?
b. a thorough survey of historical and current literature?

Methodology
Does the Methodology section describe:
a. an evaluation design?
b. sampling procedures?
c. subjects?
d. procedures for data collection?
e. instruments used?

Findings
Does the Results section contain:
a. findings relative to the stated problem(s) or purpose of the evaluation questions?
b. appropriate statistical tests?

Discussion
Does the Discussion section address:
a. practical implications?
b. generalization of the data?
c. limitations of the study?

You need to be concerned with reasonableness in all areas. Do the hypotheses or questions raised seem reasonable? Do they appear to follow what is known about the problem and gaps in the literature? If control groups are used, do they seem to be appropriate groups for comparison? Is the sample large enough for the conclusions that are drawn? Do the findings logically follow from the procedures that were used? Are there any major sources of bias or limitations that have not been recognized?

Reasonableness also applies to the length of the evaluation report. If you write a report that is too long, few people will read it. If the report is too short, important details may be omitted. My best advice is to write for *your audience.* If you think none of them will read an eighty page report, then condense. Journal articles typically run sixteen to twenty pages and manage to crowd an awful lot of information into that format. Instead of guessing what your audience will digest, pilot test a draft copy on someone representative of your audience who would be cooperative enough to give you needed feedback. Schalock and Thornton (1988) suggested a "test" where a program description or evaluation report would be considered against whether it would make sense to a skeptical, willing, careful, but generally reasonable audience.

Finally, although we have dealt with the evaluation report section by section, realize that the report should make a harmonious whole. The initial question should lead to the literature being reviewed, which should be followed by a discussion of the ways the problem has been studied in the past. These methods have a direct bearing on the procedures used in the study and the way the data are analyzed. And, the conclusions should relate to the initial question(s) being asked.

QUESTIONS FOR CLASS DISCUSSION

1. Discuss which parts of the evaluation report appear to be the most difficult and the easiest to write. Have students give reasons for their beliefs.

2. Discuss the "worst" mistake that could be made in writing an evaluation report.
3. A co-worker asks you to read a draft of an evaluation report she is preparing for an intervention program for men who batter. A nonequivalent control group evaluation design was used. Police records were checked nine months after intervention to determine if there had been a reoccurrence of domestic violence. The intervention was successful in that most men in this group did not batter again within the nine month study period. However, as you look closer at the participants selected for the intervention group, you discover that while the eligibility criteria for participation in the program was an arrest for this offense within the last three months, several of the participants were last charged over one and a half years ago. How could this affect the findings? What would you advise your co-worker to do?

MINI-PROJECTS: EXPERIENCING RESEARCH FIRSTHAND

1. Draft a short proposal for a program evaluation. Use a program with which you are familiar or make up one. This time, however, show what you have learned about program evaluation by making it an exemplar of *poor* evaluation (e.g., use too small a sample, build in obvious threats to the internal validity, etc.).
2. Find a journal article reporting a program evaluation and then critique the article using the guidelines suggested in this chapter. Write a brief paper summarizing your findings. (A recent one that may be easy to find is by Oscar Grusky and Kathleen Tierney, "Evaluating the Effectiveness of Countywide Mental Health Care Systems," *Community Mental Health Journal*, 25 (1) (1989), 3–20.

REFERENCES AND RESOURCES

Bloom, B.L., Hodges, W.F., Kern, M.B., & McFaddin, S.C. (1985). A preventive intervention program for the newly separated: Final evaluations. *American Journal of Orthopsychiatry*, 55 (1), 9–26.

Braverman, M.T., & Campbell, D.T. (1989). Facilitating the development of health promotion programs: Recommendations for researchers and funders. *Evaluating Health Promotion Programs*. New Directions for Program Evaluation, no. 43, San Francisco, CA: Jossey–Bass.

Bulow, B.V., Sweeney, J.A., Shear, M.K., Friedman, R., & Plowe, C. (1987). Family satisfaction with psychiatric evaluations. *Health and Social Work*, 12 (4), 290–295.

Carpenter, R.A., Boyenga, K.W. & Schaible, T.D. (1985). Evaluation of a prepaid mental health plan for business. *Community Mental Health Journal*, 21 (2), 94–108.

Chelimsky, E. (1987). What have we learned about the politics of program evaluation? *Evaluation Practice*, 8 (1), 5–21.

Cope, J.G., Moy, S.S., & Grossnickle, W.F. (1988). The behavioral impact of an advertising campaign to promote safety belt use. *Journal of Applied Behavior Analysis*, 21, 277–280.

Cronbach, L.J., Ambron, S.R., Dornbusch, S.M., Hess, R.D., Hornik, R.C., Phillips, D.C., Walker, D.F., & Weiner, S.S. (1980). *Toward reform of program evaluation*. San Francisco, CA: Jossey–Bass.

Dhooper, S.S. (1983). Coronary heart disease and family functioning. *Journal of Social Service Research*, 7 (2), 19–38.

Fox, D.K., Hopkins, B.L., & Anger, W.K. (1987). The long-term effects of a token economy on safety performance in open-pit mining. *Journal of Applied Behavior Analysis*, 20, 215–224.

Garfield, S.L. (1984). The evaluation of research: An editorial perspective. In A.S. Bellack & M. Hersen (Eds.), *Research methods in clinical psychology*.

Gingerich, W.J., Gurney, R.J., & Wirtz, T.S. (1988). How helpful are helplines? A survey of callers. *Social Casework*, 69 (10), 634–639.

Hendricks, M., & Papagiannia, M. (1990). Do's and don'ts for offering effective recommendations. *Evaluation Practice*, 11 (2), 121–125.

Maisto, S.A., Sobell, L.C., Zelhart, P.F., Connors, G.F., & Cooper, T. (1979). Driving records of persons convicted of driving under the influence of alcohol. *Journal of Studies on Alcohol*, 40, 70–77.

Majchrzak, A. (1986). Keeping the marines in the field; Results of a field experiment. *Evaluation and Program Planning*, 9 (3), 253–265.

McCrady, B., Longabaugh, R., Fink, E., Stout, R., Beattie, M., & Ruggieri-Authelet, A. (1986). Cost-effectiveness of alcoholism treatment in partial hospital versus inpatient settings after brief inpatient treatment: 12-month outcomes. *Journal of Consulting and Clinical Psychology*, 54 (5), 708–713.

McCuller, G.L., Salzberg, C.L., & Lignugaris/Kraft, B. (1987). Producing generalized job initiative in severely mentally retarded sheltered workers. *Journal of Applied Behavior Analysis*, 20, 413–420.

Mowbray, C.T. (1988). Getting the system to respond to evaluation findings. *Evaluation Utilization*. New Directions for Program Evaluation. San Francisco, CA: Jossey–Bass.

Roberts, A.R., & Schervish (1988). A strategy for making decisions and evaluating alternative juvenile offender treatment programs. *Evaluation and Program Planning*, 11, 115–122.

Royse, D., & Toler, J. (1988). Dialysis patients and patterns of symptom report on the Symptom Checklist-90-R. *Psychological Reports*, 62, 827–831.

Saunders, D.G., & Parker, J.G. (1989). Legal sanctions and treatment follow-through among men who batter: A multivariate analysis. *Social Work Research and Abstracts*, 25 (3), 21–29.

Schalock, R.L., & Thornton, C.V.D. (1988). *Program evaluation: A field guide for administrators*. New York: Plenum Press.

Sowers–Hoag, K.M., Thyer, B.A., & Bailey, J.S. (1987). Promoting automobile safety belt use by young children. *Journal of Applied Behavior Analysis*, 1987, 20, 133–38.

Stout, J.W., & Rivara, F.P. (1989). Schools and sex education: Does it work? *Pediatrics*, 83 (3), 375–379.

Velasques, J.S., & Lyle, C.G. (1985). Day versus residential treatment for juvenile offenders: The impact of program evaluation. *Child Welfare*, 64 (2), 145–156.

Vincent, M.L., Clearie, A.F., & Schluchter, M.D. (1987). Reducing adolescent pregnancy through school and community-based education. *Journal of the American Medical Association*, 257 (24), 3382–3386.

Epilogue

Writing a text that attempts to explain simply a complex topic like program evaluation is a challenging experience. Decisions must be made about what to include and what to leave out. The material must be organized in a logical manner that can easily be comprehended. Assumptions have to be made about the knowledge students already have and that which they are expected to acquire. All of this is backdrop for explaining some of the decisions I made in writing the text.

One early decision was to exclude material on single subject (or single-system) designs. While some teach these designs in program evaluation courses, I suspect there are two main reasons for doing this: first, single subject designs may not be taught in the research methods course, and second, it is believed to be important to give micro-intervention oriented students something that will hold their interest.

Most social work practitioners will be working in public or private agencies where accountability is a major concern. Proportionately few social workers are self-employed in a private practice. Many social workers, after several years of providing direct services, are promoted to supervisory or management responsibilities. All social workers need to have a beginning knowledge of how to go about evaluating the programs that they supervise or that employ them. I think it is crucial to focus on program evaluations.

Single subject designs are not included in this book because they cannot be used to evaluate *programs*. Single subject designs allow for the evaluation of this client or that client. They are good designs for practitioners who want only to monitor the improvement of one or two clients at a time. But when we begin to talk about whether two hundred or four hundred clients improved, these designs are clearly inappropriate. Single subject designs are unsuited for evaluating all of the clients being served by a single therapist or a larger group served by several therapists. Students or faculty wanting additional information on single subject designs should consult the references at the end of this epilogue.

Similarly, this text has not discussed Goal Attainment Scaling (GAS). GAS is a scaling technique for single-subject designs. It measures improvement or deterioration from individually tailored statements of most likely outcomes. Even though these outcomes can be given quantitative values, the methodology is still an extension of the single subject model and is not, in my opinion, useful for program evaluators. Persons desiring to learn more about this topic are also referred to the references at the end of this chapter.

Another decision was to make no mention of meta-analysis until this point. Meta-analysis is a relatively new approach to interpreting research in a given area. (Meta-analysis might be thought of as an evaluation of evaluations.) Once a database of related research or evaluations reports has been compiled by conducting a systematic survey, the investigator looks for patterns and trends in the findings of these studies. Typically, there is a quantitative assessment of the treatment effects, and then analysis is conducted on the effect sizes.

The results of a meta-analysis can be controversial. Hogarty (1989), for example, challenged Videka-Sherman's (1988) conclusions in part:

> As used in the NASW-sponsored analysis by Videka-Sherman (1988), however, few and often inappropriate representations of social work practice were included. The studies often were devoid of designs needed for legitimate inference making and of the statistical power required for testing hypotheses, were poorly analyzed, and were uncontrolled regarding crucial variables that are known to influence directly the course and outcome of severe mental disorders. Effect sizes from the better designed studies were overwhelmed by effect sizes from reports of lower quality that unduly influenced judgments of effective practice. (P. 363)

Meta-analysis may be useful for attempting to draw conclusions about such large-scale concerns as whether social casework as a technique is effective, the benefits of psychotherapy, or effectiveness of services for the mentally ill. However, meta-analysis is not a program evaluation technique; it is a methodology which uses program evaluations for its database. Because I suspect that only a small percentage of practitioners or program managers would ever want to conduct a meta-analysis, I chose not to explain this methodology in detail. You may wish to consult the references at the end of this chapter to learn more about meta-analysis.

■ Evaluation: Past, Present, and Future

Evaluation has come a long way, but it still has a long way to go. Braverman and Campbell (1989) cited a study conducted by the U.S. Department of Education which demonstrates that decision makers do not make much use of evaluation. In a survey of state alcohol and drug abuse agencies regarding effectiveness of educational programming, 93 percent of state administrators indicated sources of their judgments on effectiveness came from "professional judgment," while only 22 percent indicated the source was "formal evaluation." Is there a shortage of competent evaluators? I think the problem is two-part: there is a shortage of skilled evaluators, and too often administrators (perhaps lacking these talents themselves) fail to insist upon objective evaluations of their programs.

Goldstein, Surber, and Wilner (1984), in a review of 2,231 outcome studies reported in fifty prestigious journals between 1969 and 1979, found that slightly over three-quarters of the studies did not use control groups. Over a third used the weakest of designs—the one-group posttest-only design. The authors concluded, "Unless evaluation becomes an integral part of the treatment process, both the research and the treatments themselves will be seriously hampered" (p. 499).

Levine (1987) expressed concern that cost-effectiveness and cost-benefit analyses are only rarely used in evaluation studies. He noted that of the five hundred presentations listed in the program of the 1986 Annual Meeting of the American Evaluation Association held in Kansas City, only two indicated a focus on cost-effectiveness and none addressed cost-benefit analysis. Lipsey (1988) samples all of the evaluation research studies that could be identified in a three year period from three major abstracting services and, of 122 with a quantitative-comparative methodology (using experimental or quasi-experimental designs), concluded:

> Conventional treatment effectiveness research, speaking generally, is based on constructs that substantially underrepresent the complexity of the causal

processes at issue; it is theoretically impoverished and yields little knowledge of practical value; it is crudely operationalized and rarely meets even minimal standards for quality of design and measurement; it is largely insensitive to the very treatment effects it purports to study; and its results and conclusions are largely a matter of chance and have little to do with the efficacy of the treatments under consideration. (P. 6)

While it may be easy to be discouraged by Lipsey's observations, I think he is correct in believing that evaluation in this country still has a lot of room for improvement. On the other hand, this is not to suggest that we should stop evaluating until such time as everyone is an evaluation "expert." The best way to learn more about evaluation is by doing it. By examining what we could have done differently and receiving honest feedback about those efforts, we become more skilled.

Developing evaluation competence requires more than reading a textbook on the subject or taking a one-semester course (Sanders, 1986). Yet, competence cannot be measured in absolute terms. Usually, one practitioner of evaluation may have a little more ability or qualifications than another. When I took a course on program evaluation as a doctoral student, the instructor told my class that we would not be able to get jobs as program evaluators because we were not qualified. Yet, I was hired a short time later by an organization to be their director of research and evaluation. Relative to the other staff in the organization, I was the most competent to perform program evaluation.

A practitioner or program manager with one semester of instruction in program evaluation is certainly better off than a peer with no exposure to the topic. Any reading or course work should move the interested student a little closer to some minimal level of competence. Sanders (1986) has identified other avenues for developing evaluation competence: peer tutoring, consultation with others, mentor affiliation, assisting or doing evaluations, as well as networking and sharing experiences.

I would like to see greater use of cost-effectiveness and the more sophisticated evaluation designs, but a problem of larger magnitude is that even simple evaluations are not conducted when they are sorely needed. I was struck by this recently when I heard about a public housing agency which admitted to having fifty to one hundred vacant housing units at any one point in time—and about one hundred people on a waiting list to get housing. With such a waiting list and given the current crisis of homeless individuals, why were there *any* vacant units at all? To investigate the problems with this housing program we are not likely to need standardized instruments, control groups, or randomization—even a simple objective inquiry would be likely to provide necessary answers. A sophisticated design is not needed to evaluate every program.

REFERENCES AND RESOURCES

Single-Subject Design

Berlin, S.B. (1983). Single-case evaluation: Another version. *Social Work Research and Abstracts*, 19, 3–11.

Bloom, M., & Fischer, J. (1982). *Evaluating practice: Guidelines for the accountable professional*. Englewood Cliffs, NJ: Prentice–Hall.

Hersen, M., & Barlow, D. (1976). *Single case experimental designs*. Elmsford, NY: Pergamon.

Jayaratme, S. (1977). *Empirical clinical practice*. New York: Columbia University Press.

Kazdin, A.E. (1982). *Single-case research designs: Methods for clinical and applied settings*. New York: Oxford University Press.

Royse, D. (1990). Single system designs. In *Research methods for social workers*. Chicago, IL: Nelson–Hall.

Goal Attainment Scaling

Bartlet, R.F., & Colon, I. (1982). Implementation of Goal Attainment Scaling in residential treatment: An administrative model. *Child Welfare*, 61 (7), 424–434.

Kiresuk, T.J., & Sherman, R.E. (1968). Goal Attainment Scaling: A general method for evaluating comprehensive community mental health programs. *Community Mental Health Journal*, 4 (December), 443–453.

Kiresuk, T.J., & Lund, S.H. (1978). Goal Attainment Scaling. In C.C. Attkisson, W.A. Hargreaves, M.J. Horowitz & J.E. Sornsen (Eds.), *Evaluation of human service programs*, 341–370. New York: Academic Press.

Meta-analysis

Glass, G.V. (1976). Primary, secondary, and meta-analysis of research. *Educational Research*, 5 (November), 3–8.

Glass, G.V., McGaw, B., & Smith, M.L. (1981). *The meta-analysis in social research*. Beverly Hills, CA: Sage.

Hogarty, G.E. (1989). Meta-analysis of the effects of practice with the chronically mentally ill: A critique and reappraisal of the literature. *Social Work*, 34 (4), 363–373.

Smith, M.L., Glass, G.V., & Miller, T.I. (1980). *The benefits of psychotherapy*. Baltimore, MD: Johns Hopkins University Press.

Videka-Sherman, L. (1988). Meta-analysis of research on social work practice in mental health. *Social Work*, 33 (4), 325–337.

Future Directions

Braverman, M.T., & Campbell, D.T. (1989). Facilitating the development of health promotion programs: Recommendations for researchers and funders.

Evaluating health promotion programs. New Directions for Program Evaluation, no. 43. San Francisco, CA: Jossey-Bass.

Goldstein, M.S., Surber, M., & Wilner, D. (1984). Outcome evaluations in substance abuse: A comparison of alcoholism, drug abuse, and other mental health interventions. *International Journal of the Addictions,* 19 (5), 479–502.

Lipsey, M.W. (1988). Practice and malpractice in evaluation research. *Evaluation Practice,* 9 (4), 5–24.

Levine, H.M. (1987). Cost-benefit and cost-effectiveness analyses. *Evaluation Practice in Review.* New Directions for Program Evaluation, no. 34. San Francisco, CA: Jossey-Bass.

Sanders, J.R. (1986). The teaching of evaluation in education. *The teaching of evaluation across the disciplines.* New Directions for Program Evaluations, no. 29. San Francisco, CA: Jossey-Bass.

Index